P9-DHT-395

RANDOLPH

By the same author

Rodin – Immortal Peasant
Train to Nowhere
Love in a Nutshell
The Fabulous Leonard Jerome
Mrs Fitzherbert
Mr Frewen of England
The Life of Lady Randolph Churchill
Edwardians in Love
Francis Chichester
Cousin Clare
Madame Tussaud, Waxworker Extraordinary
The Gilt and the Gingerbread
A Story Half Told

RANDOLPH

The Biography of WINSTON CHURCHILL'S SON

ANITA LESLIE

BEAUFORT BOOKS
Publishers · New York

Copyright © 1985 by Anita Leslie

All rights reserved. No part of this publication may be reproduced or
transmitted in any form or by any means, electronic or mechanical, including
photocopy, recording, or any information storage and retrieval system now
known or to be invented, without permission in writing from the publisher,
except by a reviewer who wishes to quote brief passages in connection
with a review written for inclusion in a magazine, newspaper, or broadcast.

Library of Congress Cataloging in Publication Data

Leslie, Anita.
Randolph: the biography of Winston Churchill's son.

Bibliography: p.
Includes index.
1. Churchill, Randolph S. (Randolph Spencer), 1911-1968.
2. Journalists—Great Britain—Biography.
I. Title.
PN5123.C42L4   1985   070′.92′4 [B]   84-24468
ISBN 0-8253-0284-6

Published in the United States by Beaufort Books Publishers, New York.

Printed in the U.S.A.   First American Edition

10 9 8 7 6 5 4 3 2 1

Acknowledgements

My sincere thanks in the compiling of this book go to Natalie Bevan who was the last love of Randolph. I am also deeply indebted to the Hon. Lady Mosley and to Lady Beit, two of his Mitford cousins who were very dear to him. I also thank Kay Halle who was an enduring friend and Laura, Duchess of Marlborough who sustained him during the war years. And I must express sincere gratitude to Rosemary the widow of Michael Wolff, Randolph's chief researcher, and to Xenia Field, MBE, who helped him create his garden at Stour. I also tender thanks for reminiscences to Colonel David Stirling, DSO, Brigadier Sir Fitzroy Maclean, CBE, Lady Diana Cooper, the Earl of Longford, Nancy Lady Blakenham, Anthony Marreco, Alan Pryce-Jones, Lady Mary Dunn, Tanis Phillips and her daughter Liza Shaw. They all knew him intimately, all loved him and saw clearly what he seemed determined to do to himself.

My thanks also go to Colonel Stephan Rose, CBE, the Hon. Mrs David James, Peter Quennell, Muriel Bowen, Betty Stafford, the Comtesse de Breteuil, Lady Leslie, Kay Harvey-Miller, the Hon. Lady Aitken, Commander Michael Crichton, RN, Viscount Lambton, Peter Carter-Ruck, the late Sir John Betjeman, the Earl of Birkenhead, Colonel the Hon. Julian Berry, Major J. A. Friend, Dr Henry Gillespie, Lt. Col. William Cunningham MC, Alastair Forbes, Harold Harris and Hugo Vickers.

Mollie, Duchess of Buccleuch has elaborated on what it was like to go electioneering with Randolph and the Rt Hon. Michael Foot, MP, has described his courage in defeat. Joy Murche and Joan Forbes who were in the British Forces at Bari have helped me, and amongst his numerous researchers Alan Brien and Tom Hartman have recounted wonderful tales. Barbara Twigg who was Randolph's secretary for his final six years, Anne Sharpley who worked with him as a journalist and the Countess of Ranfurly have given their versions of a complex character. Graham Watson who was Randolph's literary agent and Charles Wintour his editor on the *Evening Standard* have offered accounts of their dealings, and the Rt Hon. Lord Home of the Hirsel and the Rt Hon. Harold Macmillan, The Earl of Stockton, OM, have allowed me to use their impressions. Then I must tender especial thanks to Christopher Sykes for an understanding story, and to Andrew Kerr who interspersed his chores as a researcher with attending to Randolph; and to Dr 'Terry' Marshall who was his doctor as well as his friend. I must also thank Martin Gilbert who inherited the biography of Sir Winston Churchill after Randolph died and who has taken great pains to help me.

Only one person did not wish to speak about Randolph and I accept his reticence with respect. Lord Boothby said that because he had been so fond of Winston's son while disapproving of almost everything he did he could not bear to talk about him.

My thanks are due to Mrs Robert Bevan for permission to use her diaries and to Laura, Duchess of Marlborough, Lady Beit, Lord Dacre, Nancy, Lady Blakenham, Mr Charles Wintour and the late Miss Virginia Cowles for permission to quote their own letters.To Mrs Michael Wolff I give special thanks for permission to quote from the letters of her late husband. The copyright of letters by the late Randolph Churchill belongs to his son Winston Churchill, MP, to whom I am very grateful for permission to quote.

For permission to quote from the following books I am indebted to the publishers:
Eastern Approaches (Cape), *The Rainbow Comes and Goes* (Hart-Davis), *Evelyn Waugh* (Collins), *The Diaries of Evelyn Waugh* (Weidenfeld & Nicolson), *The Letters of Evelyn Waugh* (Weidenfeld & Nicolson), *Evelyn Waugh and His World* (Weidenfeld & Nicolson), *The Crucible of War* (Cape), *The History of the Middle East Commandos* (Imperial War Museum), *Winston S. Churchill,* Volumes III, IV, and V and Companion Volumes (Heinemann), *The Great Saharan Mouse Hunt* (Hutchinson), *The Young Unpretender* (Heinemann).

Illustrations

Randolph the journalist *(photo by Tony Armstrong Jones)*
Kay Halle
Vote for Randolph Churchill: Election poster for Ross and Cromarty by-election, 1936
A summer picnic. Randolph with Tanis Guinness, Cecil Beaton, Oliver Messel and Mona Harrison Williams *(reproduced by kind permission of Drew Montagu)*
Diana Mitford
Clementine Mitford's wedding to Sir Alfred Beit *(BBC Hulton Picture Library)*
Randolph's wedding to Pamela Digby *(BBC Hulton Picture Library)*
Laura Dudley *(photo by Cecil Beaton, reproduced by kind permission of Laura, Duchess of Marlborough)*
David Stirling with Middle East Patrol Group *(IWM)*
Fitzroy Maclean *(IWM)*
Randolph in Korea
Randolph and June *(photo by Cecil Beaton, courtesy of Sotheby's, London)*
Winston's wedding *(photo by Anthea Sieveking)*
Randolph in the strong-room at Stour with Michael Wolff
Randolph's Stour bookplate
Randolph and Arabella in the garden at Stour
Randolph telephones from the garden *(photo by Anthea Sieveking)*
Randolph and Natalie Bevan with the dogs at Stour

Randolph Churchill was born on 28 May 1911, at 33 Eccleston Square in London, when his father was Home Secretary. Ladies did not go to hospital to have their babies in those days. A top-hatted gynaecologist would arrive in tailcoat and be shown up the stairs by a frenzied parlourmaid.

The enticing, golden-haired Clementine looked proudly at her second baby. He was a boy – and Winston shared the ordinary Englishman's belief that only males really mattered. Men could enter Parliament, make speeches, go to war – keep the world going round – but girls were for adornment. Women served their purpose but could not be considered important except in the context of their husbands. From the very start Winston could not resist spoiling his son. One must accept Randolph as a unique creature reared in unique circumstances.

Winston himself had inherited his resilience and staying power from an American mother, but the sparkling, ebullient Jennie had had to waste her talent in flirting and romances. Her dynamic strength was only to show years later when her son grew up and disaster befell him.

The little creature, with eyes that promised to be hyacinth blue, kicked and squirmed in his nurse's arms. His proud father wrote gleefully to Clementine that her new-born son, referred to as the 'Chumbolly' (he was unusually plump as babies go), must be egged on to enjoy her bosom. 'At his age greediness and even swinishness at table are virtues. . . .'

Clementine nursed her children herself, which should have created a psychic link, but in this case it did not evolve. She was more deeply tied to her husband than to her offspring and she herself said she did not have sufficient energy to support them all. She chose to be a wonderful wife to Winston rather than a loving mother to Randolph.

On 22 June, just over three weeks after Randolph's arrival, the Coronation of King George V took place. Mrs Winston Churchill pined to attend, as was her right as wife of the Home Secretary, but how could she when the ceremony lasted the entire day and every four hours her baby would be roaring for a meal? It was the King himself who learned of her dilemma and considerately made special arrangements. His Majesty announced that Clementine would be spared the hours of waiting in Westminster Abbey because he would send a royal brougham for her at the last possible moment. She could arrive after all the duchesses had been installed to watch her monarch being crowned. Then the same brougham would return her to Eccleston Square to silence the bellows of the hungry waiting baby.

During his first months of life, baby Randolph must have sucked in the violence of politics along with his mother's milk. By September he had been weaned, and Winston and Clementine together paid a visit to Prime Minister Asquith. Here it was that Winston learned he was to leave the Home Office and take up a post he had long coveted – that of First Lord of the Admiralty. This would entail leaving Eccleston Square and moving to the First Lord's residence in London, Admiralty House, which overlooked the Horse Guards Parade and backed on to Whitehall.

When he was five months old the 'Chumbolly' was christened Randolph Frederick Edward in the crypt of the House of Commons. Winston idolized the memory of his own father, Lord Randolph Churchill. The other names were those of the godfathers, Lord Birkenhead (the redoubtable F. E.) and Sir Edward Grey, the Foreign Secretary; Winston's cousin Lady Ridley stood as godmother.

Randolph's first memories were of Admiralty House and of his own importance as the son of an eminent politician. Diana, his sister, was two years older, but she did not possess his overbearing masterful ways nor his charm or beauty. For Randolph *was* beautiful. Very early on that showed. His grandmother Jennie's superb features were repeated in a chubby mask: her eyes had been dark grey and his were blue but, all the same, had he been a girl Randolph would, like her, have been dubbed a beauty – the kind that caused a ballroom to fall silent in admiration.

In the summer of 1912 Clementine wrote to Winston, 'You would have laughed if you had seen Randolph eating his pap for supper. If ever the spoon contained too much milk and not enough solid he roared with rage!' The facility to roar would never leave him.

Randolph has recorded that he could remember being taken with his sister Diana in a double pram for their daily outing in Green Park where they would enjoy the excitement of being followed by detectives who feared the attacks made by Suffragettes. Wearing white fur coats according to the taste of the day, the children could be considered adorable by those who did not think their outfits 'a bit much'.

When war came in August 1914, Randolph was three years old. He could hardly understand the excitement of his father, whose post became of yet more importance, but he must have heard the servants talking about Winston's dash to Antwerp where he had stiffened Belgian resistance before asking the Cabinet to free him from ministerial chores so that he could assume military command. On 7 October, in Admiralty House, Randolph's mother gave birth to her third child – a baby girl named Sarah. That night his father returned to London, and Antwerp fell.

Then came the tragedy of the Dardanelles – not only a tragedy for Winston Churchill, but also a tragedy for the whole human race. The conception of the landings was brilliant: Winston thought that striking at the heart of the Turkish Empire by sea and creating a direct link with Russia would bring about an early end to the war and millions of lives would be saved. Two bites were made at the orange. The British fleet which tried to force the Narrows didn't do so because of the Admiral's pusillanimity. Then came the costly landings and the horrible defeat because Kitchener thought his attack on Turkey was a side show. The Dardanelles must have cast a shadow over Randolph as a small child. He could not have helped but feel the shadow of failure.

Bitterness permeated the Churchill household as Winston was replaced as First Lord and the family had to move out of Admiralty House. Because Eccleston Square had been let, they went to live at 41 Cromwell Road in South Kensington, where Winston could strive to recuperate from the blow. They shared the house with his brother Jack, a serving officer in the army, and Jack's wife Lady Gwendoline Churchill. These were dark days. Many years later when Clementine Churchill was asked by the author (thinking actually of the Second World War) what event had most grievously shaken Winston, her whole face changed. 'The Dardanelles was the worst time,' she said. 'I thought it would break Winston's heart.'

3

Amidst all the grown-up talk of disaster and betrayal Randolph grew into a strong little boy. He knew the fun of visiting the Natural History Museum across the way in Cromwell Road and with his elder sister Diana he would skate and slide around the dinosaur skeletons. Sometimes there came the excitement of Zeppelin raids – frightening certainly, but fun also, for they necessitated the children's being carried down to the cellars of No. 41. There they saw the grown-ups quaffing champagne – as was *de rigueur* in that other war. A series of stony-hearted nurses and nursery governesses were employed, but Diana suffered more from their ministrations than Randolph. She said that one of them locked her in a cupboard all day as a punishment.

Randolph remembered his father going off to the war as a major, an operation which for a time ameliorated Winston's heartbreak over the Dardanelles. Lord Beaverbrook, who visited 41 Cromwell Road on the eve of his departure, has succinctly described the scene at which wife and mother assisted. 'Upstairs, Lady Randolph was in a state of despair at the idea of her brilliant son being relegated to the trenches. . . . Mrs Churchill seemed to be the only person who remained calm, collected and efficient.'

It was many years later that Randolph found the letter written by his father in the trenches, 'If anything should happen to me Randolph will carry on the torch.' This was the little boy who at a birthday party where a band and a musician had to entertain the children, shouted fearlessly, 'Man stop! Band play!'

Social life continued. On 1 December 1915 Prime Minister Asquith's daughter Violet married Maurice Bonham-Carter and Randolph, decked out in a little Russian velvet suit with fur, won much attention as one of the pages. And a few days later with his sister Diana and his cousin Johnny Churchill he carried the train for his aunt Nellie (Clementine's sister) when she married Bertram Romilly.

These were Randolph's earliest memories: petting by women, the knowledge he was a great man's son, and the further knowledge that his father had been wrongly treated.

The terrible losses continued. Later, in July 1916, Winston wrote to Bonar Law, 'I cannot help feeling selfishly glad that my little boy is so young.' When Major Winston Churchill, deciding he could do more good in Parliament than as a battalion commander, returned to London, Randolph saw that his mother – who had always remained dry-eyed in front of her children – was unable to hide her joy. Yet Clementine feared the ineptitude of Winston's move.

4

When Lloyd George replaced Asquith as Prime Minister he some-what belatedly installed Winston as Minister of Munitions, and for the last months of the First World War, Randolph lived between Eccleston Square (once more their home) and a country house at East Grinstead whence the children could drive to the village school by trap, and where three German POWs worked in the garden. On 15 November 1918, four days after the Armistice had been signed, Randolph's mother bore her fourth baby, a red-haired girl called Mari-gold. Randolph looked at her with interest – he was by now seven and a half, and terribly aware that something was lacking in his own life. He didn't know what it was but he felt curiously rejected. His father looked at him with affection when he thought of looking at all, but surprise at his own beauty was not what Randolph craved. It was the doting love of a mother.

— 2 —

Amidst the political turmoil of the following years, during which his father was for a time Secretary of State for War, Randolph reached the age when it is usual for a boy of the English upper classes to be sent away to boarding school. This extraordinary habit, unique to the British nation, affected Randolph rather later than most. He was nearly nine when he went to Sandroyd near Cobham in Surrey. The horrifying experiences which had almost broken his spirit at his own 'prep school' made Winston particularly careful about sending his son away. But not careful enough. Randolph has without inhibition written in his memoirs *Twenty-One Years* of the young assistant master who 'made some pretext for me to go and see him in his room. When I got there he made me sit down beside him on the bed. He undid his trousers and caused me to manipulate his organ. I was much surprised but stood in awe of him and cannot pretend that I found it particularly disgusting, or even that I had any sense of guilt until the housemaid came in without knocking to deliver his laundry.' Only then, when the master turned scarlet and jumped to his feet hastily buttoning his trousers, did Randolph realize he was doing something wrong. Randolph states that he was, at the age of ten, unscarred by this episode. When the junior master told him to answer questions as to why he had gone into that bedroom with an invented story about a lost cricket ball, Randolph innocently did so.

Other boys, younger or perhaps older and more knowledgeable, might have been deeply distressed by such an opening into sexual experience. But in England the gravitation of perverts towards vulnerable prep school boys was not discussed openly. The likelihood of unpleasant episodes was brushed aside. That young masters with little money must somehow find an outlet for their sexual urges was never considered. Winston himself had suffered at the hands of a sadist. He had in fact been younger than Randolph when his nurse Mrs Everest called the attention of his indignant American mother to the marks of beatings on his body.

But Randolph, unhurt emotionally as he swears he was, related the story during his next holidays to his sister Diana, and their nanny overheard. She told Randolph's mother who told his father and Winston hastened into the fray. Randolph relates the story:

I remember very well how my father sent for me one morning when he was still lying in bed and having his breakfast and asked me about the truth of the matter.

I told him the truth as I have always done. I don't think I have ever seen him so angry before or since. He leapt out of bed, ordered his car and drove all across country – the round trip must have been well over two hundred miles.

When Winston returned late that night having discovered that the master concerned had been sacked he simply said to his son, 'Never let anyone do that to you again.' But what happened then? Did the young master go on to some other school?

1921 was a year of mourning for the family. In April, three-year-old Marigold died. Randolph and the girls were holidaying in Scotland when the news came. Their parents were grief stricken and the children accepted her death with awe. Then in June Randolph heard that his grandmother, who had been the fabulous beauty Jennie, had died in London.

During the summer of 1922, when his father was Colonial Secretary, Randolph and his sister Diana went roller-skating one afternoon in Holland Park. They returned to find their house surrounded by policemen. Sir Henry Wilson had been shot dead on his own door-step when returning in uniform from the unveiling of a memorial to Britain's war dead. The attics, cupboards and cellars of Winston Churchill's house were being searched for assassins and for a long time Winston had to take precautions against possible assassination attempts by the IRA.

In September 1922, another baby arrived. Mary, the last child that Clementine bore to Winston, would prove to be the joy of their life, but Randolph, although still a shrimp of a boy, was already eleven years old, and he would never know his youngest sister intimately.

7

When Randolph was twelve he and his sister Diana went to stay with their Redesdale cousins at Asthall Manor. There it was that Randolph first fell in love – as only small boys can – with the pristine beauty of Diana Mitford (who was just a year older than him). This love would last through all the tribulations of their lives. Tom Mitford who was two years older than Randolph became his best friend and that also was a relationship that only death would sever.*

There was much bickering with Randolph's sister, Diana. In the heartless way that children have, the three of them would run off into the garden and hide from her. 'Chatterbox' they called the redhead because she never stopped talking. It would be many years before they realized this garrulousness was the result of deep shyness.

After that first visit to Asthall the Mitfords often came to Chartwell, and Diana Churchill was often left as odd-man-out while Randolph and Tom and Diana Mitford developed a close friendship. The fact that Diana Mitford resembled his mother added to the boy's yearning. She had the same beautiful features, and huge blue eyes that looked as if they had been carved out of sapphires. Whenever she turned her head it was a joy.

As the time approached, Winston gave his son the choice of going to Eton or Harrow. Eton appeared to have fewer rules so Randolph chose to go there. After his years at prep school Randolph revelled in the liberty allowed at Eton, though during the next four years he did not always find the college to his taste. October 1924 was the date of Randolph's arrival at Eton and soon afterwards his father became Chancellor of the Exchequer. Randolph had been taught to revere political posts, and it was a nasty blow to him when the captain of his house called upon him and said sarcastically how proud he was to associate with the son of the Chancellor of the Exchequer. However, during the Easter holidays he and Diana sat fascinated in the Strangers' Gallery with their mother while Winston made his Budget speech.

Randolph's reports from his tutor, much quoted in his memoirs, can be summarized in the judgement of the Headmaster, 'His real trouble comes in his facility. He finds it a great deal too easy to do moderately well and he is developing too early the journalist's ability to "work up" a little information or a solitary idea. . . .' That 'facility' would indeed prove a great hindrance, and his housemaster groaned at

*Lady Mosley, as Diana Mitford would become, writes to me today that 'However irritating Randolph could be Tom always loved him and so did I.'

Randolph's inability to admit he was ever in the wrong. And with a certain resentment Randolph would recount how after he had proved himself innocent of some crime the captain of games said determinedly, 'Well, you've been pretty bloody all around. Bend over. It's going to be six up.'

Randolph had not been long at Eton when he wrote a thesis on *Women and their Place in the World* which he considered worthy of a leather binding (hence its survival). This thesis begins, 'In dealing with a subject so large and so pressing as to the correct position that should be occupied by women in the world today, it does not seem to us a profitable expedient to trace their history from the neolithic age. . . .' Schoolboy Randolph went on to deplore the education of women as it made them 'dull and uninteresting' and he hoped the vote would not be extended to them because 'women are less able than men. . .' and 'the most able women are the least likeable'. Echoing his father's opinion of Lady Astor, he went on, 'Although only one per cent of the House of Commons consists of females it is a woman who is by far the most unpopular member.' Randolph ended his thesis by quoting the resolution made in 1780: 'The influence of women has increased, is increasing and ought to be diminished.'

Evidently his master approved of this diatribe for at the end he wrote in pencil, 'The whole form and arrangement of this is excellent; the treatment is thorough; and with most of the views expressed it is impossible not to sympathize.'

It was one of Randolph's Eton friends, Alan Pryce-Jones (later the eminent author), who induced him to earn his first fiver for writing an article. The boys thought this a terrific sum and masters only lifted their eyebrows in amusement. Randolph could not resist swaggering as he realized that money could be made by a lively pen. The easy success was dangerous.

At Chartwell during the holidays Diana Mosley describes Winston's words as relayed by Randolph. 'Papa says he won't be bunged up with brats,' but after the Christmas of 1926 Winston travelled over to Paris with both Diana and Randolph to leave her in school there. They had a rough crossing and Randolph was pathetically seasick. 'Poor little boy,' murmured Winston, and his sympathy was real.

But it was not always 'poor little boy', for the diary of Thomas Jones records how at the age of fifteen Randolph was allowed to stay up for dinner at Chartwell and when the ladies left the table he would remain, 'his father frequently deferring to his opinion on some phase

9

or other of the coal crisis' (which was then hypnotizing Parliament). Thomas Jones thought the boy extremely intelligent and hoped he learned something of the miners' troubles.

But how bad for Randolph those late hours must have been – and how dangerous his father's approbation was too. On occasion Winston's friend Professor Lindemann, the scientist, would take Randolph to dine at Oxford where the schoolboy found himself sitting at Christ Church high table. This sort of outing could not be good medicine for so young and vulnerable a lad. Worse still, it encouraged Randolph to talk arrogantly to his elders and betters. The fact that Professor Lindemann always sent him back to Eton with a large box of chocolates did not help.

After Christmas 1926, Sir Roger Keyes, Commander-in-Chief of the Mediterranean fleet, invited Winston, then Chancellor of the Exchequer, to view the fleet. In replying, Winston asked if he might bring along his brother Jack and his fifteen-year-old son Randolph. (He did not add that he had been scolding his son for bad work at Eton.) Winston's letter to Keyes reads, 'If we went to sea I daresay Randolph could be accommodated in the Gunroom. He is fifteen and your Middies are very little older. I should very much like him to see the Fleet, as early impressions are so important.' Keyes replied, 'Randolph can of course go and play about with the midshipmen – we've got a very good lot.'*

Having voiced his indignation at being forbidden to accompany his father and Uncle Jack when they visited the improper pictures at Pompeii, Randolph insisted they should not miss the steamer which was to convey them from Naples to the Straits of Messina. They just caught the boat and next morning they were picked up by a destroyer which took them to Malta in four hours. A few days later, after Winston, now aged fifty-one, had played the last game of polo of his life, the party set sail on the flagship of Admiral Keyes, HMS *Warspite*, to watch the Mediterranean fleet at exercise. Winston was very happy; this was where he felt he belonged. Although Chancellor of the Exchequer, he really cared about ships and unheroic money matters bored him. He and Jack enjoyed the Admiral's table and Randolph certainly made his mark with the midshipmen who, slightly older than him, were not accustomed to being talked down to.

Two years later, when Michael Crichton joined the Gunroom,

Keyes Papers, ed. Professor Paul Malpern, Vol. II, 1919–38, Navy Records Society.

Randolph's name still came up and eyes would roll to the ceiling. 'Oh God! Randy!' the midshipmen who had entertained Randolph would groan. And gradually he became a legend. None of these well-brought-up naval-officers-to-be had ever seen anything like him and they never forgot the experience.

As Chancellor of the Exchequer, Winston worried about the expense of shipping his party to Brindisi via the Corinth Canal. Admiral Roger Keyes certainly felt he could stretch a point here.

From Athens the Churchill party went to Rome and there Winston met not only the Pope but also Mussolini who rather fascinated him.

Going down to dinner from the age of fifteen was bad enough, but Winston could not resist showing off his clever talkative son. Randolph's housemaster hit the nail on the head when he wrote of 'too little concentration and too much chatter'. And of course Randolph learned to scorn formal education when he could learn politics and history from such men as F. E. Smith, Lloyd George and Lord Beaverbrook. They taught him the niceties of the English language and naturally the boy who was plunged into such brilliance grew aware that good dinner table conversation did not resemble that of the schoolroom.

When Randolph was about seventeen Winston took him to stay with Bendor (Duke of Westminster) at Mimizan, near Biarritz, where the Duke had a shooting box. On their way back to Paris by train Winston and Randolph, together with the Duke and his Duchess, Loelia, all had a meal in the first-class restaurant. Loelia has described her horror at the scene which then occurred between father and son. Having wined and dined extremely well, Randolph – the schoolboy turning now into a young man – ordered another brandy for himself. Winston said, 'No. You have had enough.' When the glass of brandy was brought by a dithering attendant Winston leaned across the table to confiscate it. Randolph would not let go and finally spilled the contents up his father's sleeve. Bendor watched with raised eyebrows and Loelia's face showed her shock, but Winston just thought the episode funny. Had he not been so great a man one would have had to blame him for ruining his son. But as things were to turn out history would only be able to sigh that if young Randolph was to be hurled on to the bonfire at least England would be led to victory.

One morning when Randolph was about to return to Eton, Winston took him for a stroll in the garden at Chartwell. As they wandered along he said wistfully, 'Do you know dear boy, I think we have had more talk in these summer holidays than I had with my father in all his life.'

Winston had never got over Lord Randolph's disregard for him. He was an emotional, loving person and he could not see the harm he was doing his own son. Randolph possessed a quick retentive mind, an unusual gift of the gab and an outstanding memory. It was natural that any boy should show off his talents whenever he got the chance, and his father was to blame for not noticing or not caring about the rage his son caused older men. And because his mother did not also admire his every action Randolph thought she must be in the wrong.

No one ever found Randolph more abominable than during the first half hour of acquaintance. But those who did not get angry had to like him even if they were annoyed with themselves at the time. What no one really appreciated was Randolph's craving for affection. His mother was incapable of giving it, and his father was so busy and so famous. It was an awkward situation to be born into and he had to learn early to hide his sensitivity, not realizing either that others could be as sensitive as he.

Chartwell was only an hour's drive from London, and all the children loved it, though they knew their mother worried at the running expenses. The eighty acres around the house gave the impression that Chartwell lay deep in the country, and when Randolph came home for the holidays he was able to run wild all day before coming down to dinner and interrupting older guests. When a tutor was engaged to coach Randolph in the subjects he was bad at, Randolph knew that all he had to do to escape was to run away and hide. Papa would laugh and pet him when he emerged. The tutor's hang-dog expression and his mother's anger made it all the funnier.

Brendan Bracken, a rising MP who had the most extraordinary hold on Winston, was always at Chartwell. This curious red-haired Irishman had become dear to Winston and had attached himself to the Churchill household for some years. Randolph had a painful memory of waiting in vain all one afternoon for Bracken to take him to the zoo – he never went, for Bracken had clean forgotten his promise. But now Randolph took no notice of him, though he liked to hear his mother scolding Winston because Bracken made life so difficult for the housemaids at Chartwell; when they descended in the early morning to plump up the cushions they would often find him still asleep on the sofa.

Diana Mitford was only a year older than Randolph, but girls grow up faster than boys and in those days the age-divide was real and chilling. There was no way of getting round this. Tom Mitford, her brother, had indeed remained Randolph's best friend, but Tom was two years older and he left Eton boasting of the marriage proposals his lovely sister was receiving. Growing up was not easy in such circumstances. To her eldest daughter Diana Clementine was downright unkind and I remember them visiting Castle Leslie together after Diana's first season. Diana sobbed to me, 'I am so unhappy and Mummy is horrid to me because I haven't been a success. I have sandy eyelashes.' This was true; in those days a debutante could not simply reach for the mascara. It was all that Clementine could do to look after her volatile Winston; the children had to lump it if they felt insecure.

Meanwhile Winston continued to revel in his son's exceptional talents. To Clementine he wrote during the boy's last year at Eton, 'The logical strength of his mind, the courage of his thought and the brutal sometimes repulsive force of his rejoinders impressed me very forcibly. He is far more advanced than I was at his age, and quite out of the common – for good or ill.'

Clementine did her best to curb her son's incessant flow of talk, but she knew that if she made a rule which Randolph broke she could never apply any sanction. He had only to run to Papa to be forgiven. And as Winston never made him apologize to older people, Randolph started to make a habit of being rude; he thought it clever.

One subject on which Winston does appear to have admonished Randolph was his handwriting, which he found indecipherable. He even suggested that Randolph attend special calligraphy classes.

During Randolph's last year at Eton a young don from Oxford, Frank Pakenham, took the place of Dr Allington, the Headmaster, for a few weeks. On arrival he found that it was to be his job to coach the senior boys and, having set them to writing Latin verse, he then thought of asking them to choose and recite the most splendid piece of English prose they knew. Among the boys who held forth with pleasure was one of unusual beauty who chose a sublime paragraph in Macaulay's essay on Warren Hastings' trial. Frank Pakenham could not but be impressed by the extraordinary memory and power of declamation shown by this youth, and on asking his name he discovered that it was Randolph Churchill – the son of the redoubtable Winston. The phenomenon of Randolph – who was already disliked because of his looks, his talent and his aggressiveness – had made a mark.

In August 1928, the proud papa drove off to see his son at the Eton Officer's Training Camp but to Winston's disappointment Randolph had been confined to camp for some disobedience and could not dine with him. It was enough to put anyone off the Army.

But at that juncture Randolph took it for granted that he would be the youngest Prime Minister ever. It seemed only too easy for a Churchill with his talent.

— 3 —

At Christmas 1928, Randolph left Eton and entered Oxford. He was young to go to a university but when Professor Lindemann told him that a place at Christ Church had become unexpectedly vacant Randolph leapt at the chance of shedding forever the trammels of a schoolboy. It was not the right term to enter a university (Winston had expected him to go two terms later) but having passed the entrance examination Randolph insisted. Sir Roy Harrod, who was to be his tutor, has deplored the Churchillian habit of just arriving and horning in, to the detriment of other freshmen who had entered in October and were already obeying the rules. Randolph did not care about rules, but as Sir Roy soon noticed he had a curious effect on other people. He intensified their *joie de vivre*.

At Oxford, Randolph found several older friends waiting for him to join their ranks – they all considered themselves to be 'the smart bunch'. No pond could have been worse for Randolph to jump into. Freddie, the son of Randolph's godfather Lord Birkenhead, and Basil, then Earl of Ava, and John Betjeman, who was to become Poet Laureate, and Christopher Sykes the future author, preened themselves unduly. They and Randolph's artist cousin Johnny Churchill soon took to giving return luncheons for clever, witty older dons. The young men all learned to imbibe far too much port. They were never abashed and when together they thought themselves more brilliant than they actually were. Randolph had always been cocky, now he became insupportable, his faults glaringly obvious. Yet it was still difficult to dislike him.

Soon after he went to Oxford he had to come to London to attend the wedding of his beautiful Diana Mitford to Bryan Guinness, the eldest son of Lord Moyne, and he accepted that he had lost his first love.

However, Randolph found solace in the company of his men friends and it was at this time that Frank Pakenham, who had been forced to recognize the extraordinary brilliance of this boy at Eton, became a lifelong friend. Once Randolph tried to explain himself and Pakenham found his words strangely telling. Decrying his own natural eloquence he said, 'I have an overwhelming urge to express myself, but the tragedy is that I have nothing to express. I am an explosion that leaves the house still standing.'

At this time the *Strand Magazine* asked him to contribute an article on famous fathers, but this Winston forbade. However, Randolph often attended the House of Commons to hear his father's speeches. Randolph considered himself no mean orator; he spoke well in debate and more easily than his father even if he missed the human touch which made Winston's speeches unique. No man could hit the nail on the head like Winston Churchill.

In May 1929, there was a general election and the Conservative Government fell. Winston ceased to be Chancellor of the Exchequer. It had been during his time in No. 11 Downing Street that Lady Houston – the eccentric millionairess – had burst into his office and offered a cheque for a million pounds to be paid into the national coffers because, being a Jersey resident, her husband had not had to pay death duties. Winston had chortled and accepted her cheque for England.

No longer being a minister, Churchill decided to go on a lecture tour of Canada and the United States with his brother Jack Churchill, whom he always found a delightful companion. Randolph and Jack's son Johnny clamoured to come also and since the tour would fall in the summer holidays Winston consented. He thought it would be a wonderful eye-opener for his son and nephew to see America while they were young.

The party departed from Waterloo on 3 August and during the Atlantic crossing Winston strove to impose discipline, making his son go to bed reasonably early. Randolph kept a diary which he refused to show his father but pretty girls were hopefully noted in it and Randolph's cheeky remarks were never forgotten by the girls aboard.

From Quebec they entrained in the special carriage which was to carry the four of them across Canada for three weeks and Randolph's diary describes his father's indignation that so many beautiful trees should be cut down to make pulp for the Rothermere newspapers!

Arriving at Toronto the eighteen-year-old Randolph, wearing an outsize carnation, was rude to a reporter and the press made much of his discourtesy – Randolph's diary noted, 'Papa was very angry with me.'

It was after seeing the Calgary oilfields that Randolph happened to remark that oil magnates 'pigged up' the whole valley and then didn't know how to spend their money; but Winston took the millionaires' side with one of his marvellous phrases, 'Cultivated people are merely the glittering scum which floats upon the deep river of production.' 'Damn good,' commented Randolph's diary.

The end of August found them all riding over a glacier. Winston, superbly attired in a ten-gallon hat and khaki jodhpurs on a white horse, was leading the party. He wrote jubilantly to Clemmie that Randolph was turning into a very strong man, apart from bulging neck and thighs. He added that Randolph spoke so well without notes, 'dexterous, cool and finished'.

After the voyage to Victoria, Winston and his party were piped in to dinner by a piper in highland dress and, said Winston, 'much petted by all parties'. Winston then addressed an enormous luncheon of some 700 people for an hour. After this Randolph tasted his own first triumph in oratory. It occurred after a long dull speech of thanks by an elderly cleric. Sensing the atmosphere of increasing boredom Randolph caught his father's eye and got up to reply. The scene is poignantly evoked by Winston himself. 'He, in a brief admirably turned debating speech of five minutes completely turned the tables upon the Dean, to the delight of the audience and also to their amazement. His performance not only showed his curious facility for spinning words but gave proof of great poise, judgement and tact. He knew exactly how far to go and how to win and help the sympathies of this audience. I could not have done it so neatly myself.' Naturally Randolph was delighted with himself.

When the lecture tour was over the party went southward into California and after staying in San Francisco and Santa Barbara the Churchills reached San Simeon, the astonishing luxury ranch belonging to William Randolph Hearst.

Here it was that Randolph encountered a lovely lady of twenty-three named Anita. Laughingly he told me this story against himself because I was the only other 'Anita' he knew. This Anita met him one evening and asked him to accompany her riding early the following morning. Randolph arose after a few hours' sleep and, booted and spurred, he paced the terrace waiting for her to arrive. She never turned up but a telegram came asking him to dinner early that night. Hoping for the ultimate favours, he reached Anita's house before six only to hear the voices of a hundred people. Far from intending to indulge romantically, Anita had thrown a cocktail party for people anxious to meet Winston Churchill's son and, even worse, had telegraphed her husband to return for it.

However, romantic compensation awaited. Tilly Losch, the Hungarian dancer, happened to be staying at San Simeon and with her – a lovely green-eyed faun – he trod paths which were much talked of but not actually explained in detail at Eton.

Back in New York, Randolph made another of his many bloomers. John Hare, who had been in the same class at Eton, had gone into an American merchant bank instead of accompanying his cronies to Oxford. To his surprise Randolph telephoned him from the Waldorf Astoria asking him to come round for a drink. John Hare found his old school chum with a glass of champagne in his hand and a large cigar in his mouth. 'What a fool you have been to select such a dreary career,' he said. The young banker was not amused. 'He was arrogant, self-assured and most eloquent,' said John Hare. This was the effect that Randolph so often had on his contemporaries.

Since the Oxford term was soon due to begin, it was necessary for Randolph and his cousin Johnny Churchill to travel back to England ahead of their fathers. Winston had been worried by Randolph's chronic cough and snuffling so he insisted the boy see an American specialist before he left. The specialist groaned at the state of Randolph's sinuses and tonsils but dictated a cure.

Lord Birkenhead (F. E.) happened to be on the same boat as Randolph, and every night he asked his godson to dine with him. This also was not good for an eighteen-year-old. Randolph has described the set up, 'My father, who was F. E.'s greatest friend, had brought me up on all the famous anecdotes illustrating F. E.'s wit, brilliance and arrogance. Without F. E.'s learning or his majestic command of language, I sought to emulate his style of polished repartee. It didn't work in my case.'*

But, alas, Randolph was more successful in emulating F. E. – who

*Twenty-One Years by Randolph Churchill.

was shortly to die of drink — in something else: the pleasures of the decanter were yet more deeply instilled on that trip, and the sight of a mere boy with a large cigar in his mouth holding forth in the vein of older, cleverer men maddened onlookers. By the time the *Berengaria* docked at Southampton much harm had been done both to Randolph and to his reputation.

Worse was to follow. Randolph did not finish his time at Oxford or take a degree. He had only completed four terms there when an American lecture bureau offered him $12,000 to tour that country. As Winston was rather broke and found it an effort to make any allowance to his son, this offer seemed extremely inviting. 'I thought it more blessed to teach than be taught,' said Randolph, and the University of Oxford saw him no more.

Sir Roy Harrod was horrified that Randolph had thrown up his education in order to jaunt around America lecturing. What could a boy of nineteen know? He could only echo the views of the men who sat at his father's table — the people who came to hear him would simply be hearing what Winston and his friends thought.

As Randolph's tutor, Harrod accompanied Professor Lindemann to Chartwell and there he heard Winston 'deploy all the resources of the English language in describing what a university could contribute to a man's life'. Harrod, Lindemann and Randolph all listened to him standing in front of his fireplace letting his splendid rhetoric flow as to why he would willingly continue Randolph's allowance rather than allow him to become a super-tax payer at nineteen. 'Phrase followed phrase and sentence followed sentence in glowing and ascending Churchillian oratory . . . he also said very nicely and modestly, with a look of appeal at Randolph, how much he had felt the lack, in political controversy, of the weapons which a university might have given him.' When Randolph left the room Winston turned to Harrod and said, 'Well, we have got down to brass tacks.'

His words, however, achieved nothing. Randolph went off to America delighted with himself.

At this stage Winston did indeed become troubled about more than Randolph's sinuses, but it was too late. The harm had been done and he would never see that in a way he was guilty of contributing to it.

It was on this first American lecture tour that Randolph fell seriously in love. The girl he asked to marry him was half-Irish, half-American and she admitted to being fascinated by Randolph, but something about him caused her to hesitate. Kay Halle of Cleveland, Ohio, was blonde, knowledgeable and a year older than Randolph. She could not but be interested in this wonderful-looking, if over-exuberant son of the famous Winston Churchill.

Winston had in fact implored Randolph to prepare lectures carefully and to build up a reserve fund of talks in case his platform commitments should be expanded. Needless to say Randolph had disdained his father's advice, feeling he did not need to study any subject, he always *knew* how to put the world to rights and audiences would lap it up. After an appalling opening fiasco at Princeton University, when he failed to time himself and caused the celebrated French author M. André Maurois to skimp on *his* talk, Kay Halle took Randolph in hand. Apart from keeping a big watch on the table before him she made him attend to his diction. 'For heavens sake speak slowly, people come to hear *you* talk. It matters much that they should do so. No one really cares what you say but they do care about the *way* you say it! And above all they want to be able to *hear*.'

This was a new angle for the would-be orator. It made sense. Randolph mulled over Kay's advice and spent a week trying to teach himself to speak slowly. He took seriously the idea that each word must be audible; he practised restraining his emotions and enunciating his vowels.

Once he had got the hang of it Randolph continued his lecture tour in fine fettle, all the while pleading with Kay to marry him. But she could not bring herself to assent – she was entranced by him, but she was very American and very independent. She could not see herself as another Clemmie, ready to wear herself out looking after a demanding, exciting husband. She would be Randolph's greatest friend for life, but to tie herself to this wilful, sparkling, undisciplined boy – that she feared to do.

Randolph stormed on across America and became known as 'England's ambassador of ill will'. He enraged the press and kept friends agog for seven months. He spoke well, and on the whole Americans were ready to be told why the British Empire was so nice, and why Randolph chose to be a Conservative. The subjects might be heavy but his spare time grew lighter and lighter. In February 1931 his mother set sail across the Atlantic and Randolph came to New York to meet her ship. Feverishly he related his great love for Kay Halle and, because she sympathized with his passion, mother and son grew closer than they had ever been.

For several weeks Clementine travelled with her son, and in Cleveland she met and was charmed by the Halle family. Clementine felt that twenty was too young for a man to marry, especially one as tempestuous as Randolph, but if he was really set on it, and if Kay could take on so strenuous a role, she would give her blessing. The American press reported that Mrs Churchill had come to America solely to put a stop to the affair but in fact it was Kay herself who refused to allow an engagement to be announced.

Sam Halle, Kay's father, gave a luncheon for Winston at the Midday Club and Randolph sat silent while his father held forth. He sat silent because Kay was listening and he did not want to spoil her concentration. But it took a forceful young woman to make him hold his tongue.

On his return to London, Randolph did not go back to Oxford but instead began to write articles for the newspapers of Lord Beaverbrook and Lord Rothermere, while at the same time earning a handsome salary editing a magazine for ICI. Thus it was that he became a wealthy man about town while still under age.

Betty Shaughnessy, whose stepfather, Sir Piers Legh, was the Prince of Wales' equerry, told me a warming story about Randolph. She had gone out to dinner before a big dance and she found herself seated, a very shy debutante, between Randolph and his friend Tom Mitford. Tom turned to her, 'Are you a deb?' he asked. 'Well, debs should not wear long earrings. You'd better take them off.' Poor Betty, who had done her best to make herself look sophisticated, quailed at this reprimand from a young man; but Randolph came to her rescue. 'Don't pay any attention to *him*,' he said. 'I was at school with him and he just can't think of anything nice to say. *I* think you look smashing.'

For a time Randolph and Tom argued across her. Should a girl of seventeen be permitted earrings or not? In the end Randolph won and on hearing that Betty was going to America he said, 'Give me your menu and I'll write on it to some friends I have there.' Betty felt her self-confidence returning and she treasured that menu card for a long time. 'Give this little girl a great hand,' he wrote. 'She needs looking after.'*

It was at this time that I grew to know Randolph well. My father occasionally took me to Chartwell and whenever we went to spend a

---

*Within a year Betty married Lord Grenfell. Later, she became well known as Mrs Berkeley Stafford.

Sunday Randolph seemed to be there too. I was immensely impressed by his garrulity and being myself somewhat juvenile and always impecunious I thought it admirable to be rewarded by him with half-crowns for telling fibs on the telephone as if I were a secretary. In fact I became what he had once been to Birkenhead's son, a fag.

The person who really enthralled me and who was exactly my age was his sister Sarah. Unfortunately we both of us found the eminent statesmen who visited Winston Churchill's table boring and, instead of listening enraptured as we should have done and writing down every prescient word in our diaries, all we did was titter in corners and plan to run away to the stage. What a waste of golden opportunities!

Once Randolph, who must have been about twenty at the time, brought a beautiful Australian debutante to Blenheim Palace with every hope of doing his worst. Patricia Richards came to stay with the Duke and Duchess of Marlborough expecting a nice weekend party. And she found the only guests were me, my father and Randolph! She was seventeen and in those days well brought-up young gentlemen did not contemplate – or were not supposed to contemplate – the idea of impinging on a young girl's virtue.

Patricia's face fell a mile when she realized the small size of the house party and I recalled my mother's description (she had often come to Blenheim Palace with my father) of girls she had known who were so bored (and so cold) that they walked to Woodstock and telegraphed friends to telegraph *them* to return home urgently!

Anyway poor beautiful Patricia who had been invited by Randolph for a jolly weekend realized immediately the extent to which she had been conned. I was not 'out' yet. I had just returned from what was, in those days, innocently termed 'finishing off' in Paris, but it was not difficult to ascertain what Randolph was up to. My father mouched off to look up letters and papers with the Duke, who was one of his oldest friends, or happily exchanged anecdotes with the eccentric Duchess. I was fascinated by Gladys Marlborough, who hated her husband and insulted him throughout every meal. She kept a vast array of Blenheim spaniels who accompanied her everywhere, their toenails tinging on the parquet floors of the vast palace.

Randolph inveigled Patricia into a walk in the rain before tea, and I well remember the Duchess asking where she was and the Duke answering (shockingly, considering I was *une jeune fille*), 'He's trying to seduce Miss Richards among the wet cabbages.' When Randolph and Patricia finally appeared for tea I noticed that she was flushed with temper as well as drenched by rain.

We went upstairs to dress for dinner together and after dolling up in the white, bare-armed evening dresses then deemed suitable for young girls I realized how thankful Patricia was to have me as her companion. We were alone in adjoining bedrooms in a wing of Blenheim Palace. The Duchess lived downstairs on her own and, unlike every other country house I ever stayed in, Blenheim offered no protective fortress in which maidens could be lodged.

During a long drawn-out tepid dinner carried from distant kitchens and served by footmen wearing damp white gloves, we girls became dazed by the wicked witticisms of the Duchess and the horror-stricken scowling of her spouse. My father listened to them both with amusement. At 11 p.m. Patricia and I went to bed. The idea of any man actually coming to one's door was too shocking to discuss but I could tell that Patricia was nervous. Randolph was of course lodged far away in the bachelors' wing but Patricia had to rely on *me*, a perfectly idiotic young girl, as chaperone.

We had cold-creamed our faces and actually donned the beribboned slumber helmets which were used at that time to keep waved hair in place, when the unbelievable occurred – a tap sounded on Patricia's door. She whispered, 'Don't leave me whatever happens.' So I remained primly under the eiderdown on her bed until the tapping became so vibrant that I had to get up and open the door. There stood Randolph looking not at all embarrassed. He knew me well enough through Chartwell visits to whisper, 'Clear off. Here's ten bob.' This was more than he usually paid me to do his chores, but such a bribe proved insufficient in the rather special circumstances – (maybe I would have heroically refused it even if he'd offered more!). In any case I ignored the proffered banknote and jumped back into Patricia's bed, snuggling with her under the eiderdown.

Randolph joined us on the bed and Patricia who had never before found herself in such a predicament kept him talking. He liked to hold forth but on this occasion he was longing for me to leave. Now that so many years have passed I remember only the gist of what he had to say, but the phrase 'when I am Prime Minister' often featured. Patricia grew desperately anxious to get rid of him and I wanted to sneak off to my own bedroom through the opened door. But having been foiled in his amorous plot Randolph held his audience captive and we *had* to listen. At long last *he* grew glassy-eyed and finally with a glower at me he departed. He had to accept there was nothing doing.

Next day Patricia Richards asked me, 'How does one get away from this dreadful place?' (She was what one called a 'top deb' and within six months she married the Earl of Jersey.) Randolph took quite a long time to forgive me for sticking it out that night.

I did not know that once in Berlin he had telephoned Philippe Barre, editor of *Le Matin*, in the early hours from some night club and asked, 'Tell me about the customs of this country. There is a lady here who interests me but her boss does not want her to leave before closing time. Do I knock him out or pay him?'

Among Randolph's London friends was Edward James, the son of the famous Mrs Willie James who had often entertained King Edward VII (Edward James told me that his mother was the King's daughter, not his mistress as a lot of people thought!). Edward James, who had enjoyed Oxford with Randolph, was himself an unusual type, arty and highly strung. For a time Edward James lent his treasure-packed house in Culross Street to Randolph and John Betjeman, who enjoyed giving dinner parties and entertaining on a grand scale there. It was in fact from this house that Betjeman launched his first book of poems (under the aegis of Edward James). What fun the three of them had when the first box of books arrived and they had to consider who might be worthy recipients of an early copy.

Eventually Edward James married Tilly Losch, the exquisite Hungarian dancer whom Randolph adored. He had enjoyed his fling with her at Hearst's Californian paradise and was somewhat indiscreet concerning the tricks she taught him!

For a time Randolph remained friends with both Edward and Tilly. He went around with them and treated their town house as his own, enjoying Edward's superb collection of modern art – especially the telephone which Salvador Dali had designed as a lobster. And he loved Tilly's broken English, encouraging her to call *All's Well That Ends Well* 'Finish Good – All Good', and to refer to moving escalators as 'rolling the stairs down'. He would not allow anyone to correct her. And her arms – those wonderful white arms with which she danced as no one had before on the English stage – those enticing arms and those great Slav eyes that turned up at the corners – who could not be entranced? Whether she stepped out of a bearskin into the darkened stage of a revue or played the nun in *The Miracle* she made your heart beat faster.

But eventually Edward James got tired of Tilly's misdemeanours and he divorced her for adultery – an unusual ploy for those days when, unless they were members of Parliament, gentlemen always took it on themselves to accept the blame. London society considered Edward's behaviour most ungallant and the case aroused much feeling – Edward's chauffeur gave nasty evidence after having peeped into Tilly's bedroom from a ladder. This was just not done, servants were supposed to be kept out of it.

Randolph took Tilly's side and attended the court proceedings, although luckily for him he was not cited as a co-respondent. Tilly lost her temper in the witness box and accused her spouse of liking boys. The judge was shocked, and King George V was sore displeased at these insinuations about a man whose mother had been high in court circles – London society disapproved of the public washing of quite such dirty linen and cut Edward James for a long time.

The night that Tilly lost her case, Randolph took her out to dinner at Quaglino's, and I happened to be there – a wide-eyed debutante entranced by the sight of my cousin comforting the tearstained indignant Tilly in public. The waiters must have enjoyed it too. Randolph looked across the restaurant at me with an expression of conceit. He was showing off and well knew that for a dismal seventeen-year-old just coming out, the situation must be absolutely riveting. Eventually Randolph slipped over to my table, 'Put this in your pipe and smoke it . . .' he said rudely and then he was back at Tilly's side while she busied herself with a powder puff, as manners permitted in those days.

Alcohol – cigars – money – *and* Tilly Losch. Being nearly three years younger I could not say a word – I just admired.

— *4* —

Bernard Baruch had once cautioned Randolph about speaking over-critically of his opponents and in 1930, Robert Bruce Lockhart wrote in his diary, 'Met Randolph Churchill, Winston's son. He is a good-looking boy with fair hair and distinguished features rather marred by a spotty complexion. Talks nineteen to the dozen and is a kind of gramophone to his father. Very egocentric and conceited and therefore very unpopular. I rather like him.'

And in November of that year Brendan Bracken wrote to Randolph, 'A brat of your age ought not to disregard the great chances given you at Oxford.' But it was much more amusing to swashbuckle around London than swat in a university. Randolph loved his father but why should he do the hard reading which Winston insisted was essential for a politician? After all, Winston hadn't gone to a university and look how he could hold the whole House of Commons in thrall.

It was actually around this time that Randolph attended a dinner after which Brendan Bracken made a speech so laudatory of President Roosevelt that Randolph shouted across the table, 'Are you going to claim him as your father *too*?' Brendan, who was a man not prone to blushing, actually turned deep red. Randolph liked Brendan less and less and, noting Brendan's new friendship with Lord Beaverbrook – who was twenty years older but shared Brendan's love of good conversation – Randolph wrote, 'Max [Lord Beaverbrook] is so tired of being flattered by paid sycophants that he's delighted to find someone like Brendan who will do it for nothing.'

Randolph first met Evelyn Waugh when they were both asked to be godfathers to the firstborn son of Diana Guinness. This love-hate relationship which started at the font would last for ever, but Randolph

26

did not notice the hate and he never tired of Evelyn's wit. He enters the famous diaries in 1930.

I can't believe all that Waugh wrote about him. I don't believe for instance that Randolph would have thrown his cocktail in the face of Wanda Baillie-Hamilton. He wasn't like that. He shouted and yelled but he didn't throw glasses at women.

Evelyn Waugh describes the incident as one that occurred on a very hot evening. He said that John Betjeman noticed liquid on Wanda's face and that she left the party in a tantrum. One can't be certain what happened and John Betjeman did not remember this occurrence. Nor need one dwell on what was at the time a famous incident when Lord Castlerosse* was so provoked by Randolph that he hurled a glass of champagne at him. It is however true that Lady Elizabeth Paget (Lady Diana Cooper's niece who became Hofmannstal) *did* empty a plate of spaghetti on Randolph's head while groaning loudly at what she called his 'ghastly good looks'.

When Randolph made a fool of himself by overspending, his father did not now hesitate to chide him. Winston's letters concerning the 'ever increasing lavish folly of your ways' hit hard, and when Papa paid up the debts incurred by Randolph's foolish betting on the election results Winston did not hesitate to write, 'If you feel yourself able to keep a magnificent motor car and chauffeur you are surely able to pay your debts of honour yourself.' Poor Randolph hung his head in shame and sold his car, but he argued that he did not just spend every penny he could lay hands on and this accusation was unfair.

When Winston went to America for a lecture tour and had a street accident in New York, my grandmother, his aunt, wrote rather a touching letter which he kept. 'Thank goodness you are all right again and with no tiresome after-effects I trust. What an escape and how lucky for you that Clementine was there. I was in hospital in Dublin myself at the same time and said many a prayer for you as I laid awake at night. Of course you have been spared to still do great things in the future and I mean to live to see it all.' She did. By the time his aunt died in Ireland in 1943, Winston had written to her, 'the tide of war has turned'.

Winston (having recovered) wired Randolph from Indianapolis again forbidding him to accept an offer to write his father's life. Winston's

*Lord Castlerosse (1891–1943), a famous gossip writer.

telegram read, 'Strongly deprecate premature attempt. Hope someday you will make thousands instead of hundreds.'

On 28 May 1932, Randolph celebrated his twenty-first birthday. Winston gave a dinner party for him at Claridge's Hotel, inviting his own famous contemporaries and their sons. Randolph's Eton friend Freddie had now become 2nd Earl of Birkenhead and he, as well as Quintin Hogg (Lord Hailsham's son), Seymour Berry (Lord Camrose's son) and Esmond Harmsworth (Lord Rothermere's son) were among the young men who made speeches which they hoped would compare well with their fathers'.

Winston listened proudly to Randolph, who spoke with assurance and polish, but his comment after the performance was 'and it is to be hoped he will accumulate a big dump of ammunition and learn to hit the target'. That was the trouble. Randolph cared so little about targets. He just wanted to fire!

— 5 —

After being taken on as a journalist by Lord Rothermere, Randolph was sent abroad to cover the election campaign of Adolf Hitler. 'The success of the Nazi party sooner or later means war,' announced his first article in the *Sunday Graphic*. But lethargy and a disinclination to face facts had descended on England. The politicians chose to do nothing. It was such a bore to arm properly . . . and so expensive.

Late that summer Winston and Hitler very nearly met in Munich. Randolph was there with his father, and he asked Putzi Hanfstaengel, an elephantine German much sought after in London society, to arrange it. Winston was agreeable but Hitler got cold feet and refused.

In March 1933 Randolph had tried to reverse the Oxford Union's verdict that the majority of its members 'would *not* fight for king and country'. He went so far as to march into the Union and tear out the page which recorded this ignominious statement from the book. Randolph failed to reverse a verdict which caused a worldwide stir and possibly encouraged Hitler in his view that whatever Germany did the English would not go to war. Meanwhile in the House of Commons Winston made a great speech about 'this abject squalid avowal'. How differently the youth of England would react when in a few years the time came to man the guns. But in 1933 people were furious with Winston when he harped on the need for readiness.

In the following year Randolph, already a well-known journalist from having interviewed the Kaiser at Doorn,* disrupted the Conservative Party by suddenly standing as an Independent Conservative in a

---

*The old emperor did not immediately realize that Randolph was a journalist, and spoke lovingly of the good Hitler was doing his nation!

by-election at Wavertree near Liverpool. The result of this ill-timed move was that he split the Tory vote and let in the Labour candidate. The Central Office never really forgave him for this misdemeanour. The Rothermere press went wild with excitement over Randolph's effort, and Lady Houston, the eccentric millionairess who desperately wanted to see a new patriotic party in Parliament, backed him financially. Her cheques made a great difference to Randolph's pocket, but her finest achievement passed into history with insufficient notice.

Lady Houston had a kind of second sight concerning the aerial warfare which lay ahead; in 1931 she had donated £100,000 to the campaign to ensure that Britain should win the Schneider Trophy outright. Because of Lucy Houston, British aircraft design excelled, and the Spitfire was developed from the seaplane which won the trophy. R. J. Mitchell, a great brain in aviation, designed the machine which was built by Rolls-Royce and piloted by a flight lieutenant of the RAF. Lady Houston had reached her eighties, but how clearly she realized the need for a proper airforce to defend England. She wanted not only to see her island rearming but also to forestall the secession of India from the Empire. She hated the National Government of the thirties and raged that Stanley Baldwin, the Conservative leader, and Ramsay MacDonald the Socialist leader seemed to be hand-in-glove and equally determined to allow the country to grow weak.

So it was natural that she should back Randolph. He was just the sort of young man she wanted to see in Parliament. Winston, however, was caught unawares by what he called 'this unconsidered plunge', and although he agreed to speak for his son he remained vexed by Randolph's sudden decision to enter the political arena. He issued a statement to the press that the step had been taken by Randolph without consulting his father.

Michael Foot attended one of Randolph's meetings at Wavertree and decided that he spoke well, though without 'the platform wit of his father'. On this occasion Randolph was haranguing his audience on the dangers of Baldwin's India policy, which was likely to put the Lancashire cotton industry out of work. 'And who is responsible for putting Lancashire where she is today?' he asked. The answer came from the back of the hall, 'Blackburn Rovers!' (the famed Lancashire football team). A roar of laughter went up.

Despite the support given to Randolph as an Independent by Lady Houston and all the Rothermere newspapers, Labour won the seat with 15,611 votes, the official Conservative had 13,771 and Randolph himself polled 10,575.

Soon after this, Sir Samuel Hoare wrote in a private letter, 'I do not know which is the more offensive or more mischievous, Winston or his son. Rumour however goes that they fight like cats with each other and chiefly agree on the prodigious amount of champagne that each of them drinks each night.'

Hoare then wrote to Lord Willingdon, 'That little brute Randolph has done a lot of mischief . . . the fact that he kept our man out will undoubtedly do both Winston and him a good deal of harm in the party.'

A few months later Randolph added to official Conservative ire by backing an Independent at Norwood. This time Winston decided that his son was now uncontrollable and refused to have anything to do with him.

However, Lady Houston still stood firmly by Randolph. She was a figure of fun at the time and was accused of wearing red, white and blue knickers as well as having a Union Jack as her tablecloth. But as events were to turn out, how right she was! She said she would continue to produce funds for any Independent Conservative who would attack Ramsay MacDonald and Baldwin, even if the Rothermere papers ceased to give support. Winston would have nothing to do with this battle for Norwood and he wrote sorrowfully to Clemmie that after sharp words, Randolph had marched out of the dining room in 'violent anger'.

By March 1935, Winston feared that Randolph – elated by the funding of Lady Houston – was ready to back anyone who would bring down the Government, even if it meant putting in a Labour member. 'I need not enlarge on the fury this will cause and its unfavourable reaction on my affairs. Norwood is the first of these essays and certainly no ground could have been more ill chosen.' Winston doubted if any Member of Parliament would appear on Randolph's platform, and the *Evening News* commented coolly, 'Now his friends are wondering whether in staging another fight at Norwood – on this occasion without the counsel and support of his distinguished father – Mr Randolph Churchill is not pushing at open doors. . . .'

Randolph was helped by his sisters, whom he had once more inveigled into working for him, but their main worry was whether their candidate would lose his deposit!

These fears proved well grounded. The final result could not have been more abysmal. The National Conservative candidate got in with 16,177 votes, the Labour obtained 12,799 and Randolph's candidate, one Richard Findley, did indeed forfeit his deposit with only 2697 votes. Then events took a turn which Randolph had never dreamed of: Duncan Sandys, the winner, had set eyes on Randolph's sister Diana (whose marriage to John Bailey had proved unsuccessful). Within a year Duncan and Diana were married. With grace Randolph had to accept Duncan Sandys as a member of his family as well as of the House of Commons.

After the Norwood by-election Randolph slunk away to Chartwell to recuperate from his failure, and Winston found him very subdued. His father reckoned it was all good for him, 'Randolph's firmness of character and courage are proof against many hard blows.'

In fact Winston was only too ready to be kind to this most difficult son; he argued that 2700 votes was not bad when Randolph had had no support from a party machine and had had to make speeches, answer questions and himself write the election address. When Randolph went off to form his own Independent Conservative Association Winston told his mother, 'The *Daily Mail* seems quite content to have him rampaging around like this.'

In April, Randolph retired to bed in the Mayfair Hotel in London with an attack of jaundice. His father visited him almost daily. As well as turning bright yellow as is usual with that unbecoming disease, Randolph grew a beard, which Winston deplored (though Randolph promised to cut it off when the fever abated).

Poor Winston wrote a pathetic letter about his family to his wife who was away. Mary's whooping cough seemed to be on the mend, he wrote, but Sarah was definitely overdoing things. She practised dancing four hours a day and then went to balls in the evening.

In May, Randolph had recovered sufficiently to depart for Bolivia, whence he wrote reports on the Chaco War for the *Daily Mail*. A telegram reached him signed 'Papa Mama' begging him to be properly vaccinated against typhus and cholera.

In December, Winston was holidaying in Spain when the Hoare-Laval peace plan caused upheaval in the League of Nations. Sir Samuel Hoare who was Foreign Secretary and Pierre Laval, the French Foreign Minister, had agreed to allow Mussolini a free hand in Abyssinia. Randolph advised his father not to hurry home and sent a telegram. 'Poor Brendan is torn between his desire to see sanctions terminated or Baldwin exterminated.'

Then Randolph decided once again to make a bid for Parliament. In this case the Conservative Association accepted him as their official candidate for a very difficult seat, West Toxteth in Liverpool. He was encouraged to contest the seat by the Beaverbrook and Rothermere press as well as by Lady Houston; but once again Randolph was to know the bitter taste of defeat. In the straight fight that ensued the Labour candidate polled 18,543 and Randolph 16,529.

In January 1936, Randolph accompanied his father, his sister, Diana, and her husband Duncan Sandys on a holiday in Marrakesh. In this Moroccan oasis he heard that the Unionist Association was ready to adopt him as their official candidate against Malcolm MacDonald, whose father, Ramsay MacDonald, had just ceased to be Prime Minister. The new sparring ground was to be Ross and Cromarty in northern Scotland. Winston spoke angrily about the inconvenience to him of such a fight. How, he said, could Baldwin ever ask him to join the Government in view of the hostility which Randolph's campaign must cause? But his son was not prepared to withdraw. Lady Houston would sponsor him, for she gladly seized on the chance offered in by-elections to have her views aired in Parliament and the country. The need for rearmament was becoming her fetish.

Brendan Bracken wired to Winston who was still holidaying in Marrakesh, 'Randolph's prospects very doubtful. Socialist win probable. More stags than Tories in Cromarty.'

But Randolph remained full of hope. He thought the fishermen around the coast would vote for him on the strength of his father's services to the Navy during the 1914–18 war.

Lord Beaverbrook wrote to Sir Samuel Hoare, 'Winston is in some doubts. He evidently wants to speak for Randolph. Brendan advises him against it. Winston is not on good terms with me at present. He is very sulky about a caricature in the *Evening Standard*.' (This caricature depicted Randolph and Malcolm MacDonald attired as babies on a doorstep while their respective fathers, dressed in women's clothes, lurked in the shadows, both hoping that Ross and Cromarty would accept their foundlings.) The election result was 8949 for Malcolm MacDonald, 5967 for H. McNeill who represented Labour and only 2427 for Randolph.

This time he could not but be downcast, but he hid his feelings bravely from the world. It was almost a relief to have other things to think about. When his sister Sarah ran away to America to marry Vic Oliver, Randolph followed her across the Atlantic – he was able to camouflage his true motive with his coverage of the forthcoming Presidential election. In September 1936, Randolph landed in New York and Sarah met him on the pier. Despite Randolph's remonstrances concerning the dangers of tying herself to an elderly Austrian citizen, Sarah joined Vic Oliver in his show *Follow the Stars* and on Christmas Eve 1936 they were married. For a time he was occupied with family dramas. Randolph couldn't help liking Vic Oliver, and Sarah's happiness counted for a great deal with him.

At the end of December 1936, Lady Houston died. She had known the pleasure of hearing Winston denounce the Baldwin Government in unique words, 'They have decided only to be undecided, they are resolved only to be irresolute, they are adamant for drift, solid for fluidity, all-powerful but impotent.' Randolph grieved briefly for the death of a splendid old lady who had always been ready to boost him.

Had Randolph been born to anyone but Winston might he have been different? One cannot know. If his father had not encouraged him to drink in his youth, he might have lived longer. Of course it would have been difficult for any son to call Winston father, but much of Randolph's egotism has to be blamed on a great man's tendency to pander to his beautiful only son. Winston could not resist holding up his famous cigar for silence at the dinner table whenever Randolph held forth. It may seem difficult to imagine Winston listening enraptured to the views of a mere boy, but so it was, and Randolph's ease of delivery and his extraordinary memory increased his father's pleasure.

Should one blame Winston for ignoring the obvious annoyance of older guests? He had seen Clementine try to restrain the boy with the result that Randolph ceased to like her. Diana and Sarah were busy with their own lives and Mary, the dearest final kitten who brought only joy to her parents was too young to have any influence on such an older brother.

All through the thirties, Randolph led a glamorous way of life which was, unfortunately for him, only too successful. He was *so* good-looking and found it easy to captivate the girls, and with his unusually sharp memory he could quote reams of poetry. Those whom he did not enrage invited him to their houses, and he always made the party go. Like Cecil Beaton and Oliver Messel he was automatically asked to stay by people who wanted to be amused – and were prepared to take the risk of Randolph's wrecking an evening with some illogical tantrum.

Both Lord Rothermere and Lord Beaverbrook spotted in Winston's son the makings of a first-class journalist. They offered him well-paid employment on their newspapers where he found it easy to produce hot political commentary. He always had his father booming in the background about the danger of allowing Germany to rearm, and Randolph would echo this theme. As his articles show, while he was in Berlin to cover the German elections, he knew only too well that it was foolish to underestimate the vital spirit animating the Nazi movement. Hitler promised all things to all his people. And the nation that had been trampled underfoot at Versailles rallied to that promise.

At this time we in England had hardly heard the word Nazi. But Randolph learnt early on exactly what Nazism meant, because the men who really understood Germany's power reported to Chartwell.

Randolph never drew breath on the subject – he loved his father and believed in him, but there was more to his passion than filial affection. He hated injustice, and when Hitler made a scapegoat of the Jews he flew into angry print. Everyone at Winston's table in the thirties knew how Churchill felt.

Meanwhile Randolph was living dangerously in other ways. He continued to copy his godfather Lord Birkenhead over-assiduously, but it was a very hopeful sign when he accepted Lord Rothermere's bet of £500 that he would not touch a drink for a year. 'Nothing will be better for Randolph's purse and his looks,' commented Winston. When in May Baldwin resigned and Neville Chamberlain became Prime Minister, Randolph telephoned the press lord from the south of France (where he was a special correspondent for the *Daily Mail*) asking for a one-day dispensation. Rothermere, tickled by the comic request, gladly gave him leave. For twenty-four hours Randolph poured alcohol down his throat with his fellow correspondents. He could mix whisky and champagne with port – and survive. Then he clamped down on himself, and at the end of the year was able to claim his bet.

When Diana Mitford left her husband Bryan Guinness (who was to become the 2nd Lord Moyne) for Sir Oswald Mosley, leader of the British Fascists, Randolph halted dead in his tracks. He enjoyed arguing politics with almost everyone, but he found it hard to face Diana. She was the one person he could not discuss politics with. Mosley had been one of the brilliant young men whom Winston had hoped to rally to his cause. Randolph had been sent to ask Mosley if he would consider joining a band of 'Tory toughs' in opposition to the Nationalist Government. When Mosley asked why Winston wanted him,

Randolph had replied, 'Because without you he will not be able to get hold of the *young* men.' Mosley liked that reply.

When Diana's father (Lord Redesdale) and her father-in-law Walter Guinness went in deputation to Mosley's flat in Ebury Street to tell him that he simply could not abandon his wife Lady Cynthia (Lord Curzon's daughter), Randolph happened to be visiting Mosley. 'What on earth are you going to do now?' asked Randolph. Mosley just laughed, 'I suppose I must wear a balls protector,' he answered blithely.

Lady Cynthia died of peritonitis soon after and when Diana married Mosley, Hitler was their best man. That seemed the end of the road to Randolph.

In the meantime Randolph had developed an extraordinary relationship with another of his Mitford cousins. He was in a way deeply in love with her, and yet simply because they had so much in common and because they became so close it made an ordinary love affair impossible. In a way they were too alike – there was no element of surprise and each always knew what the other was thinking. The ties between them were so strong that their relationship was more complicated than merely being in love.

Clementine Mitford had been a posthumous child, born after her father had been killed in 1915 in the First World War. As he was the elder son of Lord Redesdale, Clementine, had she been a boy, would have inherited the title. Her mother, the Lady Helen Mitford, had to wait six months wondering about the sex of the child she would bear, and Clementine felt that she had never quite been forgiven for being a girl. Thus the second son, the father of Tom and his six incredible sisters, eventually became Lord Redesdale.

Clementine had been sent to boarding school at the age of seven. Her mother was unapproachable, aunts and uncles and cousins were kind but no help emotionally – and she needed help. When she met her cousin Randolph they had both suffered from a lack which they found hard to analyse, and Clementine found that as well as being brilliant company – as good alone as in a room full of people – Randolph was deeply affectionate. He was what she needed and certainly he needed her.

And Clementine was beautiful in the way that her cousin Diana Mitford and Randolph were beautiful – they had the same marvellous blue gaze. It must have been very extraordinary when they looked at each other.

Sarah Churchill, Randolph's favourite sister, was Clementine's great friend; indeed she was Sarah's confidante. After Sarah ran away to America and married Vic Oliver the couple returned to London and took the flat underneath Randolph's in Westminster Gardens. Every now and again, when she returned from Berlin where she was attending the Foreigner's Institute in Berlin University, Clementine could enjoy visiting them all together.

On one occasion Randolph flew out to Berlin for interviews. Randolph did not speak a word of German and Clementine was by this time competent enough to be able to guide him. She had shed her infatuation with the Nazis and had quarrelled with her cousin Unity over the 'Jewish question'. When Randolph reached Berlin, Clementine was lodging in the home of an old Jewish couple, and when Randolph met the interpreters who were to be present at the interview next day she reluctantly agreed to be present. She feared to involve the Jewish family who were in the throes of getting their son out of the country, and was horrified at Randolph's rudeness to the interpreters. When Clementine saw Randolph off at Templehof aerodrome, he suddenly realized what he had done and turned to her with a worried look. 'I do hope,' he said, 'that I wasn't unwise and that you won't get into trouble.' For once Randolph was made to *think* of the result his acts might have.

Clementine has written me a letter about their unusual relationship.

My childhood was so odd, with no likeable stepfather. Really it was all women plus a huge girls' boarding school. When Randolph appeared in all his glory I loved him deeply. He was the best company in the world and I think he was the *first clever* grown-up person that I met. He was full of scintillating talk – quoting poetry and prose, and so funny and brave as a lion. All this, and added to it a great capacity for true affection, which he did not mind demonstrating.

I think, on looking back on it, that I filled a gap for him; he talked to me a lot about his relationship with his mother and father and did not mind me saying what I thought. The quarrels with Winston were so sad and both sides were upset. . . .

Randolph was twenty-five or twenty-six at the time and precocious – in love with sophisticated women like Mona Harrison Williams (who was a great beauty but feather-brained except in her social activities) and with a certain musical comedy actress – a great sex-pot in the theatre. His relationship with this Mitford cousin was strangely tender and urgent. She realized how desperately he yearned for what she had to give but Randolph did not realize how dear Clementine was to him till he lost her.

— 6 —

Winston may have deplored his son's foolhardy political ventures yet he continued to spoil Randolph and to weep when he was defeated. Brendan Bracken's criticism only annoyed him and it was obvious Randolph had long disliked his mother because of her opposition to his whims. Dislike? Diana Mosley says it is not too strong a word to use, yet one knows how mixed his feelings were. He had always craved the maternal adoration she could not give, and he resented her governessy if splendid qualities.

When Randolph left for the continent on a journalistic assignment in 1937, Lord Rothermere wrote to him, 'I am consenting to your going to Spain on the very strict understanding that you will under no circumstances expose yourself to any risk. . . . Regarding my bet with you – you have my full permission to drink the wine of the country and beer, but no spirits or foreign wines and never forget you are an only son.'

In March, Randolph interviewed Franco for the *Daily Mail* and in October he toured Germany with the Windsors. Occasionally he went to Berlin, where he continued to see his cousin Clementine Mitford and use her as his interpreter for the articles he sent as special correspondent. There was plenty of material, for Himmler, Goering and Goebbels were disagreeing over the Jews. They could not decide if it would be wise to persecute the big Jewish industrialists as well as the small Jewish shopkeepers. Randolph covered every facet of the German nation: from the dismissal of Marshal von Blomberg because he married an unsuitable lady, to articles on German womanhood.

Meanwhile his American friend Virginia Cowles was also making a name for herself and was to become a famous war correspondent through her book on the Spanish Civil War, *Looking For Trouble*, and Randolph enjoyed lapping up her opinions when they met.

In February 1938, Randolph made a thoughtless remark at dinner which offended Winston deeply. It concerned a present which Winston had made to Leslie Hore-Belisha, the Minister of War; too late Randolph realized that he should not have made it. A bitter quarrel resulted. When Randolph wrote to his father apologizing for his rudeness Winston replied that he found the remark 'offensive and untrue and one which no son should have made to his father. . . .'

The pain of this fracas hurt Winston deeply and he declared that he did not wish to see his son. Randolph minded terribly. He told Clementine Mitford the story and she scolded him for having said such a thing. While he was standing looking out of the window telling her the story she suddenly realized he was crying. She had never seen a man weep before and 'that was what was terrible' she writes. On her advice Randolph then went to the House of Commons to hear his father speak. Winston received him coldly, and Randolph had to bow his head in humiliation when Victor Warrender and that 'amiable flippertigibbet, Brendan' were openly preferred to him. All evening he hung around ready to apologize, but his father gave him no opening. The very next day Randolph wrote him a letter about the agony he was enduring. 'When I was thirteen and fourteen years old you paid me the compliment of treating me as if I were a grown-up. Now that I am nearly twenty-seven you treat me as a wayward and untrustworthy child. . . .' He knew that Winston loved him, which made it all the more terrible to 'crucify all these feelings by treating me with such obvious contempt'.

What had really happened was that Winston had grown afraid of his son's political ventures and of what he regarded as Randolph's indiscretions as a journalist. Randolph refuted the allegations of ever having written articles mentioning anything which he had not permission to quote; but there was no doubt that in his efforts to get into the House of Commons he had risked queering his father's pitch.

Eventually, however, Randolph cheered up enough to start writing to his father about editing a collection of Winston's speeches.*

Winston wanted to include the pleas he had made in 1919 during the Peace Conference when he had asked for the German nation to be

*This book came out in 1938 under the title *Arms and the Covenant*. In America the publisher chose the much better title *While England Slept*.

treated leniently. Harold Nicolson wrote in his diary of a late evening spent in Randolph's flat at this time, 'He is editing a book of his father's speeches which show how right Winston has always been. His adoration for his father is really touching.'

In the summer of 1938, Winston had asked the Colonel of his old regiment, the 4th Hussars, if Randolph could join the supplementary reserve. Winston wrote, 'He thinks it his duty to acquire military training and have a space marked out for himself should trouble come.'

At that moment Randolph, worn out with journalistic work, was holidaying in Greece (stopping on his way to see his sister Sarah dance in Southampton) but on his return he gladly reported for duty. During Randolph's military course, Winston indicated that he was willing to take over the column in the *Evening Standard*; he was, of course, accepted. On 15 September, Randolph wrote jauntily to his father that he was just off to Aldershot, 'to learn the goose step'. It was the very day that Neville Chamberlain flew to Munich.

Throughout October and November, at the same time as learning to stamp his feet to attention, Randolph could angrily blaze in newspaper columns through his father's only too willing pen. (Though Winston may have felt dazed at having suddenly to write the 'Londoner's Diary' in the *Evening Standard* he did it extremely well.)

The arguments between father and son about the ethics of journalism clarified their emotions, and when in December Randolph returned to Westminster Gardens he reasserted that *never* had he betrayed a confidence and that he *must* be trusted.

Tilly Losch was still a close friend of Randolph's at this time, and he took her to a number of political meetings – though heaven knows what she made of them. When Sir Oswald Mosley had his great meeting at Earl's Court Stadium Randolph sat with her in the front row – and ostentatiously dragged her off with him when Mosley said how charming Hitler was.

Meanwhile there was plenty to keep Randolph busy. With his brother-in-law Duncan Sandys he tried to start a New Movement. The *Evening Standard* published his article, 'The Revolt of the Under Secretaries', which caused a furore. Robert Hudson, Lord Strathcona and Lord Dufferin all sought to turn out their senior minister because of 'lack of gumption after Munich'!

Harold Macmillan describes a luncheon with Winston at Chartwell when news arrived of the Italian landings in Albania. 'It was a scene that gave me my first picture of Churchill at work. Maps were brought out, secretaries were marshalled, telephones began to ring. Where was the British Fleet? The considerable staff which, even as a private individual, Churchill always maintained to support his tremendous outflow of literary and political effort was at once brought into play. . . .'

Lord Halifax's first reaction to Mussolini's blow was as characteristic as Churchill's. He is said to have exclaimed when he heard of the treacherous attacks, 'And on Good Friday too.'

— 7 —

In London, Clementine Mitford continued to delight in frequent visits to 70 Westminster Gardens, and it was during one of her sessions with Randolph that a sudden realization struck her.

She was sitting on his yellow velvet sofa discussing the complexities of their feelings towards each other when suddenly she looked up and saw the portrait of Mona Harrison Williams by Cecil Beaton which hung over Randolph's mantelpiece. Mona was a well-known beauty who dominated London society as only an American woman can, and Randolph had long fancied himself in love with this sophisticated older woman. Clementine thought that nothing could be worse for Randolph than this constant hankering for the unobtainable – he seldom saw Mona and she was quite out of his reach. Suddenly the penny dropped: 'No wonder you think you are in love with her. She looks just like your mother . . . the same kind of calm beauty . . . the same wide blue eyes and marvellous features . . . she even turns her head in the same way,' said Clementine, staring at Randolph with her unblinking blue eyes – so like his and so like Mona's, so like Diana Mitford's and so like his mother's too. 'You must have an Oedipus complex,' she concluded, 'every woman you fall for looks like your mother.' Randolph remained absolutely silent while the idea trickled through his consciousness. 'A very interesting theory,' he said at last, 'I'll think it over.' Clementine tells me that she thinks she hit the nail on the head that day. Much of Randolph's trouble started with his obsession with his mother; longing for a warm relationship with her, he had discovered that in her own way she also was unobtainable.

A famous London restaurant was the scene of another incident which Clementine Mitford would never forget. They often had meals together at the Savoy Grill, and Randolph was frequently rude to waiters who spilled soup and made mistakes when serving. Clementine could not bear this habit (which was common enough in those days). She told Randolph frankly that if he ever insulted a waiter again in her presence she would walk out. Then one evening at the Savoy a new waiter slopped the soup around and Randolph let out an oath. Clementine got up and swept out into the hotel foyer, while Randolph panted at her heels, begging her to return. Everyone stared while this drama went on and eventually Clementine said, 'I'll only return if you apologize to the waiter.' He promised and, knowing Randolph to be a man of his word, she returned to the Grill with him.

'Miss Mitford says I've got to apologize to you . . .' began Randolph. 'I'm sorry I spoke as I did.' The waiter beamed, 'That's quite all right, sir.' Then Randolph, with an engaging smile could not resist adding, 'I only did so because you *were* a bloody fool.' They all started to laugh, Randolph and Clementine and the waiter too.

'I'll tell you one thing sir,' said the waiter. 'We pay each other good money not to serve you. I don't know if you've noticed how we all rush away – I was the newest and youngest today and so I got caught for the job.'

'Fancy having such a reputation – *me* of all people,' muttered Randolph.

Back in Randolph's flat, seated again on the yellow velvet sofa, Clementine once remarked to him quite casually, 'You know it's a funny thing – I've never met a Jew in England, only in Germany.'

'Oh haven't you?' said Randolph and his hand moved eagerly to the telephone. 'Henry,' he said when he got through to Lord Melchett, 'I have here a cousin who says she has never met a Jew in England, only on the continent – could you dine with us both at the Savoy tonight? Yes? Good. I've told her you are my favourite Jew.' Then he lay back on the sofa and laughed.

'I know another Jew you ought to meet; he has a lot of charm. In fact he arranged for Diana Cooper to act in *The Miracle* years ago.' Before she could stop him he had rung Rudolph Kommer and asked him the same question.

As a result of these phone calls they enjoyed a marvellous evening, but Randolph could not guess how his plan to introduce Clementine to witty Jewry would turn out.

Kommer was living at the Ritz Hotel and often gave luncheons there. He invited Clementine occasionally and it was at one of these parties that she met Sir Alfred Beit MP – and became engaged to him. Randolph minded bitterly. This wasn't what he'd intended at all.

Clementine married Alfred Beit (who like many others did not really like Randolph) in April 1939. Randolph felt himself left completely alone with thoughts he found hard to formulate. Yes, he had loved beauty and he adored the startlingly blue Mitford eyes. But he could not get out of his mind Clementine's words about falling for women who resembled his mother. In his heart he was terribly hurt and did not know where to turn. He wanted his lovely cousin to himself. She looked like him. She understood him. She had been through the same kind of trauma. And now she belonged to another man. She was truly in love with Alfred Beit, and he would keep her happy till the end of their lives. Randolph was left alone and he hated it.

— 8 —

Before war broke out Randolph met Laura Charteris at an evening party. She was married to Lord Long at the time by whom she had one little girl. This vibrant, talkative, dark-eyed girl amused him – and then he realized there was more to his feelings. 'Let's go to see Rosa Lewis at the Cavendish Hotel,' he said and the evening ended with much popping of champagne corks. Laura was married, tired of her husband maybe but legally tied to him, for in those days it was not so easy to get a divorce. Randolph had found a friend who was safe, into whose ear he could pour out his many troubles while she remained witty and funny about it all. He needed a perky listener with troubles of her own, so he latched onto her; she became his anchor really – an anchor who would last all his life – it was as if a man thirsting in the desert had suddenly found a jug of cool water.

When war broke out in September 1939, Randolph was twenty-eight and had seen much of Nazi Germany. His father was immediately made First Lord of the Admiralty as he had been in 1914, and the famous signal went out to every ship, 'Winston's back.' No one by this time could have been unaware that Hitler intended to fight, and while he inflamed his own nation with fiery oratory, London's politicians gave the Führer every reason to believe that England was disposed to acquiesce to violence. When Winston fumed in public speeches, his own countrymen called him a warmonger and the vociferous Randolph, harping on his father's views at dinner parties, often caused his host to order him from the house. Meanwhile Sir Oswald Mosley, husband of the madonna-like Diana, stuck to his absolutely opposite views. *He* thought the dangerous enemy was Russia, not Germany.

Randolph was by now a trained officer. He hadn't enjoyed what

46

had to be undergone to get a commission, but he had shown stamina in his struggle to learn the ropes. It was not easy for Randolph to stamp around the barrack square and stand to attention and salute senior officers, but he did his best, and the sergeant majors at any rate could see that he was trying. When he got to the Officers' Mess of the 4th Hussars he thought he was well liked. He did not realize that junior officers fresh from training were expected to pipe down and remain deferential. Randolph was incapable of making any effort to check himself and he kept explaining to senior officers exactly how to win the war.

Naturally Randolph took for granted, as most young Englishmen did then, that he would probably be killed. It was October 1939 when he came to London on twenty-four hours' leave, and as he pushed through the revolving door at the Ritz Hotel an old friend, Lady Mary Dunn, whirled around the other side. 'Can you have dinner?' he shouted, 'I've got twenty-four hours in town and nothing to do. . . .' Mary replied firmly that she couldn't, she had got to dine elsewhere. 'However I know someone who might,' she added, 'and I can tell you where to ring her. She's a girl called Pamela Digby who has just arrived from Dorset and I'm sure you'll like each other.' Randolph snatched the proffered number and rushed to the phonebox.

A fresh young voice replied.

'Who are you?' he inquired.

'Pamela Digby,' came the answer.

'Mary Dunn said I could invite you out to dinner. . . . What do you look like?' asked the insufferable Randolph.

'Red-headed and rather fat, but Mummy says that puppy fat disappears.'

'Will you come out to dinner with me?' asked Randolph.

Three days later their engagement was announced.

So it was that Randolph married the eldest daughter of Lord and Lady Digby. Pamela's father was the 11th Baron, and came of a Dorset family of renown. The wedding reception took place at Admiralty House, with the state rooms opened up for the occasion. Randolph asked Seymour Berry, the eldest son of press baron, Lord Camrose, to be best man. Winston and Clementine Churchill were delighted; they had gained a pretty daughter-in-law and at just the right moment. If Pamela could not make Randolph settle down, no one could.

After the honeymoon, Randolph took his wife to Beverley, in York-shire, where his regiment was stationed and there his fellow officers immediately instructed him that a certain musical comedy actress, one of those 'sex-pots' described by Clementine Mitford, should be asked to discontinue her weekend visits to see him. Randolph could never have worked out for himself what was circumspect behaviour. He listened however to his seniors in the mess and obeyed instructions.

In May 1940, after that curious winter called the phoney war, Hitler attacked France and on 9 May, when Randolph telephoned his father from Kettering where his unit was then stationed, Winston said quietly, 'I think I shall be Prime Minister tomorrow.'

While he was breakfasting in the mess next morning Randolph heard on the radio that Germany was invading Belgium and Holland. He rushed to the phone to ask his father what was happening. The answer was 'plenty'; that afternoon Winston became Prime Minister as he had predicted. His son at camp in the country could only hope that it was not too late.

In June 1940, under Regulation 18b, Sir Oswald Mosley and then his wife Diana were arrested and interned. Sir John Colville in his diaries has noted this fact, which he says 'piqued' Winston and caused 'much merriment' among his children. Diana Sandys and Sarah Oliver may have laughed but Randolph, remembering childhood days, could not smile. He suffered the blow in silence. He hated the thought of his beautiful Diana in prison.

Colville goes on to say he found Randolph coarse and aggressive at dinner and that he felt ashamed for Winston's sake. One has to accept Colville's words that Randolph, who had arrived with the pregnant Pamela, was 'anything but kind to Winston who adores him'.

Winston was always emotional, and among intimates he could burst out that if his son was killed on active service 'he wouldn't be able to carry on with his war'. But people were being killed all over England in air raids and Randolph was eager to prove his valour. He scorned danger, and anyway he felt that his father must understand his desire to make good as a soldier.

When the Conservative member for Preston died, Randolph was chosen in his stead. According to the wartime truce, vacant seats were not contested. So the Prime Minister's son – who had three times tried in vain to get into Parliament – entered the House of Commons without a fight. When Winston introduced him there was much applause – applause of course for a Prime Minister who was proving himself the greatest of wartime leaders. Randolph's entry into the House of

48

Commons was followed by the birth of a boy to Pamela at Chequers a few days later. The baby was named Winston.

Randolph made his maiden speech in the House of Commons in uniform. Winston, fearing that it might be embarrassing for a son to address the Chamber in front of his famous father, sat with his back turned to him. But he was proud all right, and Randolph hit just the right note when he started by mentioning Winston's own maiden speech and then went on to describe how the memory of Lord Randolph still lived with many members.

On 1 December his baby son was christened at the parish church near Chequers. The godparents were Lord Beaverbrook, Lord Brownlow, Brendan Bracken and Virginia Cowles, the American girl who had come over as a war correspondent and become a close friend of Randolph's. After lunch on the lawn at Chequers, Winston proposed a toast to his grandson and Lady Diana Cooper, who was among the guests, saw the great man weeping. Training planes of the RAF roared overhead, for invasion was expected at any moment. German armies were ready and waiting at the Channel ports.

When Randolph heard in White's Club that Colonel Robert Laycock was recruiting officers for Commandos he applied for a transfer. Stomping into the office of his commanding officer in the 4th Hussars, he saluted and asked permission to join Bob Laycock. What a shock it was to be told that the other officers disliked him, they were fed up with his diatribes and could hardly wait for him to get some job elsewhere. Randolph, who had thought he was well regarded, burst into tears. That was one of his endearing traits – his honest childlike desire to be loved and his amazement when he discovered that he wasn't.

Meanwhile Winston was fussing about the victims of Regulation 18b. He wanted to get Diana Mosley released, for she had an unweaned baby and Holloway gaol was a rough uncomfortable place. But he did not dare to upset the Coalition Government, and Labour would hardly tolerate the freeing of a woman held under Regulation 18b just because she was a cousin of Winston's wife. Nevertheless, Winston telephoned Holloway prison asking that Lady Mosley should be allowed a daily bath. But since over sixty women had to use the bathroom where the hot water always ran out after five or six baths, Diana felt it would be odious for her to put herself forward as the Prime Minister's pet.

That Christmas of 1940, Winston and Clemmie enjoyed a family house party at Chequers. Their four children all came and those who were married brought their spouses. Baby Winston was of course the focus of attention.

Randolph had his transfer, but he found that Commando training in Scotland wasn't all that delightful. The seaside hotels became over-crowded with loving wives and girlfriends and bills proved astronom-ical. Randolph found himself posted to be the subaltern of another MP, Godfrey Nicolson, and he complained to Colonel Laycock that he could not serve under a Member of Parliament with whom he was in 'political disagreement'. Tempers frayed, hair grew long, lap-dogs and cigars made messes. Evelyn Waugh, who had spent three months in the Marines and considered himself a real army wallah, complained that the Commandos 'wear whatever uniform they like, one very nice Grenadier can hardly be persuaded to wear any uniform at all!'

When Pamela Churchill arrived for a rather icy winter visit, Randolph, perhaps to arouse her admiration, accepted a bet that he would swim to the island of Largs. 'Unless the Colonel can be invoked, that will be the last of him,' gloated Evelyn who was also doing Commando training. But the swim never took place.

When the hotel charged £1 a week for Randolph's Pekinese, he attacked the lady proprietor. 'Do you realize, my good woman, that this is more than the interest on £2000?'

To which she impudently replied, 'What's a pound a week to you?'

Randolph then became magisterial. 'Ha – so your prices are based on what you think you can get, not on the service you give?'

And so it went on until the outraged lady was goaded into retorting, 'I should like to see you all go – there are plenty of nice people who want your rooms.'

'Nice people? I suppose you mean evacuees from Glasgow?'

'No,' she replied. 'People with estates.'

Seeing that he was getting the worst of it Randolph paid his full bill but warned the waiter, 'I hope you make sure of getting the 10 per cent charged for your services on the bill. These seem to me to be the kind of people who would cheat you.'

What a relief it was when there came a three-week course of Field Training, though Randolph soon got into trouble for heckling the instructors. But then, in February 1941, he sailed with No. 8 Commando for Egypt. David Stirling, a tall dark mysterious-looking Scotsman, joined them just before the boat left. Evelyn Waugh noted him as a great gambler, so Randolph, of course, settled down to games of chance – and lost heavily every night.

In Cape Town the inhabitants gave a festive time to all the soldiers on their way to battle. The troops were taken for mountain motorcar rides, and had peaches and cream cake thrust on them. The organizations devised to entertain the military made a great show, and Randolph even found people whom he could mesmerize by his views on how to win the war. Maybe his buddies grew somewhat restive as the ship progressed onwards up the Red Sea but he never ceased to hold forth. He did not care if he was killed now that he had a son.

The Commando organization was a bit top heavy in the proportion of officers and NCOs to men, and before reaching Suez the troopship carrying No. 8 Commando became famous for a slogan painted on the lower deck, 'Never in the history of humankind have so few been buggered about by so many.'

On reaching the Suez area, Layforce (consisting of three UK Commandos – 7, 8 and 11) found itself not altogether popular. Other Commandos already in the Middle East, Nos. 50 and 52 had already received their baptism of fire in Abyssinia and the Dodecanese islands. They regarded the inexperienced newcomers with scepticism and were inclined to demonstrate this view. No. 8 Commando could not hide pink English knees under khaki shorts, but they were all volunteers from smart regiments and somewhat conceited. Ill-advisedly some of the officers from England threw their weight about in the mess which they shared with the Commandos from regular regiments – who had in the last four months seen much fighting. To shoot a line among seasoned troops who were long-service regulars was asking for trouble.

How angry the officers and men of Nos. 50 and 52 Commando were to become later on when Evelyn Waugh referred to their action at Castellorizo island in the Dodecanese as 'discreditable'. In fact the second in command and both company commanders were mentioned in despatches. Waugh's deviation from historical truth became a very sore point, and somehow a similarly derogatory allegation found its way into Martin Gilbert's brilliant official biography of Winston Churchill.*

*The Middle East Commando Research Group has proved that No. 50 Commando behaved with great bravery at Castellorizo which it attacked before Evelyn Waugh even reached Egypt, and Martin Gilbert wrote a letter to *The Times* in 1983 apologizing for inaccuracies that occurred in Vol. 6 because of Randolph's thoughtless letters to his father.

For a time all the Commandos were grouped together at Genifa near the Great Bitter Lakes as a Special Service Brigade in the 6th Infantry Division. In April, the Germans invaded Greece and the newly designated battalions of Layforce were dispersed. B Battalion, which was Randolph's, moved to Mersa Matruh. Sitting in a sandy camp, besieged by flies, Randolph became less exuberant – and Pamela's letters about his gambling debts grew ever crosser.

Then, in May 1941, came the Battle of Crete, and many weary British soldiers who had been fighting in Greece were sent there. Off went Bob Laycock with Evelyn Waugh as his Intelligence Officer, to command A and D Battalions while Randolph's battalion remained at Mersa Matruh. When the violent Crete fighting took a turn for the worse on 27 May and British troops were ordered to withdraw (leaving the entire Eastern Mediterranean in the hands of the German Airforce so that henceforth all British ships had to go around the Cape of Good Hope), Winston sent a wireless signal asking the whereabouts of Randolph.

There was a flap. The Chief of Staff in the Western Desert asked Colonel Stephen Rose, who was in charge of the Rear Details of Layforce, to find out where Randolph was. Colonel Rose was busy meeting the wounded who were arriving exhausted in Alexandria harbour, after being bombed on the destroyers which evacuated them. But he found out that Randolph had not gone to Crete with those Commandos who had to be left behind to become prisoners of war. They had been a splendid fighting force and their feelings must have been bitter indeed.

One has to wonder what would have happened if Randolph had been with them. Would he have spent the next four and a half years as a POW or would Hitler have had him shot because he was Winston's son?

What Bob Laycock *had* done before this terrible battle for Crete – in which German troops descended by parachute and glider, and the flower of two nations fought hand to hand in the olive groves – was to arrange for Randolph to go to Cairo and dine with the British Ambassador, Sir Miles Lampson. Anthony Eden, the Foreign Secretary, had just flown in from Athens and was also staying at the Embassy. Randolph hated Eden but the bad news from Greece drew them together. Eden sent a cable to Winston and the Prime Minister in England was puzzled to receive a signal from his Foreign Secretary reading: 'Have seen Randolph who has just arrived. He is looking fit and well. He has the light of Bottle in his eye.'

The cypherine had got *one* letter wrong!

— *9* —

When Randolph arrived in Egypt in 1941, I saw a lot of him. At first he was a Lieutenant in Bob Laycock's Commando force and then suddenly he became a Major in the Press and Propaganda Dept at GHQ. At one time he appeared at our camp with a flag flying from his car which only full Colonels were allowed. One didn't like to ask too much about his postings.

Christopher Sykes has described Randolph's advent at GHQ in Cairo where Christopher introduced him to various staff officers. 'He made a delightful impression. But it was not long before my peppery chief, a former officer of the Army of India, was bursting into my room with cries of: "This damned fellow Randolph Churchill – *your* friend! What the devil does he think he's doing?" '

Well of course Randolph couldn't see why he shouldn't run propaganda in his own way and he revelled in having access to Winston's ear. Wasn't the Prime Minister his own father and in what other manner could truthful accounts be transmitted? In Cairo Randolph was permitted, like all non-regimental officers, to find his own accommodation. He settled into Shepheards Hotel and there I occasionally met him on the days when my ambulance company allowed me to leave Helmieh Camp. As Winston's son he naturally attracted a certain amount of attention and Captain 'Jummy' Friend of the 11th Hussars, a regiment of armoured cars which had been fighting in the Western Desert, often lunched with us both. For once Randolph was silenced while Jummy related his own views on the military situation. With Jummy I noted that Randolph became a good listener. 'Well, you have been fighting the real war out here ever since it broke out,' he would say. Let's hope he passed on to Winston the military assessment of a young officer who had known desert fighting with armoured cars for nearly two years.

I remember one occasion at least when the direct line to his father paid dividends. Mrs Newall was the elegant lady who headed our ambulance unit. She did not live with us in the fly-ridden sandy camps but instead shared a flat with two admirals employed in Cairo. From this nook she was better able to badger GHQ where certain generals were getting irate because we seemed to be the only girls working in the Middle East, except for army nurses. Mrs Newall chummed up with Randolph, and of course she saw much more of him than any of us who had to live behind barbed wire in the sandy camp.

Throughout that horribly hot summer of 1941 she kept sending messages to Winston via his son – messages which may have concerned our status in the army – but on one occasion she did immense good in a different way. Mrs Newall had herself retired to the 15th Scottish Hospital with duodenal ulcers, and I was laid on to carry her delicious food specially prepared by the Egyptian cook who concocted meals in her Cairo flat. By chance I happened to be present when an extraordinary figure appeared from the room next door – this was Major Orde Wingate, a larger-than-life character, who had led British forces in Abyssinia and then tried to commit suicide in Cairo because GHQ would not listen to his plans. In his room in Shepheards Hotel he cut his throat from ear to ear. The housemaid heard strange gurgling noises and summoned the head *safragi* who had a key and found Major Wingate expiring in a pool of blood. British army doctors were hastily summoned and they stitched his neck and put him in hospital, where at least he had a private room in which to think things over.

Attempted suicide was a military offence, and a court martial would probably loom when he got back to England. His voice had become most peculiar, but whether this was due to the injury he had inflicted upon himself or to the constriction of bandages, it was difficult to judge. He was a curious man, humourless maybe, but at the time he hadn't much to laugh about anyway. One afternoon I remember he led me to the bathroom to rant about the new kind of WC plug which was pushed by hand. 'Can you imagine a worse *Germ Trap*?' he remonstrated. 'Or anything more likely to go wrong? But it's the lack of hygiene I object to!' Matron, who was quite formidable, finally appeared and unsmilingly listened to him. I don't know what she thought. Officers who were not under arrest were allowed to wander round in dressing-gown or semi-uniform and one was always afraid that Wingate might pull the bandages off his throat and do it again.

Mrs Newall understood this odd bird and induced him to reveal his soul. When she told Randolph about him, Randolph relayed a version of affairs to Winston that was very different from the version of the ordinary army. When Major Orde Wingate got back to England he found the Prime Minister ready to believe in him; and so it was that he became the fabulous leader of the Chindits in Burma – which was much more helpful to our war effort than a dreary court martial would have been.

Randolph kept urging his father to set up a Minister of State for the Middle East who would have the right to decide on political and strategic direction. The first to hold this post was Oliver Lyttelton. Then in July – that particularly hot July of 1941 – Averell Harriman, who had been sent to England as President Roosevelt's adviser on Lendlease, came out to the Middle East. Randolph thought him shrewd and wonderful. He did not yet know that his wife Pamela thought the same.

Randolph often appeared at Helmieh Camp outside Cairo, where our ambulance unit was based – needless to say he thought it great fun to take out the girls on their days off. Our sergeants found themselves wondering what rank he would next appear to have reached. Stars and the crown of a major alternated on Randolph's shoulders, and we could well imagine the rage he was causing in the press departments of the Army. He always remembered to salute senior officers, but he could not cease trumpeting his opinions and older men would be seen turning purple with anger when he held forth in Shepheards Hotel.

I suppose that only I knew how forlorn he was. He would confide in me, the ambulance-driver cousin doing a stint in the desert, and I tried to help him organize himself. He was in such a difficult position and he wondered how to make the best of it. To be the son of Winston Churchill had always been awkward enough and now his father had become the greatest of all war leaders. Randolph was determined to do well as a soldier, and as a soldier one had to face the enemy. What he longed for now was exactly what his father wanted to keep him out of – without seeming to shelter him. When No. 8 Commando was dissolved and many officers went back to their units Randolph was eager to show his military worth. He never ceased to voice his admiration for the regiments who had been fighting in the Western Desert since the beginning of the war – nearly two years before. In front of me he would say longingly to officers of the 7th, 8th and 11th Hussars, 'Of course *you've* done the real fighting.' But however hard he tried, his superiors remained reluctant to employ the difficult Randolph. No one wanted to upset Winston, but his son was so talkative and, to many soldiers, insufferable. Also he was still very unfit; the effects of the fleshpots of the prewar years took a long time to fade.

Poor Randolph. He couldn't find a place for himself in all this activity. With pathetic zeal he hung around the war zones, and tried to arrange danger for himself.

Meanwhile in England, Sir Oswald Mosley and his wife remained in prison. Whenever Winston tentatively mentioned the possibility of their release, the Cabinet made it clear that no concessions could be made – and the Prime Minister realized it was all-important to maintain unity in the Coalition Government until war's end.

Dermot Daly of the Scots Guards, who had also transferred to the Commandos, was a friend of mine in those days and he took me out to lunch occasionally on my infrequent days off from ambulance driving. He had been a fellow officer with Randolph in the Commandos and I remember him describing my cousin, who was then trying to get into David Stirling's Special Group. Dermot had been impressed by Randolph's unmitigated determination and courage when they had done the training courses together in Scotland. I can hear Dermot describing him, 'We all thought he ate and drank too much and must be soft, but nothing could daunt him. When we had to lead our men at the run up to the top of a hill I really thought, "This will do for him – Randolph can't make it", but make it he did. Puffing out his chest like one of those horses you play chess with [Dermot's own words] he ran ahead of his troop shouting, "Come on, men." Looking at his purple countenance pouring with sweat I thought he'd have a heart attack or drop dead but, no, he just wouldn't be beaten – and the soldiers loved it. They thought it so funny to be led up to that hilltop by the Prime Minister's son looking as if he was about to have an apoplectic fit.'

Later Dermot was taken prisoner in the Western Desert and he did not escape until we had invaded Italy when he had to walk 450 miles to meet up with his own crowd, but that is a different story.

— *10* —

1941 was a hot, tumultuous summer in Egypt and the various outfits roving around trying to sort themselves into useful units were so diverse that one could not easily follow their intentions. However, everyone wanted to harass the enemy. Colonel Robert Laycock had left the Royal Horse Guards (the Blues) to head his Commando units specializing in attack behind the enemy lines. He said openly that he had picked most of the officers from the Brigade of Guards, recruiting many of them at the bar of White's Club in London.

Randolph and David Stirling had joined him in this way, and it was a sore disappointment to them when the unit was dissolved. Randolph's situation in the British Army seemed odd indeed. But no odder than that of a lot of his friends who were wandering around the Middle East trying to find some unit to join. But one thing was different for Randolph: he had his father's ear. He felt he had the right to communicate direct and he did not hesitate to read out Winston's long, handwritten letters describing such incidents as the meeting with President Roosevelt in mid-Atlantic. In his innocence Randolph could not see that the power which came to him so naturally through his name aroused intense jealousy.

Layforce found itself unlovingly treated but, as the Commandos had fought splendidly in Crete, the High Command thought that some units might be employed to wreck air fields and lines of communication in North Africa. But, just as this was decided, the Navy announced it had become too busy to land small parties of men along the coast and Layforce was completely disbanded. During the disruption, Randolph shared his room in Cairo at Shepheards Hotel with Bob Laycock, and what a congenial pair they made! But one had an inkling that every-

58

thing that Bob arranged at GHQ in the morning Randolph's arguments undid in the evening (offices were closed all afternoon because of the heat).

The situation in the Middle East has been astringently described by Barrie Pitt who harps on the dangers when amateurs (some of whom would become very professional indeed by the end of the war) were allowed power.* 'They used aristocratic, social or political influence to force through their ideas. . . . One of the results of this, in 1941, was the proliferation of "private armies".' The trouble was that service with these 'private armies' seemed so attractive, especially to the more romantically minded of the new arrivals in the theatre. They offered an escape from the regulation and discipline of battalion life, freedom for the young subaltern or private from the incessant disfavour of adjutant or regimental sergeant major, and they were all, at one time or another, gilded with glamour. From the point of view of the Cairo Headquarters, these formations were allowed to sprout because they seemed to promise a quick return for a minimal outlay. But too often these ad hoc units which set themselves up as a result of little but enthusiasm coupled with social salesmanship were manned by young-sters with cheerfully vague notions of 'swanning around the blue, blowing up enemy dumps etc'.

Amidst all this David Stirling worked quietly away on his own. When fifty parachutes destined for India were unloaded at Alexandria by mistake, he devised the idea of using the parachutes for raiding parties. Stirling 'experimented' with the parachutes but promptly hurt himself in a jump. During the weeks he had to lie in a hospital bed he wondered if very small raiding parties were not the right idea. They might do tremendous damage before attracting enemy attention. Instead of several hundred men, which had so far been considered the minimum number essential for any enterprise, a handful of soldiers could be dropped in by parachute – or even driven in lorries – miles behind the enemy lines. Then they could creep at night to airfields and blow up planes. David Stirling surmised that if sixty men were divided into five groups of twelve, they could attack advanced enemy airfields and explode the whole enemy airforce in Africa! The High Command didn't believe this, but decided there would be little to lose in trying out the idea.

*The Crucible of War, Vol. 1 The Western Desert by Barrie Pitt, Jonathan Cape, 1981.

General Auchinleck, C-in-C Middle East, made Stirling a captain and allowed him to recruit from the remnants of Layforce. David began to prepare for a raid on the night preceding the next major offensive.

Thus was born the SAS, a Special Air Service which up to that time had been merely a dummy force invented to make the Germans *think* that parachute troops had arrived in the Middle East. David Stirling was allowed to open a training camp at Kabrit which lay near the Great Bitter Lakes about a hundred miles from Cairo.

Randolph divided his time between being a Commando lieutenant and a major in Press and Propaganda. When not in Shepheards Hotel he stayed with Peter Stirling, David's brother, who was 3rd Secretary in the Embassy in Cairo. How security worked from *that* flat – where sleeping bags, girls and gramophones seemed piled in merry confusion – one can't imagine, but it did.

A hundred miles from Peter's set-up, David Stirling's training course at Kabrit included long desert marches and preparation for parachute jumps. At the beginning they jumped off lorries. Watching the soldiers bruise themselves enchanted the nearby naval camp. Ratings vied for places whence they could watch and jeer. As there were no parachute instructors in the Middle East, Stirling sent urgent signals back to England asking Ringway (the parachute school) to forward detailed instructions. Eventually the RAF lent a plane for several hours each day and Stirling himself jumped in the first two trials. The third time he stayed on the ground to watch. To his horror he saw two of his men hurtle down to their death with unopened parachutes. He believed that this was the result of Ringway's failure to send sufficient warning about what was likely to go wrong. Apparently the kind of parachutes issued that day was not the same as those used by the RAF. The despatching sergeant had to see the ring break away from the clips and two men died as a result before he could stop the rest from hurling themselves out of the plane. Next morning David Stirling explained exactly what had happened and he himself was the first man to jump.

Randolph felt he had every right to join Stirling's force despite the fact that No. 8 Commando had not really fitted him for this kind of work and he balked at the hard training necessary. Eventually David took him up for his first jump. Randolph, who had not even practised jumping off a moving lorry, sneakily slipped the despatcher a £5 note, 'Just in case I hesitate give me a good push,' he said. The sergeant looked at the Prime Minister's son with amusement. It wasn't often that anyone admitted to nerves. David, who did not know of this trepidation, told Randolph to follow him out of the plane to see how easy it was. After the parachute had opened, David looked up and saw an expression of rapturous relief on his chum's face. 'Thank God the bloody thing opened!' shouted Randolph and David could not resist shouting back, 'Why are you going so much faster than the others? Are you just too heavy?' Actually all the rest of the 'stick' were light and had completed their training to iron hard toughness. David could not help being amused when Randolph hit the ground hard and in an incorrect position. He raced over to the hole in the desert where Randolph lay winded, unable to get up, and put his foot on him as Edwardian sportsmen did when they shot big game. Eventually Randolph regained his breath and staggered to his feet.

When I left Egypt for Beirut in December 1941, Randolph had returned to his office in Press and Propaganda at GHQ in Cairo. He did not take part in the first of David Stirling's attempts to parachute behind the enemy lines, which was just as well, for only eighteen of the fifty-four men and four of the seven officers returned. Because of bad weather they were dropped out of the designated zone and never found the airfields they were looking for. However, after this initial failure David Stirling obtained a base at Jalo, an oasis which lay a hundred and fifty miles inland. Most of the fighting took place along the coast road so the enemy would not suspect this hideaway. He was glad to share Jalo with the Long Range Desert Group trained for desert reconnaisance (and very different to what we called the Short Range Verandah Group which had found itself many jobs based at Shepheards Hotel). With the LRDG's help, Stirling's fantastic success in destroying enemy planes began. It was not long before his little groups had blown up ninety planes on the ground in desert airfields.

Randolph became aware that it might be more pleasurable to raid behind the enemy lines than to squabble with senior officers who insisted they knew more about propaganda than he did. Winston's longing to keep him safe made him hanker for action. After all, Randolph was already half-trained as a Commando, and it was so irritating to hear of exciting forays without being able to join them. Soon after, David Stirling received permission to look around for recruits; a squadron of Free French parachutists arrived from Syria and was incorporated in his force. Then General Auchinleck gave the detachment a sort-of permission to wear their own metal cap badges

with the words 'Who Dares Wins' entwined beneath a winged dagger.*
How Randolph wanted to get that cap badge!

Fitzroy Maclean, who had been in the Foreign Office, now became one of Stirling's officers. He was an extraordinary character. When war broke out he had wriggled out of the Foreign Office to become a Member of Parliament and once in the House of Commons he had promptly joined the Army. When the 'secret' organization which had sent him to the Middle East dissolved, he had the luck to meet Peter Stirling, an erstwhile Foreign Office colleague, and thus he heard of David's SAS and went to Kabrit for the full training.

Randolph hesitated to leave his important job in propaganda – and who is to say that to madden choleric colonels is not important? On the other hand he could hardly bear to be kept out of all this 'fun and excitement' which was obviously helping to win the war far more than any office work.

When in 1942 David became still more successful Randolph suffered increasingly from envy. David had invented the dangerous adventure that he yearned for. And yet at the same time he was busy quarrelling with Sir Walter Monckton, who had sent *me*, an erstwhile ambulance driver, to run a troops' newspaper in Beirut! Randolph maintained that there was not enough newsprint for this Lebanese-run rag called *The Eastern Times*. He wanted our soldiers instead to be forced to read the *Palestine Post*, printed in Jerusalem. I did not realize the intense strain which lay behind Randolph's outbursts and kept solemnly writing to Sir Walter with serious reports on how it would be wise to allot sufficient newsprint to *The Eastern Times* so that a paper printed in Beirut could reach our soldiers in Lebanon. Monckton concurred and eventually not only newsprint but also new presses reached *The Eastern Times* from Cairo. But by that time Randolph had left his Press job.

*This badge with the winged dagger is still worn by the SAS regiment.

— *II* —

In May 1942 Randolph, who was so good at bulldozing his way to wherever he wanted to be, persuaded David Stirling to take him along to raid Benghazi harbour which lay several hundred miles within enemy country. Although he had not been through the Kabrit training course Randolph argued that he had parachuted with David and come out to the Middle East as a Commando.

David had always been adamant about forbidding men to come on raids unless they were fully trained, but Randolph would not take no for an answer. He insisted that he could get fit in a few days, and he started a series of setting-up exercises and early morning runs around Kabrit camp. In the end he won his point. Maybe David could not bear the sight of Randolph puffing around, or maybe he just turned soft-hearted. Whatever the reason he agreed to allow Randolph to accompany his group to the rendezvous and wait there during the raid as an 'observer'.

As a result of Randolph's nagging, David had to pack six men instead of five into his 'Blitz wagon' – a Ford Utility painted to look like an Afrika Korps staff car. They drove to Siwa to meet the Long Range Desert Group patrol and on the way Fitzroy discovered that although over-talkative, Randolph could also be a fascinating and knowledgeable companion. As they sat around the camp fire, brewing up each evening under those brilliantly big desert stars, Lieutenant Churchill could entrance his listeners. His unusual memory for poetry was shown at its best by the camp fire. He recited reams of Macaulay's lays and told stories with pith and humour.

It was Fitzroy Maclean's first raid, but he had completed his training at Kabrit and he spoke fluent Italian, so David regarded him as a very useful member of the group. Randolph had just been brought along because he craved danger and had begged so hard to go. But when they reached Jebel Akdar, the hill overlooking Benghazi, the very experienced Sergeant Selkings blew his finger off while checking detonators and had to be retired. With ill-concealed delight Randolph took his place.

David's intention was to drive to the harbour, blow up enemy shipping under cover of darkness, and then return to the rendezvous before dawn. Everything went wrong and the mission proved hilarious in a hideous way. The Ford's front wheels turned out to be misaligned and the vehicle made a high-pitched scream as it approached the city. Shortly before reaching Benghazi, they had to pull up at a wooden bar stretched across the road to stop traffic. An Italian sentry with a tommy-gun approached the halted car. Fitzroy Maclean's fluent Italian and the dark disguised the fact that the six men wore British uniforms. Fitzroy answered the sentry's question petulantly in Italian, 'Staff Officers and we're in a hurry.' The sentry murmured something about dimming the car lights, walked back to the barricade and swung open the bar.

The Ford drove through, and soon they were approaching Benghazi. A car with headlights full on passed them and seemed very curious, for it stopped and turned back. Afraid they had been spotted, Stirling accelerated, and with front wheels loudly screaming on the fast straight road they sped on into the city. At the first corner Stirling swung in, and switched off the car lights. He found they were in a bombed-out lot. The enemy car flashed by without noticing where they had turned in and then sirens sounded. David had arranged that the RAF should not bomb that night so he feared these sirens meant they had been detected. But whether they had been spotted or not, he felt it safer to order the two NCOs, who had been sitting with Randolph on the back seat, to slip out and blow up the car by placing a 30-minute fuse among the explosives. They could then all walk back to rendezvous in the hills on the following night.

Taking their emergency packs, the six men set off through the Arab quarter. David Stirling and Fitzroy Maclean were unusually tall and they couldn't have been more annoyed when Randolph whispered they were not to crouch but to walk upright naturally. Stumbling over bomb craters and through smashed houses they suddenly found themselves face to face with an Italian *carabiniere*. Again Fitzroy Maclean relied on his fluent Italian.

'What on earth were those sirens for?' he asked.

'Must be an air raid,' replied the man, although no planes had appeared in the dark sky.

'It couldn't be English ground forces?' asked Fitzroy. The Italian soldier laughed at the idea; it seemed hardly likely when the British were 500 miles away in Egypt.

After this conversation which David Stirling listened to without daring to join in, he felt they could risk continuing to raid the docks. With luck there would just be time to stop the car from blowing up. Hurrying back, the corporal pulled out the detonator and flung it away into the dark. They heard it go off five minutes later.

Stirling then told Randolph and one of the corporals to hide the car in the best place they could find, while he and the other three carried one of the two rubber boats to the harbour and climbed through a hole in the wire. Their plan was to row out and attach explosive limpets to whatever ships they could find, row back and drive out of Benghazi before dawn.

But to the chagrin of Fitzroy Maclean and Corporal Cooper, the boat they had brought refused to inflate. As Fitzroy pumped ever harder, the bellows made a wheezing noise which induced a sentry on one of the ships to call out asking what the hell they were doing. '*Militari,*' shouted Fitzroy, reducing the sentry to puzzled silence.

Despite Fitzroy's violent efforts with the pump, no air would remain in the rubber boat. It must have been punctured on the way. They decided to go back to the car for the second boat. Meanwhile David Stirling had not reappeared from his recce of the harbour.

On returning to the car, Fitzroy found Randolph and Corporal Rose backing it into the basement of a bombed-out house. They collected the other boat, carried it back to the water's edge and tried to inflate it. But although both boats had seemed intact when Fitzroy had tried them out prior to departure, this one must also have been punctured on the journey. Nothing could make it hold air. In despair Fitzroy realized he must give up.

He was wondering how on earth to find David and tell him when suddenly Stirling reappeared amongst the cranes and trucks. He had returned while they were fetching the second boat and, seeing no one, had gone off for a further investigation. The officers then had to decide what to do next. Only half an hour of darkness remained before dawn. They could lay their explosives on whatever they found around the docks, or they could return as they had come and trust that on some future raid a better boat might be produced by the Army. After a brief discussion, David decided to keep their presence secret and to hide all traces of this visit. They could then come back another time.

As they climbed through the wire fence intended to keep the docks safe, Fitzroy found himself face to face with a negro sentry who was supposed to be guarding the area. He has described the incident:

It was an Ascari from Italian Somaliland, I did not like the look of him at all . . . he grunted menacingly and pointed his bayonet at the pit of my stomach.

Infusing as much irritation into my voice as I could muster, I asked this formidable blackamoor what he wanted; but he only answered, '*Non parlare Italiano.*'

This gave me my opening. I have always found that in dealing with foreigners whose language one does not speak, it is best to shout. I did so now. '*Non parlare Italiano!* And you a corporal!' And I pointed to the stripe on his sleeve.

This seemed to shake him. He lowered his bayonet and looked at me dubiously. My confidence returned. Trying to give as good a representation as I could of an angry Italian officer, I continued to shout and gesticulate.

It was too much for the black man. With an expression of injured dignity, he turned and walked slowly away, leaving us to continue our progress down to the water's edge. There we stuffed the boats and explosives back into the kitbags and started on our return journey, a weary and despondent little party.

It was at this stage that, looking round I noticed that there were more of us than there should have been. Two sentries with rifles and fixed bayonets had appeared from somewhere and fallen in behind.

These were a most unwelcome addition to the party. There was clearly no hope of shaking them off in the harbour area, and, with such companions, it would be fatal to try to negotiate the hole in the wire. Alternatively to try and shoot it out with them would bring the whole place down about our ears. There was only one hope, and that was to try somehow to brazen it out.

Assuming as pompous a manner as my ten-days beard and shabby appearance permitted, I headed for the main dock gate, followed by David and Corporal Cooper and the two Italian sentries. At the gate a sentry was on duty outside the guard tent. Walking straight up to him, I told him that I wished to speak to the guard commander. To my relief he disappeared obediently into the tent and came out a minute or two later followed by a sleepy-looking sergeant, hastily pulling on his trousers. For the second time that night I introduced myself as an officer of the general staff, thereby eliciting a slovenly salute. Next I reminded him that he was responsible for the security of this part of the harbour. This he admitted sheepishly. How was it, I asked him that I and my party had been able to wander freely about the whole area for the best part of the night without once being properly challenged or asked to produce our identity cards? He had, I added, warming to my task, been guilty of gross dereliction of duty. Why, for all he knew, we might have been British saboteurs carrying loads of high explosives (at this he tittered incredulously, obviously thinking I was laying it on a bit thick). Well, I said, I would let him off this time, but he had better not let me catch him napping again. What was more, I added, with a nasty look at the sentry, who winced, he had better do something about smartening up his men's appearance.

Then I set off at a brisk pace through the gate followed by David and Corporal Cooper, but not by the two Italians who had shuffled off into the shadows as soon as they saw there was trouble brewing. My words had not been without effect. As we passed him the sentry on the gate made a stupendous effort and presented arms, almost falling over backwards in the process.'*

As the six men could not possibly drive out by daylight wearing British uniform, David ordered them to lie low in the upper storey of the half-destroyed house where Randolph had hidden the car. They had emergency rations with them, and also one flask of rum.

Each man had to take his turn on watch and Randolph was given the longest period, 'To teach him not to be lazy,' said David Stirling. At about 5 am Stirling woke up and heard Randolph grunting as he always did in the moments of intense excitement when about to gamble way beyond his means. David was instantly wide awake and let fly as at that moment Randolph flung himself on some intruder. It was an Italian sailor who had been looking for some illicit lodging, but he managed to escape leaving only his matelot's cap in Randolph's hands. The severe scolding made young Churchill very downcast. 'What on earth's the good of having you around?' asked David Stirling.

Then dawn came, and they all realized that the Arabs who lived in this part of the town only departed at night when air raids were likely. Each morning they returned. Soon the streets outside their demolished house were packed with people going about their business and the hum of Arabic, German and Italian sounded through the shutters. Randolph swore he could see booted officers striding in and out of the German Gestapo Headquarters which lay just down the street. Of course the disappointment of not being able to inflate the rubber boats kept their spirits down but if nothing else it was interesting to find out how near they could get to the enemy in British uniforms and not be noticed.

Eastern Approaches by Fitzroy Maclean.

Maybe Fitzroy's Italian had saved them; German and English accents sound rather alike when speaking Italian. And Randolph had behaved perfectly, made himself useful and for once only spoke when he was spoken to and then in a whisper.

As evening approached, David Stirling thought he would try a stroll in the dark down the main street just to see how unobservant people were. And he wanted to take a last look at the harbour to make quite certain what to try for next time.

Laughing and whistling, the men wandered through the crowds and, in the dark, no one noticed they wore British uniform. Neither did they guess that the Prime Minister of England's son walked with them! There were shops, cinemas and buses in Benghazi. It was a busy town despite the constant RAF raids. In the docks they found two motor torpedo boats tied up which had not been there the night before and they hurried back to the car to fetch explosives. But when they returned, sentries had come on duty, patrolling the dockside, and they could not risk a confrontation. David knew it was important to maintain secrecy if they couldn't find and blow up a worthwhile target, so he told his men to retrace their steps. It was time now to get back to their overdue rendezvous with the Long Range Desert Group who had been waiting for them in the Jebel Akdar since the previous dawn. In a way, Randolph had to be disappointed. It was his first raid and they had all hoped to do great things. In fact they almost had, if only those boats had inflated.

Back they drove, the front wheels still screaming horribly on the fast macadam. The wooden pole still lay across the road but the magic words in Italian from Fitzroy, 'Staff Officers', caused the sentry to draw it aside and let the Ford through the road block.

By daybreak they were back with the Long Range Desert Group in the Jebel, just twenty-four hours late. After mugs of hot tea and a breakfast of porridge they drove to Siwa Oasis.

It was on the last lap, on the road from Alexandria to Cairo when they thought, with reason, they were out of danger, that the accident occurred. The Ford Utility hit an army lorry and overturned. David Stirling had given a lift to Arthur Merton, war correspondent for the *Daily Telegraph*, who was flung out and killed. Fitzroy Maclean went to hospital with a fractured skull, Sergeant Rose had a broken arm and Randolph a crushed vertebra from which he would suffer through the years. David, who was driving, had only a small cracked wrist bone, but he had to visit his friends in hospital for weeks. They couldn't laugh about that unbelievable raid as they might have wanted.

What no one seemed to realize at the time was that, apart from the extraordinary ingenuity of David Stirling's plan, which was to lead to other forays of great value, it really had been a triumph to keep Randolph in an enemy base for forty-eight hours! How angry the Gestapo would have been had they guessed who was watching them! What a feather in their caps if they had taken *him* prisoner!

— 12 —

When Randolph flew back to England for treatment he found that Pamela had developed other interests besides himself.

This situation was not improved by a weekend they spent together with the Roseberys at Dalmeny. Unfortunately Randolph found in the bedroom a copy of his father's Life of Lord Randolph Churchill. He discovered it was superbly written, and he kept the light on whilst indulging in his favourite pastime of reading aloud. At breakfast Pamela complained to Lady Rosebery that she hadn't had a wink of sleep all night because Randolph had kept her awake by loud declarations of what he'd discovered to be marvellous passages. He could not understand that his voice might not prove endearing to a wife for hours on end.

Then, back in London, throughout a trying evening with Pamela and his father-in-law Lord Digby, Randolph tried to be jolly but his exuberance fell flat. Evelyn Waugh, who was as usual a malicious onlooker, wrote that Pamela hated Randolph so much she could not bear to sit in the same room with him. Waugh had previously described her 'kitten eyes full of innocent fun', but on this occasion the fun did not sparkle. However, Waugh praised Mrs Randolph Churchill for her method of dealing with the Americans, who, according to him, now held the position in England that the Germans had held in Italy before the war!

Ever since Averell Harriman had been sent to England by President Roosevelt, Pamela had enchanted him. It seemed natural that she should share a small house with Harriman's daughter, and when John Colville went out to look at the devastation after an air raid in April 1941 and found Pamela Churchill and Averell Harriman together examining the debris in Horse Guards Parade, it seemed more natural still. Yet Randolph became uneasy about his wife.

When Averell Harriman travelled to the Middle East, he had carried a note to Randolph from his father and Randolph wrote back to Winston proclaiming himself delighted to meet an attractive man who could tell him all about the Churchills in England. After travelling around with Harriman Randolph dubbed him his 'favourite American'.

But now that he got back to England, Randolph ceased to regard Mr Harriman in that light. It was extremely painful to him to overhear American soldiers whisper on his approach, 'Here comes Mr Pam'. He felt the knife thrust – it was not as 'Mr Pam' that he had regarded himself in Benghazi and he could not help resenting his parents' fondness for their pretty daughter-in-law. Soon Randolph longed to get back to the military scene and felt he had been forced into the wrong role – that of disregarded husband instead of wartime hero. It meant very little to be an MP during the war since all decisions were taken at the top, and only when Winston had some speech to deliver did the House of Commons fill up. Even then the number of members away on active service kept the Chamber rather empty. It was on the radio, not through Parliament, that Britain listened hungrily to its great War Leader.

When not drifting around the military hospitals trying various kinds of treatment for his back, Randolph occasionally looked into some mess which he imagined he could cheer up by representing his father. There is a description of him at Springfield, the house allotted to Air Marshal Sir Arthur 'Bomber' Harris. In Harris' campaign to gain recognition for Bomber Command, Springfield House was to play a major role. No fewer than 5000 visitors a year were entertained there, often overnight, of whom only three are still remembered as 'intolerable'.

Amongst them was Randolph Churchill who 'ranted so loudly and drunkenly against the Air Force that he had to be told he would be thrown out if he persisted'.* That was the trouble with Randolph, he didn't mean to rant and make people dislike him, but he did exactly that.

Meanwhile Winston and Roosevelt decided that the Germans be offered only unconditional surrender! No one then envisaged that the greater part of Europe would be handed over to the Soviets. Randolph

*The Bombers by Norman Longmate, Hutchinson, 1983.

heard his father say, 'I have not become the King's First Minister in order to preside over the liquidation of the British Empire.' Randolph knew that Roosevelt wished to see the end of that Empire, but he thought it would be time enough to argue about it *after* the war.

Randolph could do nothing but fret. He seemed at least to have attained the rank of Major but he longed to return to those daring raiders who were doing so much to destroy the enemy. By this time Stirling's SAS had blown up over 250 enemy planes on the ground.

Randolph kept telling his father of the exploits of David Stirling and Fitzroy Maclean. The latter had by now been sent on an adventurous mission in Persia where his job was to kidnap a General whom the Allies suspected of being in league with the enemy.

Winston was so impressed by Randolph's stories that he went out of his way to meet David Stirling in Cairo, and there he dubbed him, referring to Byron's *Don Juan*, as 'the mildest mannered man that ever scuttled ship or cut a throat'.

After this Winston had a private word with General Alexander, the C-in-C Middle East, and subsequently David Stirling's force became a brigade. But no sooner had the SAS attained that status than Stirling himself was taken POW during a raid in North Africa. He was sleeping in the desert when an Arab betrayed him for money. Randolph took the news hard. So did the entire SAS.

While Randolph was wandering around England he kept coming across Laura Long. Laura's eyes were brown not blue but she was very attractive, very vibrant and magnetic. In his lonely state he naturally became infatuated with her and she enjoyed going around with him in London.

The twenty or more love letters which he wrote her over the next two years all begin 'My darling Laura' or 'My beloved Laura' and all end 'Your devoted – Randolph'.

Randolph wrote to Laura in October 1942 before sailing from Glasgow: 'My darling Laura, I am using your beautiful writing case for the first time. . . . The place I am off to is extremely inaccessible and I gather I will have to leave for the Middle East at any moment . . . so don't expect to hear from me for some time. It will not mean that I have forgotten you. As I told you the other night it pains me deeply that I should not be in a position to say to you the things I would like to say.'

Four days later he wrote her at sea, 'I must apologise for the deception which I had to practise on you. As you may hear before you get this letter I am not really going to the Middle East. We are on a much more exciting venture of which you will soon be reading in the papers.'

On November 7 he wrote, 'We are nearing the end of our voyage and as things start popping quite soon I must bring this rambling letter to a close. . . . All my love, Your devoted, Randolph.'

One can see how anxious he had become to settle snugly into love with one woman. Unfortunately for Randolph, Laura was in love with the Earl of Dudley, a man twenty years older than herself, whom she planned to marry as soon as she could get a divorce from Lord Long.

When in Algiers he induced his friend, the American war correspondent Virginia Cowles, to write pleading his case. Her letter to Laura reads as if Randolph was not already married to Pamela Digby!

Darling Laura,
Randolph is here in Algiers and *you* are very much on his mind. He talks of nothing else.

He is looking very thin and handsome and wishes you to think seriously before taking the plunge with the Earl! Life with Randolph I am sure would be far more glamorous and exciting.

I am off tomorrow to what is known as 'the forward area'. . . .

Lots of love, much haste and why not *really* consider Randolph?
Virginia

In the same month that Virginia Cowles wrote this letter Laura obtained her decree absolute and married Eric Dudley. But Randolph's letters did not alter. He continued to write to his 'darling', groaning at her decision to marry in haste. 'I am handicapped by not being free – but what is the use of your complicating matters further by losing *your* liberty? . . . If Dorothy Beatty [the Countess Beatty] can get out here in the American Red Cross why can't you?' He asks Laura to think of him when she closes her 'shutters' (long-eyelashed eyes) each night and he made no secret of the aching void inside him.

By the time he reached Cairo the news of Laura's remarriage had arrived but he refused to take it seriously – 'My darling Laura' he still wrote.

Your long letter of 18 January has just arrived. Any letter from you will always bring me joy; but this one has made me very gloomy. But it was sweet, good and honest of you to write so frankly. I have no right to challenge the wisdom of your decision. . . .

As you may imagine I have been having a fascinating and interesting time. It has been lovely for me seeing my father again, and we have never been better friends. . . .

Two local cracks; General Montgomery when asked what he thought of General Anderson replied, 'A good plain cook!' (I think this crack tells more about Monty than it does about Anderson.)

And General Catroux' policy in Syria is said to be 'French Without Spears'. [Major General Sir Edward Spears had been sent as Minister Plenipotentiary by Winston and was unpopular with the French.]

Perhaps your two missing letters are waiting for me in Algiers? Do you remember the 'unbirthday present' in *Winnie the Pooh*? It was a present given when it was *not* a birthday – the stockings were meant to be an un-wedding present!

Good luck and bless you –

Randolph was always a good loser.

By February 1943 Randolph was in Algiers with Winston, and as the diplomatic bag remained open to him, Laura continued to receive presents. Miss Buck, who was Randolph's London secretary, would ring Laura up whenever a parcel or letter arrived. He really did not seem to care that she was now the Countess of Dudley! All he wanted was to see her in the red velvet he had bought in Cairo and watch those wonderful dark 'shutters' closing.

'Do go on writing,' he implored. 'Your letters are my only source of news from England.'

After the VIPs went home, Randolph continued to struggle to obtain useful employment at the front. It was maddening for him that everyone was so nervous of using Winston's son in battle, and that he was not considered suitable as a soldier. Eventually he found himself in charge of a lot of war correspondents. Nothing could have been worse for him than to be sent around the desert in charge of a bunch of newspaper men. Their proximity entailed much hard drinking and they played up to Randolph in entirely the wrong way, in the hope of obtaining some 'scoop' through his good offices.

— *13* —

In the spring of 1943, Winston Churchill invited Fitzroy Maclean, who had finished his Persian adventure, to Chequers for a serious talk. The Prime Minister had long been worrying about how to coordinate various Yugoslav forces who only fought the Germans – when they weren't at each other's throats. Winston decided that this unique officer could be dropped by parachute, and then he would be able to send factual reports about which side was actually doing the enemy most harm – the Chetniks under General Mihailovic, who had the backing of the royalist party in London, or the Partisans headed by an unknown Communist, Tito. Captain F. W. Deakin had already been parachuted into the country to join Tito's embattled Partisans in their long march across Montenegro and Bosnia.

By July 1943 Fitzroy Maclean found himself appointed brigadier and head of the British Military Mission in Yugoslavia. The few British officers who were already spread throughout the country would report to him on the state of their various territories, then Maclean would report direct to Winston Churchill. The situation might have been easier to assess had the British officers not been living far apart in wooded mountains with wirelesses that seldom worked. But Maclean knew he could coordinate their ideas and in September 1943 he and his party of British soldiers parachuted into Yugoslavia.

Meanwhile Randolph, eager for employment, acted as a liaison officer with the Highland Division in Sicily. There is a vignette of him, strolling unconcernedly through a stream of bullets to inform the SAS that they had done their bit and were to return to North Africa for a fresh assignment.* Then he tried to be of use representing the enemy on army manoeuvres, but to his rage he was 'captured' by Nicholas Mosley, the son of Sir Oswald Mosley and Cynthia (the daughter of Lord Curzon). Nicholas was a very young officer who had just arrived in camp near Algiers. To his father in Brixton prison he wrote, 'I captured an enormous Captain in some hush-hush job whose face seemed vaguely familiar. Unfortunately I treated him with great respect, for it later turned out to be Randolph Churchill. If I had known earlier, I would have hurled him into a dungeon full of syphilitic Arabs. I am sure he would have enjoyed a taste of the Brixton atmosphere.'

Randolph moved on to Malta where he bumped into Lt Col. Laycock who asked if he would like to join the landing at Salerno. So he found employment in Italy. How much better he was among fighting men than in the Ritz Hotel! If only he could get a definite military job.

Hitler had by now realized the worth of David Stirling's boys and had issued an order: 'Captured SAS troops must be handed over at once to the nearest Gestapo unit. These men are very dangerous and the presence of SAS in any area must be reported immediately.' It may have comforted Stirling that he had made his mark with the Germans before his capture, but all his attempts to escape from prison failed – partly because his height of 6ft 5in made him so conspicuous.

When Bari in Italy had been conquered by the Polish Colonel Peniakoff, Brigadier Maclean travelled there from Yugoslavia by naval launch and boarded a plane for Cairo. There he handed a written report to Anthony Eden, newly arrived from Moscow. Maclean's conclusions would be passed on to Winston.

Brigadier Maclean told the Yugoslavs that all British help in the form of ammunition, boots and stores would in future be dropped to the Partisans and not to the Chetniks. Rather sadly it had to be accepted that aid to Mihailovic must cease because his forces seemed determined to wait for an Allied landing. Maclean now had to bring a Partisan delegation to Egypt. Alas the delegation tried to fly out in a small German aircraft they had captured but they had been betrayed and just before their take-off a German plane bombed them. One member of the Yugoslav delegation was killed and so were two of Fitzroy's best British officers. When weather permitted he set out again in a Dakota surrounded by American fighters. The plane managed to land on the snow-covered field in Bosnia where fires had been lit to

*Special Air Service by Philip Warner, Kimber, London, 1971.

signal the lie of the runway. It seemed a triumph to get his party back to Italy but as no one expected them in Bari they were only too glad to fly on to Egypt with their wounded.

When they landed in Alexandria an ambulance swept off the wounded Yugoslavs to hospital and Maclean discovered that a luxurious villa had been laid on for him and the delegation.

After leave in London Randolph returned to North Africa, travelling part of the way with his father who was on his way to the Cairo Conference for talks with Roosevelt. On 15 November 1943 he wrote to Laura, 'Only scent in good supply! You know what decision I pray that you will reach, although I feel it would be wrong of me to press you to it. We could be divinely happy together.'

Along with stockings and a belt, Randolph sent Laura another letter saying, 'In Cairo I met your friend the Regent of Iraq. He told us of his activities at Himley [Eric Dudley's country house] and Winston said to him, "I hear your Royal Highness is very fond of hiding in the same place when playing hide and seek!" The little man was astounded that Winston should know this about him. Winston pointed out that he always had to keep well informed.' This succulent news item had of course reached Randolph through Laura, who had had the Regent to stay at Himley.

Randolph caught up with his father at the Teheran Conference where Churchill and Roosevelt met Stalin – and from where Randolph sent Laura a belt and more stockings! Perhaps he was glad that one person at least existed to whom he could pour out his heart, for he minded deeply when he and his father had rows.

On this jaunt to Persia, Randolph had taken pains to keep his name out of the papers. Winston did not want it to look as if he was travelling around with his whole family. Despite occasional bickering with his father, Randolph enjoyed himself in Teheran. He liked meeting the bigwigs – President Roosevelt and Stalin and all the admirals and generals. He could stomach the banquets too!

He wrote to tell Laura of the new secret – that he was hoping to join Fitzroy Maclean – adding, as if she was not another man's wife, 'My sweetest darling, I love you. . . .'

In Cairo, Fitzroy lost no time in making his way to the Churchill villa near the Pyramids. Here Winston received him wearing an embroidered dressing-gown and could not resist asking Brigadier Maclean, who had been in the Cameron Highlanders, if he wore his regimental kilt when parachuting. Then Winston settled down to business and said he had been very impressed by Fitzroy's report on Yugoslavia and definitely decided that all support must be given only to Tito. This meant that Mihailovic must be abandoned. Not only would supplies to the Partisans now be increased but also the number of aeroplanes employed in dropping them. The Prime Minister also confirmed that the scope of the British mission was to be extended and the officers employed therein would be dropped to Partisan formations throughout Yugoslavia as Maclean directed. Owing to the snow-covered mountains, there was no way of entering the country in autumn and winter except by parachute.

When Brigadier Maclean got back to Cairo he looked around for the right type of officer for his very special mission. Peter Stirling's flat offered a good recruiting ground. Adventurous young men were always congregating there.

When David had been taken prisoner his elder brother Bill took command of the SAS regiment and Peter had remained on as 3rd Secretary at the Embassy and there, in the famous flat, the Brigadier could take his pick. Randolph was of course fretting at not being able to get nearer the fighting and he soon began to badger Fitzroy Maclean to go to Yugoslavia. It didn't take long to get fit, and hadn't he been useful on the Benghazi raid? The Brigadier made his decision, 'I weighed up the pros and cons and despite massive resistance from all sorts of quarters, decided to take him. I knew that with Randolph there wouldn't be a dull moment. Not that life with the Partisans was ever dull. I just thought the two would go together.'

Randolph was of course in seventh heaven at being accepted. He minded his ps and qs, started every peroration with 'Permission to speak, sir?' and never failed to defer to his commanding officer's rank. Fitzroy Maclean got rather tired of the constant saluting and 'Brigadier may I have a word . . . ?' but he felt it was safer to keep Randolph very subordinate.

Soon after the Cairo Conference, Winston got pneumonia and retired to Marrakesh to recuperate. So that Fitzroy could continue to explain the Yugoslav situation, General Alexander took him there in his personal plane – and Randolph accompanied them.

On the way they looked in on the Duff Coopers in Algiers. Duff was now British representative to General de Gaulle until such time as he could become Ambassador to France. The Coopers had just arrived and found their 'British Embassy' to be a Moorish house set in jade green gardens. However, the house had no hot water and nowhere to cook. Lady Diana has described Algiers at the time, 'streets and streets of shuttered shops. I slept in my fur coat, shaking it out vigorously for day wear.'

It was quite a relief to her when, after taking a nap in Harold Macmillan's villa she suddenly heard 'Randolph's clarion call. He had just arrived with Brigadier Fitzroy Maclean, the Partisan hero.' As the pair of 'fierce fighters' were on their way to see Winston in Marrakesh, Lady Diana did not lose the opportunity of ordering Randolph to tell his father about the British Embassy's plight, and that Air Marshal Tedder and General Wilson had far better houses than the Ambassador. 'After all, why should these warriors, who are supposed to be fighting a war in Italy, loll in luxurious immunity, while we permanent missionaries are left nothing but sties?'

So Winston then knew that not only was he supposed to attend to running the war but also see that his representatives had cooking facilities and hot water. Soon after this, Harold Macmillan offered the Coopers a daily hot bath – and Lady Diana predicted that he would eventually become Prime Minister.

When they reached Marrakesh, Fitzroy and Randolph found Winston – wearing a bright blue boiler suit – installed in the Villa Taylor, a superb copy of a Moroccan palace in its own great garden. By this stage, Fitzroy Maclean had no wish to know more about the decisions being made at the top than was necessary; as he wrote, 'In a few days time I was due to be dropped back into enemy-occupied territory where the possibility of being taken POW could never be excluded, and, with the Gestapo's methods of interrogation it was advisable to know as little as possible about the future conduct of the war.' He realized too that it would be extremely disagreeable if Randolph were captured, but they had both resolved to take that risk.

Before Randolph took up his job with Brigadier Maclean he wrote to Laura telling her that he could not give her a clue to his whereabouts, but hinting that he had at last the chance of doing useful and exciting work. He assured her that he himself kept no secrets from her, but his father's secrets were different.

On 17 December 1943, he wrote to Laura, 'Owing to Winston's illness the little gifts I wrote of in my last letter will not reach you for some time, so I'm cramming a few stockings in this letter so that something at least will reach you for Xmas.' On 21 December he wrote openly, 'I am just off to Italy to join Fitzroy; so this is the last "rapid delivery" letter you are likely to have. . . . Winston is much better. He is a very unusual patient. He selected 10 pm last night as the time to get up for the first time. We played bezique for an hour and a half. When his nurse came in at 11.30 he demanded solicitously, "Have the doctors gone to bed? . . . Good," he said, "I hope they sleep well." I'm very much excited at having something useful to do at last and it will be great fun being with Fitzroy.'

On Christmas Day 1943, Randolph told Laura that 'Winston really is much better. He is celebrating his Xmas by presiding over an immense military conference.' This included the Supreme Commanders, General Maitland Wilson and General Eisenhower, General Alexander and Admiral Cunningham. Even Randolph found his convalescent father's energy 'fantastic'.

While they were in Marrakesh, good news of the Partisans' military successes arrived and Winston felt that the mysterious leader called Tito might need encouragement. He wrote a letter which Fitzroy Maclean was to hand over personally when he could find Tito in the forests.

All this time Randolph kept writing to Laura hoping she would leave her new husband Lord Dudley – although at the same time admitting it would be 'wrong of me to press it'. The affair was psychologically important to him, although conducted in cloud-cuckoo land. As long as she cared for him a little, and as long as he could think about her every night, that was good enough. What he could not bear was the thought of losing her completely. She remained his sheet anchor.

As 1943 ended, Randolph flew to Bari with Brigadier Maclean where they had to spend a fortnight before being dropped in Yugoslavia. He still remembered to call Fitzroy 'Sir', and tried his level best to behave as a major should.

At Bari, Air Vice Marshal William Elliott, who commanded Balkan Air Force and was crucial to Maclean's effort in Yugoslavia, had the idea of giving what he imagined would be an interesting political dinner party. He invited Randolph, an MP, to meet another MP. Randolph greeted his fellow member of the House of Commons with the cry of, 'You traitor . . .'. Actually the gentleman in question (who was killed shortly afterwards) had enlisted in a fascist movement before the war. The Air Vice Marshal soon realized that his dinner party was not going to be all that delightful. Half way through the meal Randolph stood up and asked to be excused. 'I can't sit at this table any longer,' he spluttered. Then saluting bravely (after a few drinks he did not realize he had no cap on), he stepped backwards, fell and crashed his head against a cement ledge. 'Oh God, the Prime Minister's son has killed himself! How on earth will we break it to Winston?' cried the Air Vice Marshal. But Randolph was not dead. Carried away unconscious, he woke bright as a button on the morrow. Air Vice Marshal Elliott did not give any more political dinner parties for a very long time.

Then Brigadier Maclean met two brothers who had become friendly with Randolph at the recent Salerno landings. Tom and Jack Churchill were no relations of Randolph but both of them were Commando officers and they invited Fitzroy and Randolph to a New Year's Eve party in their mess to celebrate the advent of 1944. During the revelry Fitzroy and Tom Churchill crept away to discuss the possibility of installing a Commando garrison on the Isle of Vis, where supplies could be landed for the Partisans. Thus was born the idea of a Headquarters for the Yugoslav fighting movement.

Meanwhile the weather continued to be bad for parachuting at night. Eventually Fitzroy Maclean was allotted a Dakota and an escort of a dozen Thunderbolts. With Maclean travelled his own trusted Sergeant Duncan, who was a wireless operator, two new wireless operators and an American who had been in the British Army since the outbreak of war. Randolph was the new boy. They flew in clear sunshine over the Adriatic. When the 'despatcher' signalled them to be ready, Fitzroy's hand strayed under his parachute harness to make certain that Winston's letter lay safely inside his tunic.

He had decided to jump first, with the others following in a 'stick'. The doors were opened and the despatcher motioned them to get into place. As Maclean looked down, the houses of the village beside which they were to land appeared unpleasantly close – he hoped there would be time for their parachutes to open. But he did not warn Randolph who was to jump next. Then the lights turned from red to green and Fitzroy Maclean had to hurtle into the air followed by Randolph.

— 14 —

Randolph's satisfaction at seeing his parachute actually billow out above his head changed to disgust as he met the ground with a severe jolt. For a few minutes he sat in the wet snow of the Bosnian mountains worrying about his vertebrae. Then he looked around and saw he'd just missed a telegraph post. The others had landed all over the valley, and the reception party ran wildly around greeting them. They wanted to draw up a Partisan guard of honour for the Brigadier. Then horses appeared and all set off at a gallop to the village while the guard of honour turned to collect the supplies which had been dropped in containers over a wide area.

A splendid meal had been prepared in the hamlet and to this the parachutists did full justice, although their Partisan hosts innocently described it as less good than the one they'd prepared the day before and then eaten themselves when the plane did not appear.

Towards dusk, in falling snow, Maclean left on horseback to meet Tito for the first time at his secret hideout in the woods. It was midnight before he arrived. He found a group of huts constructed from the trees in the forest. Maclean handed Winston's letter to Tito. It was a most flattering gesture, for the great man himself had written on 10 Downing Street paper and sent a signed photograph in another envelope. Churchill harped on the fact that he had sent his only son to serve on the British Mission. While Maclean was assuring Tito that in future he could rely on ammunition, food and boots by air-drop, the self-made Marshal explained that he hoped before long to move his headquarters to Drvar, a village in Bosnia which had often proved a haven for Partisan forces. As for the islands off the coast, they had all by now been occupied by the Germans and it would be a *tour de force* if Vis could be kept as an Allied base.

Towards dawn, Maclean left Tito and followed a soldier through the snow to the hut prepared for him. A moustachioed Partisan attached himself to the Brigadier and explained that he was to be bodyguard, cook and batman. Wearily Maclean filled the canvas bag which had held Winston's letter with straw and using it as a pillow lay down to sleep.

Several days later Tito announced they would move to Drvar. After an extraordinarily difficult journey they arrived there several hours before dawn. One house had been arranged with double-tiered sleeping shelves to accommodate the entire Mission and the old peasant/owner proudly explained that one end was 'specially reserved for President Churchill who was to arrive on a State visit to Marshal Tito'. As several of Tito's strangely attired fighting men had already been made 'Cabinet Ministers', Maclean did not press for exactitude. But a few days later, when Randolph and the rest of the Military Mission arrived at Drvar, Fitzroy wondered how to explain to the naive peasants that Randolph wasn't actually Prime Minister of England. It was all very well having him along but Randolph's sleeping habits were not pleasant; and Maclean felt that he could well dispense with the honour of sharing a room with this particular 'President'. The other officers were after all juniors and they could simply sleep off the effects of too much slivovic, whereas Maclean had to *think* and *organize*.

The Partisans seemed delighted to stop German troop movements by blowing up the Trieste–Lubliana railway viaduct. With the approach of spring it became easier to drop supplies at night, although the whole of Yugoslavia seemed to consist of jagged mountains and narrow valleys, so signal fires always had to be lit for landing planes. Randolph and the other British officers would run to retrieve the bundles thrown, but sometimes bad weather would stop the aircraft and they had to wait all night in vain. Maclean described it in *Eastern Approaches*:

Some pilots would let go their loads from a considerable height, and the parachutes, caught by the wind, would drift a mile or more from their proper destination, often ending up with the enemy. Others, with more experience of the job would edge their aircraft right into the valley and make the drop from a couple of hundred feet above the fires, banking steeply immediately afterwards so as to avoid hitting a hillside. Sometimes they came in so low that, looking up we could see for an instant the figure of the despatcher, outlined against the dim light of the open door, as he rolled out the containers.

As the shortage of parachutes became more acute the RAF took to making 'free drops' of supplies. This called for considerable agility on the part of those on the ground.

Fitzroy Maclean continually explained to the Yugoslavs under his command that meteorological conditions in Italy could prevent the RAF making their drops, but the Partisans were incapable of understanding that weather might be different across the Adriatic. They always attributed short supplies to 'Capitalist Intrigue'. At one stage rations became very short indeed, but the slivovic, which was locally made, continued to enhance diminishing repasts.

While Brigadier Maclean strove in vain to impart some technical knowledge of new weapons to the Partisans, they remained absolutely convinced that they knew everything about everything that explodes. Then, as snow melted, food became more plentiful. Randolph did his best to be useful. His fiery romantic nature appealed to the Yugoslavs, and it was good for him to learn how other people had to live rough and go hungry.

Throughout February, Randolph kept writing to Laura. On 9 February 1944 he pressed her 'Would you be very sweet and order me some good cigars. . . . Yesterday I rode across the mountains for 3½ hours on a charming white pony.' Fitzroy Maclean was busy and kept disappearing to other parts of Yugoslavia, but for Randolph there was little to do. Towards the end of the month he wrote,

Still surrounded by snow on all sides. I have been teetotal for exactly a month except for two or three days when I got hold of some slivovic. I find the enforced water wagon all right. More serious is the shortage of cigarettes.

Our pastimes here are simple. I have just been making tea and whiling away the time washing my pillowcase and some handkerchiefs. The bright red slippers I bought in London are a joy – they remind me of home!

I started to keep a diary here – like a schoolboy's, 'got up, washed, went to bed'. But when I could not even chronicle that I had washed I decided to give it up! . . . . But I enjoy writing to you even when there is nothing to say.

Two American officers have just arrived and share a room with me. It is very small and untidy. We have nothing to do but wait! Do you ever have time to think of me or are you too busy sitting under apple trees with a lot of other guys, infatuating them with your 'shutters'. You always get into trouble when I go away. Last year you got married. What will it be this time?

Then the Russians gave a sumptuous dinner party. Randolph wrote it was the first good tuck-in he had had in 'this primitive and hungry land. Immense quantities of the best smoked salmon, caviar, black

Persian sardines, *pâté* and sausages to start off with! I brought away one chocolate biscuit to send you but got so hungry that I ate it later!'

The Americans made it possible to have a four for bridge. 'Money has no meaning here, so we play for a cigarette a hundred. We all over bid and have lots of goulashes. My partner is Sir Andrew Maxwell, a cousin of David Stirling's. He is a very agreeable addition to our party.'

But oh how dull it was! Partisan cook batmen were not all that marvellous and the war seemed very far away.

On 21 March the first batch of mail for months reached Croatia and to Randolph's delight contained four letters from Laura. 'Bless you darling,' he wrote, 'your letters, but luckily not the books, arrived riddled with bullets. They got shot up on the road coming here by a German plane. I am worried about my back. It has never really got right since I broke it eighteen months ago in the car crash with David. The three jumps I have done since then didn't seem to affect it at all but I have found recently that after quite a short walk or even sitting upright for long, it tends to ache. It doesn't hurt much but enough to be troublesome if we had to do any long marching.'

The spring weather improved. Every morning the sun shone and a wonderful scent arose from the valleys that lay at the foot of the snow-covered mountains.

At a party for Tito and the Russians – they were to be shown the film *Desert Victory* 'in order to persuade them that someone else has done some fighting apart from themselves' wrote Randolph. The British set to preparing a great blow-out in the mess. Randolph knew it would not be possible to provide as sumptuous a repast as the Russians, but capitalist countries could hardly hope to vie with 'the luxury of officials of Communist Russia'. However, the British had a lot of bully beef, and they traded all their remaining parachute silk for lashings of the local slivovic.

After the film, Randolph 'had a long talk with the Russian General. He became very confidential and asked me, " 'ave you got a woman 'ere?" I told him that unfortunately I had not. He said he hadn't either . . . . Actually we had asked all the local girls to our party. But none of them are pretty and they all wear uniform and pistols which I find very unsexing.'

Fitzroy Maclean was in London reporting to Winston and looking around for suitable volunteers for Yugoslavia, when in May the news arrived that German parachute troops had launched a massive air attack on the village of Drvar where the Missions were situated, and that although Tito seemed to have escaped capture, heavy casualties had been inflicted on the Partisans and the peasants who had sheltered them.

Randolph had, like the other British officers with him, been asleep when the cry of '*Avioni!*' woke him. He and the rest hurried out into the orchard around their cottage, and stood for a time staring at the sky. First came the whistle and crack of bombs, then parachutists and glider troops hurtled down out of the sky to shoot their way into the village.

As usual Tito was sleeping in a cave in the mountains which served as his HQ. This cave looked down on the village and its entrance came under fire. Luckily he and his companions managed to escape up the rope which lay up a waterfall at the back. Drvar had to be abandoned and the inhabitants left to their fate.

For several days Tito's guerillas and Randolph with the Allied Missions had to keep on the move through the forests. They had to hide by day and only dared to travel at night. Eventually they halted to build an airstrip and get their wirelesses to work. Planes then found them and evacuated them to Bari.

Despite the terrible cruelty of this type of warfare Randolph excelled when danger – real danger – occurred. He was in fact recommended for the Military Cross for his resourceful conduct during the retreat, and was awarded the MBE. Care had to be taken that Winston's son was not decorated too easily!

When Fitzroy Maclean got back he learned sorrowfully that many peasants whom he had known and liked had been shot. The Germans had forced old men, women and even children to carry ammunition for them. When they had done so, and were of no more use, the Germans shot them. Furious at having missed Tito and the Allied Missions the enemy could but take it out on the peasants before trailing through the forests where they could only hope more important game might be hiding.*

Eventually Tito and his staff reached Bari, and the new HQ was installed on the island of Vis.

The only letter from Laura to Randolph which I have been able to lay my hands on, shows what reason he had to be avid for news from

---

*It must be remembered that the atrocities committed by Serbo-Croat-speaking German troops were usually the work of Germans who had been settled in the north of the country two centuries before.

England. It is dated 19 May 1944 and must have been written about the time of the German attack on Drvar.

Darling Randolph

Judging by your letters from Yugoslavia life at Himley [the Dudley family home] and Birmingham is a razmatazz of excitement in comparison. People are blown up in the streets and by Eric at the bridge table – where the stakes are not for a cigarette a hundred! Don't go on about my spelling – it's boring, a thing you don't tolerate – nor will I. As for the numbered letters it's hard to remember for my life is much more hectic than yours. We *do* have caviar (two sorts, grey and black), also smoked salmon but NOT I am glad to report as a gift from a Communist totalitarian regime. I couldn't and wouldn't eat from that kind of a hand. Keep on writing about your American Colonel with a Cockney accent and I will do my best to scribble you anything that might be of interest. At the moment I am horribly busy with a meeting tonight about my forthcoming Red Cross fete in August which as you know I hope your father or mother will open. Thank you for several letters received via Miss Buck – mostly informing me of your leisurely way of life.

Take care.
Much love as always.
Laura

PS. A longer letter will follow.

— *15* —

By now the newly created RAF formation, called Balkan Airforce, was well established at Bari, and while Fitzroy Maclean and Tito were arranging the Partisan HQ on the island of Vis Randolph was sent home on leave to England. Before he left he complained to Brigadier Maclean, 'There don't seem to be any of my intellectual equals in your Mission. Couldn't I bring a few amusing chaps back with me to Yugoslavia?' Fitzroy Maclean only wanted fighting men who were capable of doing a job properly, but he liked Randolph and appreciated his very real courage so, as he had other things to attend to, the Brigadier gave him permission to recruit officers who could be useful and were allowed to leave their jobs. With a beatific smile Randolph flew away.

He passed through Italy on the way home, saw his brother-in-law Duncan Sandys in Naples and met his old friend Tom Mitford. He had not seen Tom for three years and the ache of knowing that Tom's sister Diana Mosley was still with her husband in prison, made the meeting very moving. Winston had tried his utmost to alleviate the discomforts which Diana had to face. In the end, the Prime Minister arranged for Oswald Mosley to be incarcerated in a house in the prison yard with his wife and then, as Mosley's health deteriorated and no British Government could want a martyr to the Fascist cause, they were driven to their country home and merely restricted from travelling. Tom was bitter enough about their plight, especially as he himself was a serving officer and his sister Unity, who had imagined herself in love with Hitler, was slowly dying of a self-inflicted bullet wound. This was in fact the last time that Randolph would see his great friend.

During the few days he spent in newly liberated Rome Randolph sought a private audience with the Pope, and as Winston Churchill's son this was accorded him. Because Fitzroy Maclean's mission was accredited to Tito and Randolph's future part was to be concerned mainly with Catholic Croatia this was a wise move, but the conversation with Pius XII dragged – Randolph tried to keep it going with talk of Evelyn Waugh who had dedicated his first war novel *Put Out More Flags* to 'Major Randolph Churchill – Fourth Hussars, Member of Parliament'. But the Pope had never heard of Evelyn Waugh and Randolph made one of his most inept comments, 'I thought Captain Waugh's reputation might be known to Your Holiness because he's a Catholic too.'

On reaching London, Randolph had two ideas in his head: first he wanted to see Laura Dudley, and then he wanted to find those witty pals whom Fitzroy Maclean had said could return with him to Yugoslavia. The first on the list was Freddie Birkenhead who proved hard to winkle out of his job in Political Warfare Executive where he was very useful and well liked. Randolph also asked to see Evelyn Waugh, who seemed more difficult to trace.

In his Life of Evelyn Waugh, Christopher Sykes has succinctly described the month of June 1944, the time of the Normandy landings. Waugh had just finished his novel, *Brideshead Revisited* – for which he had been given months of leave by the War Office who couldn't think what else to do with him! This unique privilege had been extended by his Colonel, who also could not think how to employ such an extraordinary character, but the allotted time had now expired. The novel was finished and the Military had him back on their hands.

On 15 June Waugh notified Colonel Brian Franks, who commanded the SAS regiment which had developed out of No. 8 Commando, and to which he really belonged, that he was ready to return to active service. Christopher Sykes was with Colonel Franks when he received the letter at his Headquarters in Perthshire. Colonel Franks 'was dismayed. "What on earth shall I do with him?" he groaned. "I can't very well tell him to take another three months' leave and write another book, which is what I would like to do." We all bent our minds to the problem, which was not an easy one, for Franks had set an absolute condition on any solution. "I'm not going to allow him near the men," he asserted. "Get him up here and see what he wants to do," I suggested. "I know exactly what he wants to do," said Brian. "He wants to mess up the men and the regiment, and the brigade, and the Air-Borne Corps." '

Christopher was at the time Operational Intelligence Officer and he suggested that with the Second Front just opened in Normandy and voluminous enemy documentation becoming available, Evelyn might be useful on the staff. The Chief Intelligence Officer turned pale at this suggestion. Evelyn had to remain in Scotland while everyone scratched their heads wondering what to do with him.

On 28 June, Christopher Sykes was sent to London on military business, and after a busy morning at Combined Operations Head-quarters, he went to White's Club in St James's Street for refreshment. He had not been there many minutes before he heard the loud and unmistakable voice of Randolph Churchill at the bar saying: 'Where the hell is Evelyn Waugh? I've tried everywhere! No one can tell me. I need him immediately.' Christopher was an old friend. He went quickly to the bar crying, 'Randolph, did you say you wanted Evelyn? I think I can help you. What's it for?'

Randolph then explained his job under Fitzroy Maclean in Yugos-lavia. He said, 'Fitz agreed before I left that I could try to get Evelyn Waugh and Freddie Birkenhead. It's all very secret,' he added, his voice rising a little in volume, 'So don't tell anyone. But where the hell *is* Evelyn? How can I get him?'

Christopher immediately responded, 'Randolph if you just stay where you are, I think I can get him for you. Don't go for five minutes. . . .'

Sykes then rushed to the phone booth and put through a priority call on the military line to Scotland. At the other end Colonel Franks heaved a sigh of relief. He sent Evelyn down by the night train, only too thankful to be rid of this officer who was even more difficult to place than Randolph. So it was that Captain Evelyn Waugh reported to Major Randolph Churchill at the Dorchester Hotel and joined the Military Mission to Yugoslavia!

Waugh's diary hints that Randolph asked him to go with him to Croatia 'in the belief that I should be able to heal the Great Schism between the Catholic and Orthodox Churches – something with which he has just become acquainted and finds a hindrance to his war policy'.

Within the week Randolph announced they were both to leave and the two of them set off by air via Gibraltar.

On 6 July they reached Algiers and Randolph rang up the Duff Coopers. Diana Cooper, who adored Evelyn Waugh, welcomed them there – although there still wasn't hot water she reckoned that Waugh's conversation would compensate. Duff, who was extremely busy, groaned at the prospect of political diatribe at every meal and Lady Diana proceeded to write to her son, 'Randy is thin and grey, keen and sweet. Evelyn is thin and silent. I have put them on improvised camp-beds in the unused dining room. Evelyn came up and sat in a grey, dejected heap, without a word, a smile or a nod. Later, when alone I asked him why . . . he said he was never so happy in his life, he had just written a book that he thought a masterpiece [*Brideshead Revisited*], he had no money troubles, a wife he adored, three fine children, splendid health and now an active life calling him to Yugoslavia with his beloved Randolph. His serenity knew no bounds. I said I wished he could reflect his happiness a little.'

A few days later Randolph and Evelyn reached Bari and met Fitzroy Maclean. Randolph's new protégé immediately dubbed him, 'dour, unprincipled, ambitious, probably very wicked, shaved head and devil's ears'. Brigadier Maclean was a serious soldier and he had been carefully recruiting officers who would be a real help to his Mission and their integrity was of paramount importance.

The plane taking Randolph and Evelyn to Yugoslavia crashed on 16 July, and the accident is described in his diary as Waugh remembered it. They had boarded a Dakota in the evening at Bari, and were pleasantly sustained by peaches and grapes which the Russian military passed around. As the plane came in to land in Croatia it crashed, and Waugh, who was seriously concussed, only remembers walking in a cornfield by the light of the burning plane.

'The next thing I knew I was sitting on a stretcher in a hut, Randolph in tears because his servant had been killed. A good deal of confused talk about who had escaped and who hadn't.'

Randolph found himself lame in both legs and shouted for morphia. His spine however was what really mattered and that much-jolted vertebra seemed to have survived the latest jogging.

An ambulance took those who were still alive to nearby houses. When Evelyn came to visit Randolph, he found him lying side by side with 'a hurt Communist commissar of Asiatic appearance'. Later they travelled back to the airfield by ambulance, with Randolph grumbling at being moved at all and a badly injured RAF officer apparently dying on a stretcher. Randolph, according to Waugh, now started shouting orders. Eventually they got back to Bari where all were placed in a military hospital.

Randolph, never a good patient, could not be expected to behave well. According to Waugh he never ceased 'drinking, attacking the night nurse, wanting everyone's medicine and every treatment, dictating letters, and plastering the hospital with American propaganda and photographs with Serbo-Croat captions'.

What a relief it was to get him sent off to Algiers ten days later! Lady Diana Cooper then wrote to her son on 27 July 1944,

On this day of all days Randolph staggered in looking like the man that was – grey-haired, ashen-faced, black pits harbouring dead blue eyes, emaciated, with perished thighs and bandaged knees. I was really alarmed. His story was horrible. The pilot had miscalculated the runway on landing in Yugoslavia, had tried to rise, had lost speed, stalled and crashed. Randy was in the tail with Evelyn and Philip Jordan. The plane took immediate fire, though Randolph can't remember seeing flames. The door had buckled and wouldn't open; by tugging at it they made a kind of gap through which four of them slipped. Ten were killed. Nine saved. Evelyn's hands are burnt, Philip Jordan is also burnt a bit. Randolph's injuries are water on knees, jolted spine and obvious shock, yet his spirits are as ebullient as ever. He lies in a hot cupboard upstairs and is carried to the sitting room by four Wop gorillas [Italian POWs].

It's like a madhouse these days. Randolph stumbles in at 8.30 when Papa is still in his bath and says: 'Can I have my breakfast here?' I say yes. A few minutes later Victor* lollops in, tray in hand, and plonks it on the end. When Sweeney [the soldier servant] arrives with Papa's tray, there is no place to put it. Papa leaves his contiguous bathroom, gives one look, renounces his coffee and leaves the house. . . . The boys 'light up' and quarrel across me, I get the trays taken away, hoping the boys will go with them. No! 'Can I lie on your bed?' Randy says. 'Yes'. They remain even when I get up (so that I have to dress in the bathroom), sprawling in bath-towels or underpants. Once I've gone they jump into my bed and put their dirt-encrusted feet on my sheets and sweat into them, cover them with ash and burn them with butts. I love them both but oh, I'm tired and get no moment to write or read or think.

The doctor came at noon and thinks badly of Randolph's legs. He is not to put them to the ground for a week, and is to have electric treatment.

Before leaving Algiers, Randolph wrote wistfully to Laura Dudley. It was five weeks since he had said goodbye to her in 'gloomy circumstances'. Despite daily massage his knees were very slow in recovering. However, it was wonderful to be at the Embassy instead of in some military hospital, and he thought the Coopers were coping brilliantly with the Gaullist French. Then he relapsed into his old style. . . . 'I love you so much in that you are so tremendously English, so when I am away nostalgia for England makes me love you all the more. . . . I only

* 'Victor' was Lord Rothschild, who was also staying with the Coopers.

have 5 per cent of you! I wonder if you were free if you could pin the other 95 per cent? . . . Bless you even for the 5 per cent – I love you with all my heart. Your own, Randolph.'

In August 1944, Tito flew to Italy with Brigadier Maclean for talks with General Maitland Wilson about the military endeavours of the Partisans. Then before they could meet Winston, Fitzroy had to keep Tito hanging about in Rome and Naples; for security's sake, until Winston arrived all had to be kept secret. Tito finally met Winston for the first time in Naples on 12 August 1944, in a villa overlooking the bay. Through an interpreter Winston told the Partisan leader the sort of things he would like to hear and he lamented that owing to his advanced years he could not himself land by parachute in Yugoslavia.

'But you have sent us your son,' Tito exclaimed. At that moment tears glittered in Churchill's eyes. Tito later told this story to his delegate, Vladimir Dedijer, and Tito was not the man to invent tears.

Randolph reappeared from Algiers still hobbling from the air crash. He wrote to Laura not only about the perfume he had despatched to her but also revealed that once again he had become good friends with his father. 'I am very happy,' Randolph wrote. But it was really Winston who suffered from these family feuds. He found it hard to accept that his son was unhappily married, and had become an impossible husband into the bargain.

Lieutenant Colonel William Cunningham, who was General Alexander's military assistant describes a dinner that Winston and Randolph attended at General Alexander's camp. Winston held forth in his characteristic rolling tones. 'Do take care not to be captured,' he told Randolph, 'The Gestapo would only try to blackmail me by sending me your fingers one by one – a situation I would have to bear with fortitude.'

Before going to Corsica on sick leave, Randolph drove with Evelyn Waugh to see the desolation of Monte Cassino. Months of shelling had turned it into a blackened mountain covered with ruined houses and a few branchless trees – looking like gallows – surrounding the old monastery. There were notices everywhere that transport must not stop; but Randolph drew up their car, and descended to make water in front of a group of peasant women.

'Why do you choose this spot?' asked Evelyn.

'Because I am a Member of Parliament,' answered the insufferable Randolph.

On reaching Rome they found that Lady Diana Cooper had arrived at the Grand Hotel, which she regarded as having been turned into a sort of Kremlin with guards standing with tommy guns at every door.

After ten days in Corsica, where Randolph tried to improve his knees with swimming, the two of them returned to Croatia by plane. It was September 1944 by now and Evelyn had decided that what Tito's Partisans really wanted was to oust the Germans so that they could continue their own special kind of civil war.

During the summer a few planes were able to fly into Croatia, and the British officers there found themselves billeted in a wood of chestnut trees at Topusko. The work proved insufficient. There was far too much hanging around hoping for wireless news – and heavy drinking continued unabated.

Evelyn does not record his own alcoholic intake but it had always been his habit to consume more than was good for him and now his diary recorded that Randolph had little to do except get 'fighting drunk'. There was plenty going on in Serbia where Fitzroy Maclean and other members of the Mission were, but officers in Croatia had to hang around taking wireless signals.

On 16 September Randolph wrote sadly to Laura that he had found a mass of mail waiting for him in Bari but only *one* letter from her – he and Evelyn were trying to make themselves comfortable but as there was no typewriter he found it difficult to compose.

While Randolph roared at whatever Communists he met and attended their drunken dinner parties, Evelyn busied himself going to Mass and trying to assess the religious fervour of Croatians, so that he could 'tell the Pope'. When planes came in to the airfield, Randolph and Evelyn hurried to meet them. Loud were their lamentations when, after peering longingly at the sky, they heard plane engines roaring away into the distance in the grey mist because they were unable to land. That meant no mail from home. As the autumn fogs increased, landings became fewer and fewer. Time dragged slowly despite news of occasional small-scale battles, and the morale of the British Mission to Croatia deteriorated sadly.

On 13 October Evelyn Waugh's diary recorded, 'Randolph and I at dinner, I wonder how long I can bear his company, even he I think faintly conscious of strain. . . .' Then came a telephone message from the airfield, to announce the arrival of Freddie Birkenhead. His second-ment from the PWE had taken months because, unlike the case of Evelyn Waugh, no one had wanted to release this amusing and attractive officer who made friends so easily – and who did not rub up ordinary soldiers the wrong way.

When Freddie arrived with Major Clissold, who spoke Serbo-Croat fluently, Randolph and Waugh both fell over each other in their eagerness to welcome them.

Freddie did not pretend that he had enjoyed the flight from Bari in an aged plane piloted by a Russian who, as he adjusted the passengers' parachutes, indicated in mime and with guffaws that they were unlikely to open in case of emergency.

Randolph, being in charge of the four-roomed farmhouse which was British HQ, had allotted one room to Evelyn, another to Major Clissold and, as one room had to be kept as office, he told Freddie they would share. 'This was a privilege of the most dubious kind and my heart sank,' wrote Lord Birkenhead in the chapter he contributed to *Evelyn Waugh and His World*.

Randolph may not have noticed the effect he was having on Waugh, but Waugh noticed only too clearly the effect that Freddie's arrival had on Randolph. According to Evelyn, who became suddenly prissy, the two of them encouraged each other to drink too much and went singing to bed. Evelyn says he had to make excuses for Major Churchill who was due to dine that night with the Russian General commanding Croatia, and Freddie had to remain in bed all the next day. As he had been ill with dysentery on the way out he at least had some excuse. But Randolph had none.

Birkenhead tells a slightly different story. But not all that different.

We found pleasure in one another's company provided it was not too constant. Randolph had been dropped into Yugoslavia to appear as a *deus ex machina* – the Prime Minister's son, a visible symbol, as he was paraded through stark and battered villages. . . . His almost insolent and contemptuous courage was indeed never disputed even by his worst enemies, whose numbers were not few. To me, the difference between him and Evelyn in this respect was that Randolph was liable to be stimulated by danger to a delicious excitement which accentuated a natural tendency to hysteria, while Evelyn remained calm, glacial and unmoved. But I was uneasily conscious that during all the years of our friendship I had never spent more than a few days in Randolph's company without some cosmic upheaval, and the idea of being under his command for an indefinite period in a small outpost was one for sombre reflection.

Major Clissold retired to his room intent on his Serbo-Croat translations, determined to take no part in the quarrelling. In fact he was only too thankful to be alone and out of all the emotionalism. Freddie did not immediately realize how bad things had become. When he arose from his bed of pain and was walked around Topusko town he did notice that Evelyn did not accompany him, but Randolph said he was just sulking. Freddie was forced to wonder. He had known them both for years and he knew that Randolph could be an 'entrancing companion, vibrant with an energy and warmth which seemed like an explosion of pagan mirth'. And yet how much could anyone stand of him?

Later on, Evelyn Waugh asked Freddie if he would not like another stroll around the town. Waugh took this opportunity to confide that being confined with Randolph had 'lacerated his nerves' and Freddie recalled that Randolph had said exactly the same thing about Evelyn a few hours earlier.

During the next weeks Freddie had to listen to them both arguing about Winston's *Life of Marlborough* which Evelyn rudely described as being 'the special pleading of a defence lawyer'. The outraged Randolph burst out, 'Have you ever noticed it is people who are most religious who become the most mean and cruel?' Evelyn Waugh replied, 'But my dear Randolph, you have no idea what I would be like if I weren't a Catholic.'

Meanwhile, the approach of winter caused planes to behave with increasing unreliability. Sometimes those hoping to be evacuated – Jews who were fleeing from Yugoslavia and injured American pilots – waited in vain for long hours on the icy airfield, only to be returned to their billets when no planes arrived. Randolph sent many a petulant signal to the Air Commander at Bari marked 'personal' but these had no effect. Lights often failed at night and the three of them, Randolph, Evelyn and Freddie Birkenhead were locked up together with nothing to do but argue.

Fitzroy Maclean, guessing the Germans were going to evacuate the Balkans, had gone off to Serbia to organize attacks on main roads and railway lines. A few weeks after Freddie Birkenhead's arrival the British Mission in Croatia was woken at dawn by an enemy air raid. Randolph tumbled out of bed to rouse Freddie shouting, 'Get up, you fool. The Germans are overhead and trying to get me. They've got this house pinpointed.' Randolph then pulled on his trousers and ordered all under his command into a trench at the back of the farmhouse. Zora, the old peasant cook, pulled Freddie down on top of her, 'Cover me

Lord,' she cried. And the Earl of Birkenhead wondered if it was such a good thing to be a peer.

Meanwhile Randolph was noisily recalling the air attack on Drvar. He half hoped that a parachute attack would take place in which it would be possible for him to prove his fearlessness.

But Evelyn was imbued with the same idea. He wanted to prove *his* bravery and had donned a white sheepskin coat which made him an obvious target. Randolph roared at him to take cover like the others, and above all else to 'hide that bloody coat'! But Evelyn threw his coat on the ground where it could be spotted by attacking planes. After spraying the farmhouse with machine-gun bullets, the planes turned for the village and dropped bombs which killed a number of Yugoslavs. Then they flew away.

As Freddie noted, Evelyn's behaviour had endangered them all. Throughout breakfast Randolph did not try to conceal his anger. But eventually he said he was sorry to have been so abrupt during the attack. Unforgivably, Captain Waugh replied that it wasn't Randolph's manner that worried him, it was his cowardice!

This insult was followed by days of not speaking. Evelyn Waugh's diaries paint a sombre picture throughout November 1944 when the heavy rainfall started. Randolph and Freddie lie in bed because there is little else to do. Then Freddie becomes morose and, to Evelyn's annoyance, Randolph wakens at eight in the morning, two hours earlier than usual, and begins his eager telephoning and typing and 'clucking' over the signals. The airfield is pronounced unusable until there is a gap of at least three days without rain. Evelyn wonders again how he can bear it. As he wrote to his wife, 'I have got to the stage of disliking Randolph, which is really more convenient than thinking I liked him and constantly trying to reconcile myself to his enormities.'

The diary recorded,

At luncheon Randolph and Freddie became jocular. They do not make new jests or even repeat their old ones. Of conversation as I love it – a fantasy growing in the telling apt repartee, argument based on accepted postulates, spontaneous reminiscences and quotation – they know nothing. All their noise and laughter is in the retelling of memorable sayings of their respective fathers or other public figures; even with this vast repertoire they repeat themselves every day or two – sometimes within an hour. They also recite with great zest the more hackneyed passages of Macaulay, the poems of John Betjeman, Belloc and other classics. I remarked how boring it was to be obliged to tell Randolph everything twice – once when he was drunk, once when he was

97

sober. Two hours later in a fuddled state, with a glass of raki in his hand, he came to my room to expostulate with me for my unkindness. Later he cooked kidneys for Zora making loud appreciative kisses and whistles when the dish appeared – these, his American slang, his coughing and farting make him a poor companion in wet weather. At least I have not to endure his snoring as Freddie must.

To escape from this party Major Clissold struggled over 500 miles of snow-covered mountains and crossed the enemy lines to get to Brigadier Maclean. 'I think they may kill each other,' he reported.

— 16 —

The drizzle went on and on. Waugh had lost all patience with Randolph, who kept appealing in vain for kind words. 'It left me unmoved,' wrote Waugh, 'for in these matters he is simply a flabby bully who rejoices in blustering and shouting down anyone weaker than himself . . . however as we are obliged to live together I must exercise self-control and give him the privileges due to a commanding officer.'

Poor Randolph – his ego was so easily pricked. He could not help minding that his friend no longer even pretended to like him. Stuck indoors, with contrary signals pouring in, Randolph suddenly fancied himself as a cook. He dumped on the plate of each indignant companion 'one enormous raw potato with a hard egg embedded in the centre'. The novelty of the occupation did not last long however and soon he and his cronies were back at the bottle.

Meanwhile Brigadier Maclean, with his Yugoslav HQ now based on the island of Vis was having a most interesting time with the Partisans in Serbia. The operation called 'Ratweek' was designed to smash the German withdrawal routes; the Brigadier had surmised that the enemy was going to evacuate the Balkans and was determined they should not do so without heavy losses. Main roads and railway viaducts were to be attacked throughout Yugoslavia.

The local Partisan commander of each area was made responsible for individual targets within his territory and British liaison officers had to send their reports to Rear HQ at Bari where the RAF and the American Air Force kept bombers waiting. As Croatia was cleared of enemy forces, Randolph and Evelyn found they had even less to do and Evelyn's diaries present a doleful picture of the life they led.

Meanwhile Winston and Supreme Commander General Maitland Wilson had given Tito permission to remain based on Vis for an indefinite period, and Fitzroy Maclean was congratulating the Partisans on their splendid advance through Serbia when a signal reached him with the horrid news that Tito had disappeared from the island. All that anyone knew was that an unidentified Russian plane had landed and taken off from the airstrip without leaving a message of any sort. Churchill was fuming in London and General Wilson was fuming in Italy. Fitzroy had to leave Serbia and make his way back to Vis to investigate. No response whatever could be elicited from the locals about Tito. 'He is sick, he is busy, he has gone for a walk,' they answered. Tito had vanished without trace.

The Brigadier, seeing that he wasn't going to discover anything from questioning the Yugoslavs, returned to the fighting in Serbia. He did not want to hang around sharing Allied consternation. If Tito chose to behave like this there was nothing anyone could do about it.

When Belgrade fell to the Partisans, Tito reappeared there to head the celebrations – just as Maclean had expected. Making a shrewd guess where the truant must have been, Maclean asked him slyly if he had enjoyed Moscow. The answer, after some shilly-shallying, was yes! He had met Stalin for the first time – and didn't understand why Churchill had been offended by the way in which he had vanished without saying a word. After Fitzroy Maclean had carefully explained that it was the manner of his sudden disappearance which had alarmed London, Tito seemed genuinely distressed. 'Only recently,' he argued, 'Mr Churchill went to Quebec to see President Roosevelt and I only heard of this visit after he had returned!' The Brigadier decided not to pass on this particular remark to Churchill.

The guerilla war against the Germans was over. The Partisans and Chetniks could now fight it out for themselves.

On 4 November Evelyn wrote ill-naturedly, 'Randolph, with ostrich cunning, stayed in bed hoping to give the impression that he had been ill, not drunk, the night before.'

Waugh continued to deplore Randolph and Freddie's encounters with the bottle. The last straw was when Stari, the Yugoslav handyman attached to the British Mission, emulated his masters – and then begged Randolph not to send him back to his unit under arrest because he would be shot!

The sojourn at Topusko in Waugh's diary wrings one's heart: 'Mud under foot, grey skies overhead, intermittent rain, drizzle, mist. . . .

Mass at 8, to baths at 11, where the water was not as deep or as hot as I should have liked. . . .' Then news came that no plane could possibly appear for a week. On 10 November the sole entry was, 'Snow and thaw.'

On 11 November Waugh records a celebrated event: 'Thinking the money well spent if it would keep Randolph quiet, Freddy and I have bet him £10 each that he will not read the Bible right through in a fortnight. He has set to work, but not as quietly as we hoped. He sits bouncing about on his chair, chortling and saying, "I say, did you know this came into the Bible?" or "God, isn't God a shit".'

Whenever escaping Allied pilots reached Topusko, and asked the way to the British Military Mission, to their amazement they were led to the wooden house inhabited by this astonishing party. They found it yet more bewildering, after their long struggles over snowy mountain passes, to be assured that Winston Churchill's son commanded the Mission and to be marched into the presence of Randolph who sat with a cigar in one hand and a glass of raki in the other reading aloud from a large Bible!

By 18 November Randolph was still hard at it. Waugh's diary records petulantly that, 'Freddie, having doubled his bet, is now anxious to win it, so that instead of purchasing a few hours' silence for my £10 I now have to endure an endless campaign of interruption and banter, both reader and heckler drunk.'

During the next week, as heavy snow fell outside, Randolph found that he preferred drinking to reading. Evelyn himself could not listen, for he was busily correcting the page proofs of *Brideshead Revisited*. The sight of his friend at literary work drove Randolph to compose verse. But to Waugh's rage he grunted as he counted the syllables out on his fingers.

Randolph did not return Evelyn's ill will. He was himself incapable of resentment, and Evelyn's crossness merely hurt his feelings. Randolph remained an uncontrollable child. Full of hope, he would go out to the airfield to see what goodies his father might have sent him from England – boxes of whisky or cigars would be shared with his pals as if they were receiving tuck at school.

Joan Thompson, who was Fitzroy Maclean's ATS G.III Operations at Bari, recalls the fuss that Randolph caused whenever he appeared there. Evelyn Waugh was very 'snobby' and did not deign to speak to her because Captain Thompson 'held no social standing', but the staff found Randolph friendly and lovable – when not causing consternation.

Bombers now operated from Foggia, harassing the enemy throughout Yugoslavia, and Balkan Airforce HQ used a Dakota to bring letters and stores to Topusko. The plane usually left at night and would land when a path of flares had been laid out, but all this air activity was, of course, 'weather permitting'. Major Churchill occasionally appeared at Bari to throw dinner parties in the Hotel Imperiale, but on his way back he had words with the conducting officer, a captain who was in control of boarding. 'Do you know who I am?' bellowed Randolph when made to wait his turn. 'Yes,' answered the conducting officer. 'You're Vic Oliver's brother-in-law.' Randolph looked deflated, having never thought of himself thus. This exchange was much quoted in the Mess.

Then Freddie Birkenhead was recalled by his Political Warfare unit. He wondered what sort of atmosphere would prevail in that little hovel in Topusko after he left. It was with genuine regret that Randolph saw Evelyn Waugh depart for Dubrovnic to a new job which consisted of urging the Partisans to fight the Germans rather than their fellow nationals. There was a real danger that all Yugoslavs would become sidetracked by their own civil war. With the zeal which only a Catholic convert can show Waugh was also eager to tidy things up for the Pope.

When Randolph sent him a cheque for the bet lost over failure to read the Bible, Waugh called it 'dubious-looking'. We would have heard more if it had bounced! But Randolph's cheques did not bounce. Waugh might complain that Randolph had only just learned of the Great Schism between Rome and the Orthodox Church but he couldn't complain that Mr Churchill did not pay his betting debts!

That Christmas of 1944, Winston flew to Athens to deal with the Communist rising and Randolph joined him there, thankful to escape from Yugoslavia. Later, when Tito had taken over the White Palace in Belgrade and organized a series of magnificent entertainments there, Randolph appeared for the ball given in honour of General Alexander. He much admired the beautiful palace. It had been built by Prince Paul a few years before the war in the style of an English Georgian country house, and the furniture, books and pictures were all in charming taste – which, happily, the Marshal had decided not to change. Fitzroy Maclean, heroically running the British Embassy until a real ambassador appeared, went every day to the palace to argue heatedly with Tito, much as he had done in the forest cave six months before. Here it was that Randolph, prancing on the dance floor, felt his injured knees begin to play up. He flew to Rome for an operation and as he was carried into the hospital, who should run into the gasping stretcher-bearers but Evelyn Waugh, now busily engaged in Catholic affairs and more successful than Randolph in his private audience with the Pope.

Waugh had contributed an official report to the Foreign Office about the situation in Yugoslavia, one succinct paragraph of which reveals his feelings about the political situation and the character of the people: 'The Yugoslav Army of National Liberation, popularly called "Partisans" is an organized revolutionary army whose main characteristics are extreme youth, ignorance, hardiness, pride in the immediate past, confidence in the immediate future, intolerance of dissent, xenophobia, comradeship, sobriety, chastity.' In vain Evelyn Waugh pleaded that it should not be Allied policy to destroy one illiberal regime in Europe in order to substitute another. This was not at all what the Foreign Office wanted to hear.

Randolph remained fidgety. He knew the war must be drawing to a close and he had not made the martial impact he desired. Then there came a great blow: the death in Burma of his friend Basil Dufferin, 3rd Marquis of Dufferin and Ava. Randolph felt the jar of sudden bereavement when the news came. Basil, though so brilliant and sensitive, had achieved little in life. He sought and found relief in being killed in action – and, perhaps by chance or perhaps not, he died near the city of Ava in India from which his grandfather had taken his title.

And then five days later came a yet more bitter blow for Randolph: the news that Tom Mitford had died of wounds in Burma on 30 March 1945. The loss of these two old friends choked him. He could still see Tom as the handsome fair-haired boy at Eton, his closest friend throughout the years. How did one live without such companions? What was the use of staying alive when they would come home no more? He mourned deeply, but being Randolph (and therefore made of India-rubber) he then perked up. A general election was due. Taking good care of his injured legs he flew back to England.

— *17* —

Randolph arrived in his own country as the Germans conceded defeat in Europe. He had the excitement of being at his father's side during those breathtaking days of triumph in May 1945.

Obviously there was nothing more he could do as a soldier. Nothing more could damage a dead Hitler, and with his crushed vertebrae and his knees in a parlous condition, no unit could even try to pretend that it had a use for Randolph in the Pacific, where the Japanese seemed to be ready to fight on indefinitely. So the Serbo-Croat dictionary was put away, and Randolph decided quite reasonably to immerse himself in politics. There, he thought, must lie his future – making witty speeches on the floor of the House of Commons and eventually becoming Prime Minister. He still hoped for that – he knew how good he was in debate and a general election was soon to be fought.

Prisoners of war came pouring back, David Stirling among them, and he went straight to his SAS regiment. While Winston remained Prime Minister Stirling was eager to interest him in the SAS philosophy and he thought that small bands of dedicated men could harass the Japanese. Through Randolph he got himself invited to luncheon with Winston – just the great man, Randolph and Randolph's five-year-old son. David Stirling was determined to resurrect Winston's interest in the SAS and had several schemes in mind. Before Winston arrived the little boy practised throwing cushions at the door, and when the Prime Minister arrived one caught his cigar and the child ran and hid under the sofa. Winston started to growl at Randolph, 'How dare you throw cushions? Will you never grow up?' Before Randolph had time to reply, giggles sounded from behind the sofa and Winston realized who the culprit was. 'What a wonderful aim you have for a little fellow,' he beamed and all was forgiven.

David Stirling poured out his plans for harassing the Japanese and Winston took it all in, but David could not account for a curious lack of real enthusiasm. Of course Winston was waiting to see if the atom bomb would explode as it should. Only he and the President of the USA and a few top generals knew about it.

When the Big Bang occurred at Hiroshima, David Stirling knew his job as a soldier was over and he left the Army as quickly as possible.

In 1943 Randolph had already asked Julian Amery to replace the other Conservative Member of Parliament for Preston, who had written frankly to the chairman of the Preston Conservative Association saying that he could not bear Mr Randolph Churchill – and 'on personal and public grounds' he refused to run in harness with him again.

Julian Amery parachuted into Albania soon after agreeing to stand with Randolph and he had half-forgotten his application to be a Member of Parliament when, nearly a year later, a letter reached him to say he had been accepted. This news arrived when he was on the run in the hills of Albania. In his own words, 'It is easy enough to drop mail with explosives by parachute but there is no equivalent method of catapulting back replies.'

It was two months before Amery returned to Bari and was able to write a formal letter of acceptance to the Preston Conservative Association. As he said, 'I had liked Randolph from our first meeting. . . . He had a very quick intelligence and an astonishing memory, and his provocative views and uninhibited curiosity made him the most stimulating of companions.'*

Now the two of them, both returned warriors somewhat tousled by the fray, sought to contest the two Preston seats side by side. They thought themselves undefeatable – for they had returned from the war carrying youth and valour emblazoned on their shields and the name of Churchill had become famous throughout the world.

Randolph immediately taught Julian not to look at notes while speaking, and after an initial tiff on this subject Julian Amery learned how right his mentor was. Tutored in the past by Kay Halle, Randolph believed that the public did not want to listen to read speeches. It would rather watch the orator thinking and hesitating or, like Winston, openly referring to notes. Randolph had made a fine study of the art

*From *The Young Unpretender* edited by Kay Halle.

of electioneering. He even asked the local zoo if they would hire out elephants, so that he and Julian could parade through the streets shouting through loudspeakers with their howdahs decked with party placards. The zoo acquiesced, but though the cost was not great, the local Conservative Association said it did not want candidates who behaved as if they were part of a circus. Randolph lost his temper and abused the committee calling them narrow-minded provincials. 'No imagination and no guts,' he said rudely. The Association had disliked the idea of a 'stunt'. They disliked the candidate still more and soon they wondered if they should ever have risked accepting Winston Churchill's son and his friend Julian Amery.

Colonel Robert Laycock spoke for them and Winston himself made a twenty-minute speech at Preston. The Prime Minister drove from the station with Julian and Randolph sitting on the hood of an open car and the crowds shouting 'Good old Winnie' when he gave the V-sign. Winston was certain that officers in uniform had the best chance of being elected. Randolph doubted this, but he was quite certain of his own seat and of Julian Amery's too.

As long as it lasted, this kind of electioneering remained a riot of fun, and as thousands trooped into the theatre which the Conservative Association had been inveigled into hiring, the two young men took it for granted that they must have won. Deafening cheers drowned their speeches and after the meeting they were chaired down the street to the Conservative Club. Both Randolph and Julian had heard the troops mutter about Socialistic hopes but they still thought they themselves would be safely elected.

Next day they drove in a procession of open cars behind a loudspeaker van blaring slogans. Barmaids came out carrying trays of cooling beer and each buxom girl was rewarded with a kiss from Randolph. But despite the jubilation, the songs and the laughter, neither Randolph nor Julian were elected and a Labour Government replaced the Conservative. Many of the returning soldiers were so ill informed that they did not realize their voting Labour would mean that Churchill would cease to lead the nation.

It seems surprising that after such sour squabbles in Yugoslavia, Evelyn Waugh should have been eager to share Randolph's house at Ickleford near Hitchin when his own had been let out to nuns. At least it seems surprising on Mr Waugh's part, for Randolph hardly noticed when people were annoyed with him. Without blinking an eyelid Evelyn accosted Randolph when he found him playing billiards at

White's Club, and arranged that his six-year-old son Auberon should share little Winston's nanny at Ickleford. Those were the days when nannies were still expected to smile if another child was placed in their charge. When Evelyn Waugh drove down to Hitchin to see the house, he found it only half-furnished because Pamela had taken everything she fancied for her town flat.

Nevertheless Evelyn moved in, and he proved a good friend during those despondent days, for the Churchill family inevitably took the political disaster hard. Randolph, although dazed at losing his own seat, did have experience at losing by-elections; but the hurt to his father was deep and grievous. Winston would never get over the experience of winning the war and then having his party kicked out. He had not realized that all the returning troops thought of was better jobs for themselves, and it had been Labour who had promised them most in 'Civvy Street'. Lord Beaverbook had put pressure on Winston to hold an immediate election. Now his Lordship spoke much of the joy a Leader of the Opposition must feel. But Winston remained sombre, 'If this is a blessing in disguise – it's very well disguised.' He was unmoved by a tiff in the press concerning his own popularity. All that mattered to him was that he had led the nation in combat, and now found himself unable to arrange the boundaries of a shattered Europe.

Of course Randolph minded losing at Preston, for he, who was so voluble on so many subjects, had never managed to make a speech in the House except that one maiden speech in 1940. But he braced himself for the struggle to contest some by-election in another constituency. His friend Julian Amery would go on to be a Minister in the next Government, but however hard Randolph tried, he was always unlucky. If he held a fete to raise party funds it would pour with rain and the tents would be swamped. The middle class of England, whom he consistently mocked, said little; but they didn't like him or his ideas. And Randolph slowly realized that all Conservative Associations were becoming loath to adopt him as their candidate. They could not forgive his prewar heresies, they hated his ideas about hiring elephants; and besides, an applicant was expected to keep his temper at committee meetings and be polite to the chairman. No political association was ready to risk scenes. It was Randolph's bad manners that kept him off the short lists. He ruined himself by lack of self-control.

He would have been splendid in Parliament but Randolph never managed to get back into the House of Commons. It was a shame to keep him out, for the excitement of politics ran in his blood and he would have added pith and humour to the House. He would have been brilliant at debate and at shooting down other people's balloons. As it was, he had to fall back on journalism as a career. American newspapers pronounced themselves eager to print his articles and remunerative offers came pouring in, first perhaps because he was Winston's son, but also because his writings always showed perspicacity.

There was a last family party at Chequers and then the Churchills had to move out. Attlee, who succeeded Winston as Prime Minister, was unable to fight for the millions of displaced persons as Churchill had been prepared to do. It was Europe and the refugee camps which suffered most from the political changeover in England.

On 6 August 1945 came the news of the atom bomb in Hiroshima. Evelyn Waugh, who had been exhorting Randolph to 'grow up or perish', watched him as he heard the news. Randolph kept talking about redressing the balance of power till Waugh asked him testily, 'If we knew early this year that we had this power, why did we betray Poland to Russia?'

This pertinent question Randolph could not attempt to answer. The fact that the Poles, who had fought so magnificently and been lauded in 1938, were now not allowed to march in the Victory Parade through London in case Russia was offended did not bear discussion. Randolph quickly changed the subject.

When Evelyn Waugh eventually got his own house back and departed from Ickleford, Randolph plied him with cigars, hinting that Nancy Mitford might relay Paris gossip through him which Randolph could weave into articles for America. A fascinating correspondence resulted from this, but by ill-chance it was later destroyed.

With the end of the war, restrictions for Diana Mitford and her husband Sir Oswald Mosley were automatically lifted. Randolph wrote asking if he could visit them at their country home; he wanted to talk to Diana about the death of her brother only a few months before. But Sir Oswald Mosley refused to allow him to enter the house. He was afraid that Randolph would not be able to keep off politics, and exhausting arguments might ensue, for Sir Oswald still maintained that Soviet Russia was more dangerous than Nazi Germany.

Diana's mother Lady Redesdale, knowing that Tom Mitford had been Randolph's greatest friend, asked him if he would like to come to her home and choose a few of Tom's books. To her amazement

Randolph took the whole lot – even the German ones by Nietzsche and Goethe which he could not read. Lady Redesdale found it puzzling that he should have made off with volumes which Tom who read German easily had prized. How curious was the connection between them? Did Randolph simply want to own the pages which had been Tom's? To stare at the words which meant nothing to him but had been so dear to his friend?

Now that Winston was no longer Prime Minister and Pamela had made it clear that she did not intend to remain his wife, Randolph made desperate efforts to persuade Laura to divorce Lord Dudley and marry him. But his efforts were in vain.

After the war Laura and Eric Dudley, whose house had been weakened in an air raid, were forced to live in Claridges Hotel for six months. They occupied separate bedrooms because Lord Dudley snored so loudly; but Laura allowed him to stride around her room while getting undressed. One night he was holding forth about money, a topic which interested her not at all. Coal had been nationalized so he could not think where to invest his millions. She listened to him for a time and then drove him off to his own room, to reach which he had to cross a sitting room. No sooner had he gone than to her horror she saw her wardrobe door open and Randolph got out doubled-up with laughter. 'How dare you . . . ?' Laura started to say but she found herself dissolving in laughter too. Randolph had tipped the hall porters, who knew him well, to let him into the Dudleys' suite. There he dispensed drinks, taking one himself. Then, having assured the porters that he was expected and would wait, he had hidden himself in the huge wardrobe, 'To listen to the love-birds,' he said, tears streaking down his cheeks. Laura did not know how to get him to go without raising her voice. 'I don't think this is funny . . .' she kept whispering. But of course she did.

On 11 May 1946, a year after the guns had been silenced, he wrote to her from Dover:

Laura darling

This is just to thank you for last night.

If the power to confer happiness on others makes people happy themselves you deserve to be the happiest person alive. Every minute last night was sheer enchantment. I only wish I could do one tenth as much for you as you did for me. I know beyond any doubt that I would like to spend my whole life with you. Please think about this before you make any plans. I love you my darling more than ever and shall always pray for your happiness.

Bless you,
your devoted
Randolph

But when Laura decided to leave Lord Dudley it was not to Randolph that she turned. It was in the arms of Michael Canfield, a young American, that Laura found happiness. Randolph had to accept the crumbs that fell from her table . . . that 5 per cent which he knew was all she was prepared to give him. The other 95 per cent he could but dream of. But it was something to feel he would always be welcome in her house. Maybe he liked being told where to get off and assured that he would make the most dreadful husband. Maybe his other friends were less truthful.

Lady Diana Cooper describes a row that occurred in the Paris Embassy during the Nuremberg Trials. Duff Cooper had a temper and he never liked Randolph as much as she did. On this occasion he let fly. A film was being shown in the Embassy's small private cinema which depicted the trial of Stauffenberg and the generals involved in the July 1944 plot to kill Hitler. 'Exactly what we are doing at Nuremberg today,' remarked Randolph thoughtlessly. Duff Cooper, His Majesty's Ambassador, leaned forward and slapped Randolph hard on one side of his face with a folded programme and then still harder on the other. Even Lady Diana could not induce them to make it up. Duff Cooper sent Randolph 'storming from the house', and himself sizzled with rage for a long time.

Around this time Sir Winston Churchill was introduced to a well-known French lady who bore the name of Pol Roger, which happened to be Winston's favourite champagne. The old man had grown slightly deaf and could hardly believe his ears. 'What is her name again?' he asked. After it was repeated he turned back to her in admiration. 'A most beautiful lady,' he said in his inimitable way, '*and what a beautiful name!*'

Randolph met Madame Pol Roger soon after and immediately paid court to her. But Randolph's methods of flirting tended to be rather crude. When she refused his pleas he asked her the reason why. Laughingly she replied that he carried too much weight. 'How much would you like me to lose?' inquired Randolph. '*Un peu près douze kilos,*' answered Madame Pol Roger and thought no more about it.

But Randolph took her literally. He travelled back to England, banted hard and at last he obtained a weighing-machine ticket that proved he had indeed lost fourteen kilos. Back to France he hurried, and, according to Madame Pol Roger, arrived while she was reading quietly in her garden. She had long forgotten her demand and to her horror and amazement Randolph snatched her up, and proceeded to carry her into the house looking for her bedroom. He really thought she'd made a promise. Madame escaped with difficulty and Randolph was very hangdog. The Pol Roger family dined out on this story for many a long year.

— *18* —

1946 found Randolph separated from his wife, bereft of a seat in Parliament, and famous only as Winston Churchill's journalist son. Maybe his ego was slightly soothed by a flight to Moscow to attend a Red Army parade from which he wrote descriptive articles. The Russians had never been able to understand why Winston Churchill had allowed himself to be deposed in the summer's election and when Randolph was invited to make a speech, he attempted to give them the facts about parliamentary procedure. Unhesitatingly Randolph criticized the USSR and defended the democratic system which allows a country to throw out any party it does not want. Interpreters may have altered the meaning, for at the end of his tirade a Red Army officer offered him a cigar and asked him to pose for a photograph. Randolph was nothing loath and later he carried a huge bucket of caviar back to London. This he proudly produced at the dinner given by those who had been in No. 8 Commando to Colonel Robert Laycock at Bucks Club. How tender and nostalgic grew the memories of those old days when they could all squabble together, and then turn on a real enemy. Who was the real enemy now?

The Germans had become the object of diplomacy rather than hostility. In 1946 the Congress of Europe took place at The Hague, at which Randolph and his friend Alastair Forbes were kept busy drafting resolutions. It was all very well to win a war but then something must be done with the victory, and that proved very difficult. Randolph and Alastair scribbled away in corners while Anthony Marreco, who had been in the Fleet Air Arm during the war, found himself relegated to the role of 'Chaperone-Nanny' to Dr Adenauer, who was the first German to be allowed to attend an international conference since Hitler's defeat. At the end of the proceedings Sir Winston made a terrific speech in a thunderstorm which he enjoyed as it enabled him to quote *King Lear* ('Blow, winds, and crack your cheeks! rage! blow!') which lightened the atmosphere. Winston, like Randolph, had a prodigious memory and he always enjoyed being able to recite some relevant verse. Marreco then had the tricky task of arranging the handshake. Duncan Sandys and Randolph were not keen that Winston should tender his hand to the German delegation. However, Marreco was told that if he could induce Adenauer's party to fall in in two ranks, Winston would shake all their hands. The Germans refused to comply with this arrangement, so in the end Marreco had to bring Churchill and Adenauer together in a private room. The complexity of all this may seem strange now, but for years after the war feelings were still very tender.

Soon after the war Randolph went to stay with his old friend Tanis Guinness who had by now married her second husband, Howard Dietz, and was living on Long Island. They went shopping together in New York, and Randolph enjoyed selecting records in a music shop. He chose over thirty and eventually the assistant asked where he should send them. 'To Mr Churchill . . .' began Randolph. But the man destroyed his sang froid by asking, 'How do you *spell* Churchill?' Randolph blinked in amazement and then roared, 'If you don't know how to *spell* Churchill I'm damned if I will buy any records off *you*.' Tanis hurried him away. Although she always put him up during his tours of America she says frankly, 'I was always so pleased to have him arrive but *greatly relieved* to see him go.'

On one occasion her house was full so she asked her neighbours, the Herbert B. Swopes, who were old friends of Winston, to allow him to sleep there. Randolph returned late and mislaid the key which Mrs Swope had given him. Eventually he decided to sleep on a glass table outside the house, but this disintegrated beneath his weight. Mrs Swope heard an unholy noise and telephoned the police to say that the house was being broken into. The police arrived and arrested Randolph, blood-stained from glass splinters, and took him off in their van protesting violently, 'I'm the son of Winston Churchill and a guest in that house. . . .'

'We've heard that one before . . .' muttered his jailers.

It was dawn before Randolph, bandaged, confused and indignant, reached his own bed.

Randolph was noisy and violent on more than one occasion while in America. Sir Isaiah Berlin describes Randolph in Washington interviewing Spruille Braden, who had been American Ambassador in the Argentine. During Randolph's interrogation, Braden passed remarks about the disappearing British Empire at which Randolph took umbrage. Behaving somewhat unlike the usual journalist, Randolph proceeded to punch him in the face. Mr Braden retaliated and it was a very dishevelled young Churchill who returned to the British Embassy, with a black eye, but still sure he had been in the right. Anyone who attacked England in his presence deserved all they got. The newspaper for which Randolph worked was not impressed; this was not the manner in which it expected its employees to behave.

But despite such incidents Randolph maintained his reputation as a journalist throughout 1946, although he failed to reinstate himself in the Conservative Party.

Besides this, he was lonely, for he had lost his wife and he could not really count on his beloved Laura. She gave him understanding and affection and found him fun to go around with, but the men she fell in love with were quite different.

There were moments of compensation for Randolph. Early in 1947 he attended the wedding of his sister Mary and Christopher Soames. And there was always America.

It was perhaps just as well that America existed for Randolph; it was such a large country to jaunt around in giving lectures, – and Randolph remained excellent on the platform if not in private life. Once again Kay Halle tried to reform him, and he confided to this most loyal friend that he could *feel* whenever an illogical tantrum was going to overwhelm him. He described it as a physical sensation that arose from the earth. 'If I can stop it before it reaches my knees I will be all right, but once it gets above them a black fog envelops me and I just don't care what I say.' Kay tried to train him to check this crazy creeping temper at the ankle stage. But it was no good.

Randolph's last letter to Laura, or rather the last one she kept, he wrote to her in early September 1947 while flying from Rangoon to Singapore, where he had been commissioned to write an article.

... In Calcutta I went and had a talk with Gandhi. I had to squat on the floor beside him while he did his ablutions in a bowl held for him by one of the least gabby dolls I have ever met. From Calcutta to Rangoon we had Lord Listowell and his goodwill mission on board. He is a nice but very unimpressive little man. A sort of 'poor man's' version of his brother.

I see in the papers that our wonderful Government have now forbidden all travel at home or abroad. You had your holiday just in time. . . . My fellow travellers are very dreary. Two very plain dolls out of the lower middle drawer and some rather tedious businessmen.

This is a very dull letter; don't let it serve as a model for yours. . . .

Please remember how much I love you now and always.

Bless you my sweet
Randolph

And there we have to leave it. Laura's own letters to Randolph written during the war he kept in a box in his bedroom but they have disappeared, all except the one I have quoted. Maybe someday in a dusty attic that box will be found and opened. Then we will have the description she sent to the Prime Minister's son of what it was like to be a nurse when England was fighting.

Despite his own propensity to be unfaithful, when Randolph failed with Laura he tried to induce Pamela to return to him. He was still looking for a nanny for himself – a nanny who looked like his mother. He hated living alone in Dolphin Square, where he rented a flat after the war, and later in the large house he took, 8a Hobart Place. Kay Harvey-Miller, who was his secretary at this time, describes him as a very sad man. Kay fretted at the discomfort of never finding a table suitable for a typewriter and having to produce her work sitting with the machine perched on her lap. But just as she felt she could not stand another minute Randolph would do something endearing – he would bring her back four pairs of nylon stockings from America, or a specially blessed cross from the Pope, or he'd drive her home to her own flat, when petrol was severely rationed. So she did not hand in her notice as she had intended, not even when he ordered her to join him in Paris and she arrived there to find he had not bothered to book her in at his hotel. Little Winston often came to lunch at Hobart Place, usually in the charge of his grandmother Lady Churchill or with Duncan Sandys who remained a good friend to Randolph. Kay's heart was wrung by the sight of the little boy, who was obviously trying hard to please and endeavouring to eat with the right fork, just like the grown-ups. He always said, 'Good morning father,' very nicely. But Kay knew that his parents' marriage was at an end. In late 1946 it was legally dissolved.

In 1948 Randolph became engaged to June Osborne, the only daughter of Colonel Rex Osborne, DSO, MC. Little Winston, the precious only child of Pamela, had often spent long periods with his Digby grandparents, and their youngest daughter Jaquetta was in fact only eleven years older than him. She describes how upset the small boy became when this engagement was announced. He could not understand the role June would play in his life and asked Jaquetta pathetically, 'Everyone says she will be my stepmother but what happens to Mummy?'

Aunt Jaquetta, herself only nineteen, explained that one can only have one Mummy no matter how many people one's father married.

'But how?' asked the child.

Jaquetta then stepped in with what she describes as a 'lucky inspiration'. 'You know where you came from and you can't have been in two people's tummies so you can only have *one* mother. It's the one who *bears* you that counts.'

June was ten years younger than Randolph, very attractive and lively, not intellectual and not what the Churchill family called 'a political animal'. Maybe she didn't know what she was doing when she married Randolph but for a time she created for him a joyful atmosphere and a sense of security. Despite his prejudice against divorce, Evelyn Waugh wrote to June with much feeling about Randolph, 'I have known him for a long time; perhaps before you were born, certainly before you could read and write, and have always felt that he had a unique natural capacity for happiness, which, one way and another has never been fully developed. I am sure you will be able to do this for him. He is essentially a domestic and home-loving character who has never had a home.'

One might think the 'home-loving' facet of Randolph's character would have been somewhat shaken by the ghastly lovers' tiff which Evelyn describes later. June had been inveigled into going to a party when she had flu. Instead of letting her remain in bed, Randolph filled her up with benzedrine and then encouraged her to drink wine. The result was disastrous. Randolph, obtuse in such matters, failed to see how sick she was as he took her back to his sister Diana's house in Chester Row. According to Mr Waugh she then said she'd lost the key and would commit suicide and 'legged it for the river pursued by Randolph. He caught her on the Embankment [quite a long run] where she struck him three times with the clenched fist, called the police and gave him in charge for indecent assault. Five policemen appeared in a flying squad car and Randolph harangued them.' Policemen on the beat must have *some* fun, and one only wishes one could see their notes concerning this episode.

June does not seem to have been very seriously affected, for later that night she was back in Diana's house, weeping on Evelyn Waugh's shoulder while Randolph kissed and petted her before going off to White's Club with Mr Waugh for a few drinks.

They honeymooned in the house at Biarritz which Tanis Guinness lent them, and within a year of the marriage June bore a daughter, Arabella. On the night of the baby's arrival, Randolph had organized a bridge party and Tanis with her new husband Edward Phillips (a very handsome man who had long pursued her) and Lady Bridget Parsons arrived at the small house in Westminster where Randolph and June were living. Randolph opened the door with a champagne glass in his hand. 'Welcome,' he exclaimed. 'We have just had a daughter.' Cries of appreciation went up from his guests but they thought they should leave immediately and not disturb the new mother, 'Not at all — you must stay as arranged,' insisted Randolph. More corks popped and one by one they were taken up to see June who was lying exhausted. 'Poor girl — I don't expect she wants to see anyone,' remonstrated Tanis, but upstairs they all had to troop. Later on that night, when they had settled down to bridge, the nurse kept appearing to scold them. 'Mrs Churchill can hear your voices,' she complained. 'What do you mean by ordering me to be quiet in my own house?' Randolph would answer and they all saw that the excitement of fatherhood was going to his head along with too much champagne.

After Arabella's birth, June and Randolph looked at many houses with the idea of settling contentedly in the country. But Randolph grew ever more brash and assertive. Frank Pakenham invited him to dinner with the man who had been head of W. H. Smith in Cairo. He thought they would interest each other but to Pakenham's dismay they just quarrelled. Eventually Pakenham's friend said, 'Well, I shan't vote for you at the next election.' Randolph replied grandly, as if he was a senior statesman, 'As you are resident in Egypt — I can well do without your support.'

When Sir Alfred Beit bought Russborough — a most beautiful Palladian house in the Wicklow hills — Randolph took June to stay there. As hostess, Clementine Beit watched the couple fearfully because already they were quarrelling. Sir Alfred, her beloved husband, just said, 'I told you so.' He expected Randolph to behave badly and the bickering that took place merely justified his suspicions.

When the 1950 war in Korea blew up, Randolph was flown out as a war correspondent for the *Daily Telegraph*. According to Alan

Whicker, who was on a television team there, he appeared too convivial to be a successful reporter but Whicker couldn't help liking him and listened sympathetically while Randolph poured out his soul. 'If I achieve anything they all say it's because of my father, and when I do something badly they say "What a tragedy for the Old Man!" I can never win.'

The highest accolade which Alan Whicker could give Randolph was this: 'One good thing you could say for him was that he was as rude to ambassadors as he was to waiters.'

Randolph happened to arrive in Korea at a crucial moment when the hard-pressed United Nations forces were engaged in desperate fighting. He promptly wrote dispatches praising the weary American 24th Division and the US Marines. These forces were grateful for his appreciation of the way that they were saving the situation on the peninsula until the other UN troops could arrive.

Eager to get his report telegraphed from Tokyo, Randolph hitch-hiked back to Japan in an empty transport plane. Thus he missed being in the jeep which ran on to a landmine and killed Christopher Buckley, the other *Daily Telegraph* correspondent, and Ian Morrison of *The Times*. When he reached Tokyo the news had arrived and no one wanted to be the one who had to tell Buckley's wife. It was typical of Randolph that he should brace himself for such an occasion. 'I'll tell her,' he said and taking the bull by the horns he drove to her hotel – Randolph's warmth and sincerity in such a moment helped to make the situation less unbearable. Mrs Buckley was glad that it was he and not some stuttering diplomat who brought her the news.

By the end of August, Randolph was back in Korea. He and Frank Emery, the representative of the International News Service, decided to accompany a crack unit of the US First Cavalry Division on a night patrol across the Naktong river.

This river became low in the dry season and, having waded across, the patrol split into three parts, one part remaining near the bank to guard the rear and the other two fanning out through the jungle. It was reminiscent of the old days in Yugoslavia and Randolph, over-excited by the proximity of danger, never drew breath. In vain the American sergeant in charge of the expedition begged Mr Churchill to lower his voice; Randolph had to explain loudly how the Partisans would reconnoitre. Soon a series of mortar shells began to land along the sandy banks. They had been overheard. Soldiers of the patrol with which Randolph had elected to go were wounded and then Randolph himself received a shell-splinter in his leg. It was, in fact, all his fault but it remains typical of Randolph that he insisted upon writing his story and arranging for it to be flown back before he would submit to emergency dressings. When he was lying on a stretcher a GI asked with open curiosity if he was really Winston's son. 'Well, I'm certainly not one of Attlee's offspring,' Randolph retorted.

As soon as he was able to hobble, Randolph flew to Hong Kong to see the British troops arrive, and then returned to Korea just before the dramatic Inchon landings of the UN forces under General MacArthur's command.

Seventeen war correspondents were killed during the Korean fighting, and Randolph was not the only journalist to be wounded. When his flesh refused to heal he returned to England and Evelyn Waugh visited him in hospital in April 1951. 'No sign of June at the bedside,' he wrote, and 'his legal and financial difficulties are huge.' Naturally such difficulties would always be 'huge' with Randolph – huge but unimportant. He could never really care about such details.

In 1951 came the general election which restored Winston to power. But it was too late. He had needed so desperately to retain high office in 1945. Thousands, maybe millions had died in labour camps in the previous five years, and he had only been able to galvanize the Western world into understanding by his talk in a college gymnasium at Fulton; it had been called 'The Sinews of Peace' which became famous as the 'Iron Curtain' speech. Unfortunately no one bothered to take a tape. The students simply did not think of it. But the free world listened. Eventually the Churchill Memorial was built there, with a fine Wren church carried stone by stone from bombed London to the shores of the Mississippi.

With his father once again Prime Minister, Randolph made his next election bid at Devonport, a division of Plymouth. The ordinary man's feeling was against him and a splendid old Cornishman, the landlord of the *Shipwright's Arms* at Helford, complained to Anthony Marreco, ''Tis the moral *turpitude* of the man. . . . ' Everyone knew what he meant.

Plymouth was a marginal constituency, the sitting MP was a Socialist of repute and a local man – Michael Foot. Randolph felt nervous as never before. He could not bear to remain while the counting of votes took place and left the hall trying to quell his wild hopes. An exhausted town clerk had given him mistaken figures and so he felt entitled to reassure the waiting Conservative committee. But finally it was revealed that his opponent had won by 2390 votes. Michael Foot recognized a brave adversary when he saw one, and he felt compelled to compliment Randolph on the way he accepted defeat. No one could know how much it meant to him – this ousting from the House of Commons. Hiding his bitterness, Randolph tried to put a good face on it as he caught the train back from Plymouth to London. Evelyn Waugh wrote to Nancy Mitford, 'Nothing he has ever done deserves such punishment.'

Randolph analyses the news – his favourite photograph of himself, presented to Natalie Bevan in December 1958

Kay Halle

Vote for Randolph Churchill! Randolph's election address to the constituents of Ross and Cromarty in 1936 included the following forthright statement: 'I have been brought up to believe that the British Empire is the highest expression yet achieved of mankind's genius for civilization and government . . . I shall resist all defeatist tendencies calculated to dissipate the labours and achievements of our ancestors who gained for us this glorious heritage'

ROSS AND CROMARTY BY-ELECTION.
Monday, February 10th, 1936.

RANDOLPH CHURCHILL,
THE UNIONIST CANDIDATE.

A summer picnic. Left to right: Cecil Beaton, Tanis Guinness, Oliver Messel, unknown, Mona Harrison Williams and Randolph

Diana Mitford

Clementine Mitford's wedding to Sir Alfred Beit, 1939

Randolph marries Pamela Digby at St John's, Westminster, October 1939

David Stirling greets a Middle East patrol group
on its safe return to base, January 1943

Fitzroy Maclean in Yugoslavia

Laura Dudley

Randolph in Korea in 1950, discusses the military situation with an American second lieutenant. Randolph reported the war for the *Daily Telegraph*

Randolph and June, April 1953

Winston Churchill's wedding. In the foreground left to right: Randolph, 'Minnie' d'Erlanger, Lady Churchill, Sir Winston, Winston and Arabella

Randolph at work on his great biography of his father. Present also in the Strong Room at Stour are Michael Wolff, his chief researcher, and the archivist Miss Harryman

STOUR

Randolph's bookplate at Stour

In the garden at Stour. *Above*: Randolph and his daughter Arabella. *Below*: Randolph at work on the telephone

Randolph with Natalie Bevan on the terrace at Stour. At Natalie's feet are Orlando the spaniel and Captain Boycott the pug

— _19_ —

In 1952, Evelyn Waugh and Randolph held a tipsy but undoubtedly sincere argument about Clarissa Churchill, brought up as a Roman Catholic, who had announced her engagement to Anthony Eden, a divorced man. Randolph kept to the line, 'What business is it of yours? You are not the Cardinal Archbishop or the editor of the *Tablet* or even like me, a cousin.'

To Clarissa herself Waugh wrote that he was appalled at her decision to ignore the law of her church. Concerning his row with Randolph he added at the close of this letter, 'I know and love Randolph too much ever to think better or worse of him.'

It was around this time that, during one of his frequent visits to Tanis Guinness's house at Biarritz, Randolph happened to coincide with Noël Coward. Tanis and her husband Edward Phillips were living there with her teenage daughter Liza Dietz. Tanis always tried not to have the high-powered Noël and Randolph to stay at the same time, they were too wearing and witty in their different ways, but on this occasion Randolph arrived early. Tanis thought it would be a good idea to drive her guests off for lunch in the hills with a charming old Spanish lady. As they arrived Randolph bent forward getting out of the car and the zip of his fly burst open. Noël Coward held his panama hat in front of the offending place, but this made their movements extremely peculiar. The moment they were shown the garden, they bolted behind the greenhouse and tried to find a remedy. Their Spanish hostess saw them through the glass panes twisting around in strange-looking attitudes, and whispered to Tanis, 'I always heard Noël Coward was like that, but Mr Churchill too?'

A year or so later Tanis decided to give her daughter Liza a 'coming-out' dance in London. A friend lent her very grand house for this affair but Liza, who had been brought up in America, knew no one. White's Club had been combed for the right sort of gentlemen but as Liza remarked wistfully, no one knew who she was or asked her to dance. Of course Randolph did not fail in this duty. He was only too delighted to find a pretty young girl whom he had known since she was six years old standing bewildered amidst the throng.

'Come and we'll dance away,' he said. And then he added, 'Remember the times in America I tried to debauch you? I used to ask you if you smoked . . . if you drank. . . . Now I'll ask you another question . . . have you ever been to bed with a man?'

Blushing, Liza could but shake her head.

'Why not?' Randolph demanded.

But he never knew because the next moment he asked her, 'What about a game of bridge?'

She knew what *that* meant, and it was the last thing she wanted. What a way to spend her own coming-out dance!

As Randolph's journalistic career continued, he realized that he could not cope with the amount of work offered him and so he looked around for assistance. He was lucky to hear of Alan Brien, who was only just beginning to make his name as a writer. Brien was first interviewed at Randolph's Westminster flat, and Randolph's interviews tended to be unlike those of other people. All he really wanted to discover was how congenial the interviewees were to him personally. Immediately realizing that this tough, lively youth would fill the book, Randolph asked Brien what money he wanted. Brien couldn't think what he might be worth. Neither could Randolph. Eventually they decided that Brien was to take 15 per cent of any work he did. His first job was a book on the Coronation, and Brien found it most amusing to report the state of London streets to Randolph at White's Club.

At one meeting Evelyn Waugh joined them and somewhat nervously Brien asked him if he had really disliked a 'Profile' he had written on him in the magazine *Truth*. Waugh took umbrage, 'I've never heard of the rag,' he snarled. 'How curious – someone called Evelyn Waugh has written complaining of inaccuracies,' said Brien humbly. Thenceforth Waugh refused to address the young man directly, and insisted on speaking only to Randolph, who finally burst out, 'If you belong to a club for gentlemen you must behave as a gentleman, and the first requirement is that a guest should not be insulted. Speak direct to my friend.'

Waugh continued to address Alan Brien through Randolph, and in the end the three of them departed in varying degrees of fury. After this Brien soon realized how easy it was to grow fond of Randolph, and he enjoyed writing articles for him despite the author's astute criticisms. 'I'd never use this phrase,' he'd say, 'it's not my style. It's good but it's *you* not *me*. I'm terribly sorry, but we'll have to cut those sentences – you see I'd just never say it like that myself.'

Brien and Churchill were complete contrasts, and worked well in harness. Alan Brien came from working-class stock and was proud of it; he hadn't been to Eton, he didn't belong to White's Club and he said that Randolph opened his eyes to another world. Before meeting Randolph he drank beer, ate at pub counters, scraped a living writing as a freelance for any magazine that would accept his work. Randolph changed all that. Champagne became a sort of daily tonic to be sipped between meals. 'My working-class, puritanical instinct that said it was indecent to stuff yourself unless you were sure there was enough for tomorrow dissolved, and never returned.'

Brien was good for Randolph and Randolph was good for Brien. 'It was not so much that he would erupt late at night in loud-voiced blow-ups, calling me a Communist coward, as that he would not allow me to insert one tiny word into the molten flow of his rhetoric.' 'Must I be interrupted in my house?' he would trumpet. Or alternatively: 'Am I not your guest and entitled to courtesy?'

Alan Brien did not want to become a gentleman, but like it or not Randolph taught him that 'no gentleman remembers what he says after midnight'. And so Brien had to learn that it was no good sulking at breakfast over three-in-the-morning arguments. And no good sending for a taxi to make a dramatic get-away. No one would notice. It was better to tuck into the kidneys or kedgeree, smile and forget it.

Of course Alan Brien enjoyed attending grand occasions with Randolph. He had never before met anyone so absolutely fearless. And he never forgot the first time he saw Randolph sweeping into an assembly to confront the horrified Esmond Harmsworth, now the 2nd Lord Rothermere. 'How can you make so much rotten money by appealing to the basest instincts in the human race?' was his opening gambit.

Lord Rothermere, who had known Randolph since boyhood, swallowed but could not answer. 'Why do you just stand there like a flogged jellyfish?' Randolph went on using what had become a favourite phrase of his. 'I hate flogging jellyfish.' Alan Brien, pulverized, watched these two gentlemen in white ties behaving in quite a different fashion to that in which he had been brought up.

It was about this time that Randolph's fancy turned towards other issues. He looked around him and noticed that England was a country of wonderful landscapes studded with exquisite houses in which *grands seigneurs* of the eighteenth century had collected furniture and pictures from all over Europe. England itself had even produced some great English painters – Lawrence, Hoppner, Gainsborough, Raeburn and Sir Joshua Reynolds. In fact England could be considered a treasure trove. He started to educate himself. Never having previously taken note of his surroundings, he now dug into the history of those great mansions which had always been open to him for weekends. He decided to write a well-illustrated coffee-table book – what Waugh deprecatingly termed a 'popular book' – but this venture entailed 'fun'. Instead of pursuing guests at weekend parties Randolph now got out his notebook and read guidebooks. The result was the publication of *Fifteen English Houses* and in July 1953 he sent an early copy to Evelyn Waugh who replied somewhat dampeningly.

Dear Randolph,
I do not think you have chosen a subject well suited to your genius. You have no appreciation of architectural beauty or of the paintings, decorations and treasures which enhance it. . . . I do not know what reader you seek to interest. Certainly not the specialist or the amateur.
Forgive my bluntness. This is not your proper work. You need hot, whisky-laden contemporary breath, the telephone, the latest gossip, the tang of the New World to bring out what is lively in you. History and culture are for gentler creatures.

Such criticism did not deter Randolph at all; he was searching now for some biographical subject which would prove to his father and his father's trustees that he was indeed capable of writing the life of Winston Churchill – capable and also worthy of so great a task. One day in White's Club, Randolph was moaning on this issue with young Lord Derby, who said, 'Why don't you do my grandfather? We'd give you all the papers at Knowsley.'

Brendan Bracken had written of Lord Derby when he died in 1947, 'Eddie Derby died today. Death has been merciful to him. He was . . . a man who greatly enjoyed and made good use of his position and wealth. He liked the company of pretty women and they greatly enjoyed his gaiety and benevolence. The war ended all his fun. He had to spend the remainder of his life cooped up at Knowsley with some very fractious domestics. His successors will never know the happiness he inherited. . . . '

Graham Watson of Curtis Brown acted as Randolph's literary agent for the book, which eventually emerged as *Lord Derby: King of Lancashire*. In all the years they worked together Randolph never had a row with Graham Watson. That was what was so maddening about Randolph. If he liked a man in a certain way and knew that a row would interfere with their relationship he behaved himself.

At Oving, the great eighteenth-century house near Aylesbury which Randolph rented and thought his trustees would buy for him, Randolph seized on the idea and began the long and arduously researched political tome which was to prove him worthy to write his father's biography.

Alan Brien helped him devise an orderly method of assembling material and dealing with Lord Derby's voluminous correspondence. He put everything in the right folders and documents were carried around in laundry baskets. By trial and error Randolph learned how to depict accurately a political period. When the book came out it was much praised as proof of Randolph's scholarship and judgement.

Unfortunately there had been some misunderstanding about Oving and Randolph's trustees began to demur over the moneys which would be needed to do up the house with its fine plasterwork. For much of the time Randolph found himself left alone there with little Arabella and he would ring up Hermione Ranfurly* who lived not far away and beg her to bring over her daughter Caroline who was the same age as Arabella. 'We have a swing on the lawn and it really does swing quite high,' he would tempt her with childish delight. And Hermione, who had known Randolph during the war, would feel the pathos of this man whom women would accept only as a lover or for the glamour of the Churchill name.

While the little girls played together on the green sward Hermione would watch Randolph with her eagle eye – how much he wanted to be loved for himself alone. And how difficult he made it after a few drinks.

*The Countess of Ranfurly who had been personal secretary to General Sir Maitland Wilson in the Middle East and Italy.

After the trustees insisted that Randolph should leave before he became over-involved financially, Lord Camrose bought Oving and its park for his son Michael Berry and his daughter-in-law the Lady Pamela (sister of Randolph's friend, Freddie Birkenhead). Sore put out, Randolph, with June in tow had to look elsewhere for a suitable establishment.

From this moment on he was determined to buy some lovely country house into which he could, as he optimistically termed it 'settle down'.

Randolph was never his best at balls. He drank too much, and champagne made him more than usually pugnacious. Maybe it had not been entirely his fault when soon after the war Maureen, Marchioness of Dufferin and Ava, attacked him on the dance floor for not having written when Basil her husband was killed. Lady Weymouth, the hostess, watched appalled while Randolph's ears were boxed. He spluttered but could not really answer, because he had cared deeply for Basil Dufferin. Indeed that may have been the reason he had not been able to bring himself to pen a note. Anyway a scene occurred the like of which seldom occurs at a London dance.

Far worse was to come, and in this case Randolph was entirely to blame. He came in after a dinner party at which Lady Pamela Berry was one of the guests. The host, Leo d'Erlanger, had retired to bed because banking demanded his attention in the early morning. After he had gone Randolph blew in, having had as usual rather too much to drink. He joined the general conversation and then took Pamela to task about Oving, which had now become her home. A most unseemly row started. In vain the hostess tried to impose peace between the contestants. Finally, in a thoroughly peeved state, Randolph shot a parting rejoinder at Pamela, who was a very dark beauty (*very* beautiful and *very* dark). As she turned away eyes flashing he said, 'Look here my girl . . . . You'd better go home and have a shave – you seem not to have used that electric razor given you for Xmas.' The Lady Pamela took umbrage at this ungallant remark and vowed loudly that she would never speak to Randolph again. (And, though she had known him since childhood she never did.) The other guests were, of course, horrified and the hostess near to swooning. Next morning, her husband, who had missed the fracas came down and said, 'What a successful dinner party it was last night, we must give a lot more. . . .'

Randolph never understood why Pamela minded his remark so much. He told me this story himself with a puzzled expression. Later on when he had the opportunity to visit Oving by helicopter he rang up to ask if his party could land in the daffodil field. He could see no reason why cucumber sandwiches and tea urns should not be carried out to him and his friends. But Lady Pamela remained obdurate. 'Don't come if you value your life,' was her sole reply. And so he had to fly over the house that once he'd lived in, peering down crossly and unable to understand exactly why he would never be made welcome.

In September 1953, Randolph attended the Literary Luncheon given by Miss Christina Foyle at the Dorchester Hotel. He took the chair and, although speeches were *de rigueur*, no one expected the blast which issued from him as chairman. After a momentary intake of breath the guests loved it. Randolph seized this heaven-sent opportunity to stand up and attack the pornography of Fleet Street in general, and poor Lord Rothermere in particular. He accused Lord Rothermere of being the owner of a group of newspapers which built up their sales with sexy photographs and headlines. During this diatribe Randolph stated, 'I have known Lord Rothermere all my life but I can only confess myself baffled that so rich and cultivated a man should hire people to prostitute newspapers in this way – it must be a case of pornography for pornography's sake. He has no need to do it to earn a living. . . . ' Lord Rothermere had not attended this luncheon, but the guests, accustomed to platitudes interspersed with carefully chosen jokes, pricked up their ears. At last they had got something to talk about.

The following month, in a speech to the Manchester Publicity Association, Randolph went yet further. He knew so well how to 'trail his coat' and how to get laughs. Specifically, now, he attacked Lord Rothermere's group of newspapers which, he said, made no bones about increasing their sales by lurid presentation. 'Lord Rothermere desires not only what his father was accused of – power without responsibility, the prerogative of the harlot throughout the ages, but the cash that comes from the sale of pornography, without the shame attached to this squalid way of life.'

Randolph gloried in nice usage of the English language. When the speech was relayed to him, Lord Rothermere can hardly have revelled in the title of 'Pornographer Royal' – but Randolph had enjoyed himself exceedingly, and made his audience see the joke of flailing a group of publications which included *Horse and Hound*, *The Hairdresser's Journal*, and *Debrett's Peerage*.

In 1953, Tito (inelegantly labelled by Moscow 'the lackey of imperialism' when he diverged from Soviet policy) came to London. He was welcomed by Churchill, now again Prime Minister, and taken to lunch with the Queen at Buckingham Palace. Fitzroy Maclean was an MP, Julian Amery was an MP, but for Randolph there still seemed to be no opening in politics. He could but work on as a journalist – and he minded.

In June 1954, Evelyn Waugh wrote from his home, Piers Court, 'Randolph and June turned up here yesterday in a decrepit taxi and whisked us off to Bath, where they are buying an exquisite miniature palace. A fine staircase, a really splendid ballroom, a good secondary ballroom, two attics, terraces leading to a public cemetery.'

This delectable enterprise did not come off, but later in the year Randolph discovered the house of his dreams and purchased Stour at East Bergholt in Suffolk. It was a large pink eighteenth-century house, beautifully situated with views over the river Stour towards the square tower of Denham Church (made famous by Constable, who had been born in East Bergholt). Around the house lay seven acres of tangly garden, full of splendid old trees – planes, oaks, chestnuts, limes, ilex and cedars, and a sheltered walled garden ready for vegetables. Randolph was wild with excitement. But it was with mixed feelings that John Hare, who had known Randolph well at Eton and in Tunisia, received the ecstatic telephone call telling him that Randolph had purchased Stour and would henceforth be his neighbour in Suffolk. As John Hare wrote, 'I had always retained my affection for him in spite of his infinite capacity to wound those nearest to him.' And during the next six years, while Hare was a member of the Government, his telephone would ring unceasingly. Randolph's questions were always pertinent and interesting but Hare, whenever possible, tried to switch the conversation to gardening.

In time John Hare became Lord Blakenham. His wife Nancy, who had been born a Pearson, sister of Lord Cowdray, has written me the following account of life in Suffolk:

I didn't know Randolph until he came to live in East Bergholt. He often used to come over to lunch and dinner. Quite early on I went on strike about dinner, because I wasn't prepared to sit up half the night. When sober, Randolph was the best company I have ever known. He never moderated his language or his stories in front of the young, so they adored him.

I also loved him dearly (on and off!). There was a six months 'off' period on my part after he published in the *Evening Standard* a letter I wrote to him concerning his book on Anthony Eden, with all my spelling mistakes included!

What I would call his 'rages', he called 'warming to the subject'. There may have been some truth in this. By normal standards he would appear to be in the throes of a blood row, but if you came in during one of these performances to say lunch was ready, he would turn it off like a tap, and by the time we got to the dining room he would be talking about something else.

One weekend when my brother John Cowdray was staying with us, Randolph and Dick Stokes [Labour MP for Ipswich] came to lunch. Dick was quite a talker, so there were, as you can imagine, few pauses in the conversation. My brother, however, contributed nothing. I asked him afterwards why he'd been so silent. He said he'd been at Oxford with Randolph, in fact Randolph had the room directly above him, and he, John, had learned many years ago that the only way to deal with Randolph if you didn't want to have a row, was to remain silent, which John did.

At a later date Randolph said to me, 'I always found your brother rather a dull dog.' So I told him why. Randolph took this in quietly and obviously minded, for afterwards my brother said that whenever he met Randolph in White's Club, he would go out of his way to make polite conversation.

Randolph's love of creating controversy, and his irresistible urge to arouse passions without discrimination were his undoing I think.

Some years ago I remember Freddie Birkenhead was being interviewed on TV. He was asked if he thought Randolph reliable. He answered with a dead-pan expression, 'As reliable as a rattlesnake!' One other thing I remember very vividly. He loved his garden and showing people around it. He talked to his trees and shrubs as if they were human beings, always giving them a gender; thus to a rose, 'She has a lovely stink' (Randolph's language not mine) or to a fallen elm, 'You bastard, how could you do this to me?' The ease with which he could quote from the classics, ought, he knew well, to have been shown off in the House of Commons. As he couldn't get there what was there to do but air his talents in his garden. The trees and shrubs must understand.

— 20 —

In January 1954, Duff Cooper died and Randolph's genuine emotion gave some comfort to Lady Diana Cooper, who had to fly her husband's body back from what had been intended to be a holiday cruise. She told me that she had never had a row with Randolph, and the many times he had caused Duff to get what she called 'veiny' (when the veins stood out on his forehead with anger for Duff was a very hot-tempered man) were forgotten. Randolph had so often stayed in her various houses and now in what she called her darkest hour he did not hesitate to hold out a comforting hand. Randolph's genuine warmth penetrated all shadows – Diana had always loved him, and never more than now.

When it was decided to raise money for a literary prize in Duff's memory Randolph headed the organizers, but he almost lost Lady Diana's gratitude when he admitted to having lost the list of subscribers. 'The dropsical brute has two secretaries and a ghost writer,' she complained. However, the sum he eventually raised caused her to forgive him. Poor Randolph, he was so easy to see as dropsical or drunken but his brain ticked on.*

In the meantime Randolph settled into his country house with June. He had run up big gambling debts at White's Club and he wanted to get away from London, 'out of the temptation of the tables,' as he put it.

Stour offered every delight. But the whole house had to be redeco-

---

*The first Duff Cooper Memorial Prize was awarded to Alan Moorehead for his book on Gallipoli and Winston, when presenting it, was able (after many long years of bitterness) to make a joke about the Dardanelles.

rated; and though the rose garden had only been planted fifteen years before, the seven acres of strangely enticing slopes covered with wonderful trees which reached down towards the river needed a great deal done to them.

Randolph thought that at Stour he could retreat from a life which had treated him roughly, and while writing articles he could await the summons which must surely come. For he had to suffer at the delay. Would his father *never* ask him to be his biographer? Surely he had proved that he knew how to handle loads of documents and that he could reconstruct the politics of a period? For what other reason had he slaved at Lord Derby's Life? What could Winston be waiting for? With the special pride that was Randolph's he could not bear to *ask* his father to allot the task to him. He simply wondered how much more he had to do to prove himself.

Beside the front door Randolph affixed a plaque, made by his friend Denzil Reeves the artist, with Constable's words: 'I am come to a determination to make no idle visits this summer, not to give up any time to commonplace people. I shall return to Bergholt.'

For a time June kept herself happy decorating the rooms, and perhaps Randolph did not notice how much she minded his tantrums. He forgot about them. Why shouldn't others? There were curtains to be hung (yellow velvet ones downstairs), flock wallpapers chosen and chairs bought ('those things you sit on'). And overhead on the first floor Arabella's nursery was chosen to overlook the famous Constable view.

After a year of frenzied interior decoration Randolph discovered that the crust of the earth is inclined to burgeon in its own way if not held in check by human beings. He had never really noticed that men laboured with wheelbarrows and mowing-machines at Chartwell. Now he suddenly realized the big lawn in front of his own house had become a hay field and all the other lovely acres had turned into jungle. Only the fairly new rose garden had been tended and mulched. Being Randolph he thought he could learn it all in a few days and meanwhile be able to direct quite knowledgeable people.

One person he did listen to; Xenia Field the expert gardener, responded to his appeal and helped him to lay out and embellish the slopes around the house. The splendid old trees looked approvingly down at the flowering shrubs being planted at their base. All he had to do was to use his imagination – and of that Randolph had plenty. But to create a new garden it is also necessary to use a shovel and dig.

Mrs Field has described the beginnings: 'I bought him a box of pink button-daisies from Colchester and gave him the know-how for planting them. He'd rush off into the garden with a trowel and tremendous enthusiasm to put them in, and hovered around the plants with a watering-can in hand throughout the weekend. It was a great misfortune that not a pink daisy survived.'

Head gardeners came and went while Randolph's enthusiasm showed no signs of abating, the weeds grew as weeds do, rather too fast and well. When an overdose of fertilizer burnt the grass Mrs Field received a piteous telegram. 'Lawn ruined. Grass funeral black. My summer wrecked. Come as soon as possible.'

Later on he devised the brilliant idea of clearing his lawn by holding a competition for local children. Those who dug up plantains with the longest roots were to be awarded prizes. That took up a merry Sunday but the root-measuring entrusted to Arabella did become a little complicated and caused squabbles, and Randolph had not got a natural touch with children when they argued about root length. Between struggles with polyanthus, roses and honeysuckle Randolph wrote an essay on flowers. *A Book of Gardens* was published by Cassell, and his contribution is called 'Reconstructing an Old Garden' and even now, reading through it, one feels oneself scampering around under his direction. It is so full of 'go'.

'The first rule is "Do it yourself",' he wrote. 'On no account fall into the hands of a landscape gardener. . . . My own principal plantings have been willows, poplars, two white weeping wisterias, walnut, almond, three magnolias, flowering cherries, eucalyptus, a mulberry and a balsam poplar which Vita Sackville-West gave me when I visited Sissinghurst a year or two before her death. I have twice planted a tulip tree. They both died. I mean to have another go.'

How excited one had to become when the white wisteria dreamily, mystically, came into bloom. 'It's had lots of lovely grub,' Randolph would murmur. 'It ought to say it's grateful.' He discovered a fine bank of rhododendrons protected from winds by high laurels and Scots pines. The rock garden in front of it had to be abandoned but this needed only a firm decision.

A garden is a place to walk in agreeably, said Randolph and with this in mind he began to clear paths through his jungle. Or rather he hired men to clear them for him. 'Invitation, mystery, surprise,' was Randolph's slogan and several people, great gardeners in their own right, wrote to tell him with what excellence he expressed their own views.

For a short time June wondered if she could not accept life in this glorious home. Then she realized that no woman on earth was cut out to be Randolph's wife – girlfriend maybe, for he was loving and generous and pathetically eager for attention. But wife – no!

They quarrelled hideously in London, for she easily lost her temper and she had not the nanny-like quality which alone could hold Randolph in check. Laura, who was by now happily married to Michael Canfield, heard with misgivings from her nearby flat the sounds of June pitching her belongings into the street as she threatened departure. There was a dreadful evening at Chartwell staying with Sir Winston and Lady Churchill. Randolph had had too much to drink at dinner, and kept vilifying Sir Anthony Eden until Winston turned white with annoyance. Finally Randolph stormed out of the room and found that June, who had grown sick of the subject, had gone to bed. He dragged her from the sheets saying, 'You have got to dress and pack. We are leaving this house forever.' June demurred and then poor old Winston came padding along the corridor in his dressing-gown to make it up. He tapped on the bedroom door, entered and said, 'I'm going to die soon. One must *not* have family rows. Let's kiss and forget it.'

Randolph quietened down and June lay in the dark beside him wondering how much more she could stand.

The turning point may well have come at a ghastly dinner party given by the brilliant John Sutro, whose conversation could enliven any meal – a description has been written for me of this lamentable affair by Christopher Sykes who arrived at Sutro's flat to be told that having asked Randolph and June as well, Sutro had booked a table at the Queen's Restaurant in Sloane Square.

Randolph was late because he had arranged to meet June at their home and he had had difficulty in getting someone in the house to hear him as he hadn't the key. All of which had put him in a bad humour. The subsequent quarrel did not cease quickly owing to the fact that Randolph had been drinking. As things got worse Randolph turned to abuse his wife, describing her among other things as 'a paltry little middle-class bitch always anxious to please and failing owing to her dismal manners,' and other endearments of the same kind. All this was shouted in a loud voice in the restaurant and as Randolph was recognized as the son of our great Prime Minister, it caused a great deal of interest among the customers and Randolph soon had a large appreciative audience.

During this painful scene I had said nothing, nor had Sutro, but as it went on increasing in violence and arousing yet more interest amongst the people in the restaurant, I felt I must intervene, or I would feel a worm for the rest of my life – so when Randolph next paused for breath in his denunciation I said in a conciliatory way, 'Randolph you really should not talk to your wife in that way. . . . ' For a moment Randolph was silent. Then he roared out, 'What the hell do you mean by butting in to a private conversation?' I could not think of a witty rejoinder so said, 'I'm sorry but I thought you were having a public conversation.' John Sutro saved the situation by starting to laugh – with some embarrassment I admit.

Randolph had been oblivious to the fact that he was in a restaurant, shouting in front of a riveted audience, he had really imagined he was giving June a dressing down out of earshot. She, meanwhile, sat blinking back her tears, unable to swallow the dinner ordered. In the following year she left him. Randolph never understood how appalling his behaviour had been, and he lost two old friends that night, as well as his pretty if unsuitable wife. But who was suitable for Randolph?

Arabella, a lovely little girl, disappeared with her mother but later came down to Stour for weekends. No matter how remorseful he might be, Randolph had to face the fact that he had lost June. From now on he had only himself and his garden and his fertile mind. These ought to have been sufficient, but deep inside Randolph two things kept nagging – the fact that he would probably never grace the House of Commons and the lack of any message from Winston inviting him to write his biography.

Back at Stour Randolph always employed two young girls as typists and, as Alan Brien says, they often had nothing to do and grew bored. There were no cinemas or dance-halls in East Bergholt, so Alan would give them some pages of Lord Derby's life to retype and as the type-writer keys began to tinkle a satisfied smile would spread over Randolph's face. 'How nice it is to hear work going on,' he would say. 'Now let's find a drink for ourselves.'

During all this period Randolph worked as a freelance, and his journalistic talents improved. He produced articles for various period-icals and occasionally some newspaper would send him off as a special correspondent.

In 1954, Charles Wintour, Deputy Editor of the *Evening Standard* noticed the force of a scorching article penned by Randolph for the

Spectator. Wintour telephoned to ask if he would comment on the Crichel Down affair, which was bringing the Ministry of Agriculture into disrepute. So it was that Randolph started once more to work for Lord Beaverbrook, and the fact that his father was still Prime Minister added power to his pen. Soon Charles Wintour offered him a contract on the *Evening Standard* at £65 a week – which in those days was a pleasant salary to receive. Randolph signed with glee. Not only would he contribute regularly, but in addition he agreed to write two articles on the forthcoming general election without extra charge. How useful › those personal telephone numbers which he had collected assiduously over the years now became! This large array of secret numbers had to be yet more jealously guarded. At four in the morning Randolph would feel no compunction whatever in ringing people. His voice could become so seductive when trying to elicit information, the tone changing to an insidious purr very different from the raucous shouting used at dinner. Many a sleepy statesman was cajoled into revealing some impropriety in the early hours.* The *Evening Standard* knew it was on to a winner.

In May 1955, came the general election. Winston resigned the leadership, for the old warhorse was beginning to feel the strain. Stephen Carson, then a young MP, relates how Churchill had stopped him in a corridor to ask if he could find a black swan to replace one at Chartwell. 'I'll see, sir,' said Carson. A few weeks later he met Winston again and proudly said, 'I've got the black swan for you.' 'Don't bother me about black swans,' said the Prime Minister 'ten minutes before I have got to make a speech.' Anthony Eden became Prime Minister. On the day this was announced Randolph consoled himself somewhat alcoholically at White's Club and when he tottered down the steps he saw to his indignation that his car, which he had left outside, was getting a parking ticket; a policeman was heartlessly affixing a summons on the windscreen. 'So the Eden terror has begun,' growled Randolph as he slid into his seat and drove away.

---

*Randolph's secret telephone book has survived in the care of Mrs Michael Wolff. In its unimpressive brown paper covers one can read names and numbers which are *very* impressive indeed – almost everyone who mattered at the time is listed from the Kennedys in America to the Prime Ministers and Cabinet Ministers of England. Only my own father is inscribed as having *no* number – there was in fact a telephone at Castle Leslie in Co. Monaghan, but it was tucked away in a room where the ringing of its bell could not be heard.

— 21 —

It remained a tragedy that Randolph was not able to get into the House of Commons, many MPs thought he excelled Winston in debate and fast repartee. His successes in court when he was able to reduce trained barristers to mincemeat corroborate this theory. Winston had always had to work hard at his speeches. Randolph was a natural answerer back.

But let no one doubt that he remained passionately loyal to his father. He thought that since war's end Anthony Eden had shown undue impatience to become Prime Minister. Randolph had long ago accused Eden of being responsible for the British Government's truckling to the League of Nations, and now he saw Eden jockeying himself into a position to replace Winston. Randolph resented this eagerness, this 'ill-concealed impatience' as he called it. And he considered Eden unworthy of succeeding Winston Churchill as Prime Minister. The fact that Eden had married his first cousin, the madonna-like Clarissa Churchill, only added fuel to the flames of Randolph's dislike and distrust. He never missed a chance of placing his father's successor in the pillory.

Randolph possessed not only courage but also the rhinoceros-hide quality of his fellow reporters. In January 1956, he crossed the Atlantic on the same ship as the new Prime Minister and throughout the voyage never stopped badgering him to give an interview. Both Anthony Eden and his Foreign Secretary, Selwyn Lloyd, had to resist the importunities of Randolph all the way to New York. 'Very curious behaviour' was all that Randolph would say to the American press concerning Eden's refusal to speak to him.

On 2 February 1956 the *Evening Standard* carried a blistering report on the conference which was being held in Washington to hammer out an Anglo-American agreement on the Middle East. 'When statesmen and politicians can't think of anything else to say,' wrote Randolph, 'they always drag in God. Last night's declaration did it twice over, both in preamble and peroration.

'It was obvious from the start of the conference ... that as no planning had been done by either side, no joint plan could be produced. The declaration and the communiqué were full of pious platitudes and impeccable opinions.'

In the following month Selwyn Lloyd was stoned in Bahrein, Randolph heartlessly noted that it was 'not to death like a martyr'. Then with Julian Amery (now a prominent politician and son-in-law of Harold Macmillan) who happened to be staying at Stour, Randolph descended on R. A. Butler, Lord Privy Seal, to press him to organize an immediate Cabinet meeting, in which Britain's disastrous situation in Arab countries could be discussed.

On subsequent days Randolph's political column in the *Evening Standard* added to the growing disquiet which the House of Commons felt at the leadership of Sir Anthony Eden. Under the headline 'Britain in Danger' Randolph wrote, 'I was told ... that the Prime Minister was doing his best. I do not doubt it, and that is why I am sure there has got to be, and quickly, a change in the occupancy of 10 Downing Street.'

In the following debate Eden was taunted in the House of being afraid of 'the Churchill pen'. 'Frightened? Frightened?' – Sir Anthony's voice shot through octaves of indignation and his flushed face showed how near to the bone this sally hit.

In July came Suez. Randolph, from his special vantage point, embarked on newspaper diatribes against the Prime Minister who was making such a mess of things and fulminated about how much better his father would have done. In November Eden resigned.

From 1955 to 1959 Randolph worked with passion for the *Evening Standard* and although Charles Wintour was irritated by certain of Randolph's tricks he decided to accept them. Maybe it was just Churchillian arrogance that made Randolph always hand the newspaper a carbon copy of his articles, keeping the top copy for himself. However, for a year or so all went smoothly – or fairly smoothly. Living in the peace of Stour he felt no urge to gamble at White's Club, yet he was able to dash to London and 'keep in touch by telephone' as he put it, and at the paper's expense he could dart around Europe.

For a time he produced a weekly column for the *Spectator* as well, but when Iain Macleod, the editor, cut a few lines, 'not in any spirit of literary criticism but simply to make it fit the page', Randolph blew up in fury and *that* job ceased. Iain Macleod remained his friend, however, and occasionally went to Stour. He has written, 'It is a hopeless task trying to explain to people who did not know him how overwhelming was Randolph's charm.' One night at Stour, Macleod and Randolph kept up an argument together. 'It became more and more heated, more and more thunderous until suddenly we noticed that we were alone.' Worn out by the debate all the others had melted away. Randolph looked around, momentarily puzzled. The fact that his guests might have been outraged or perhaps just tired, never struck him. 'Damn fools,' he remarked and returned to the discourse.

Randolph revelled in the law. Sir John Foster, QC, who took his most famous case in court describes him as a dream litigant. 'Have we done our prep?' Randolph would ask his legal advisers and once when his solicitor referred to a paragraph as bad taste Randolph snapped his head off. 'You advise on law,' he said, 'I am the judge of taste.'

He brought a case against *Private Eye* and won it. 'No good having an apology in *that* paper,' he said. 'What we need is a full-page advertisement in the *Evening Standard* withdrawing the libel and expressing regret.' This he obtained by means of a 'mandatory injunction' – not a very common method of approach but one which Randolph, who was never tired of exploring the labyrinth of English law, discovered could be used.

The greatest of his court-room successes occurred in October 1956. The newspaper *The People* had unwisely referred to him as a 'paid hack, paid to write biased accounts'. When Randolph wrote asking the editor for a retraction, his letter was published in truncated form. Thereupon he sued for libel and acquitted himself brilliantly in the witness box.

Randolph, who was forty-five by now, revelled in being cross-examined. He knew he could show off his wits and get away with it. When asked if he had not referred to the *People* as 'the lowest mongrel cur in Fleet Street', he answered coolly, 'That arose out of the saying, dog don't eat dog. If you use metaphors from the canine world you naturally use other metaphors drawn from the same world, otherwise you complicate the issue and do not carry your audience with you.' The learned counsel who sought to get under his defence found himself constantly floored by Randolph's quickness and exactitude of phrase.

The *People*'s omission of the final paragraph of the letter which Randolph had asked them to publish meant that their retraction was no retraction at all. Michael Foot gave evidence on Randolph's behalf. So did Ian Gilmour, who had become editor of the *Spectator*. Randolph's own counsel hit the right note in his concluding speech when he asked for heavy damages, 'I have yet to meet a British jury who will stand for hearing a man who has been brave in war and peace called a coward, and I am sure I will not meet one today.'

Maybe the *People* had thought that Randolph could be provoked to unendearing rudeness in the witness box but he kept his head throughout and his speedy replies came like machine-gun bullets. He won the case and it cost the *People* £5000 plus costs to have used those words 'paid hack'.

What Randolph objected to was not criticism but lies. When interviewed on TV concerning Hochhuth's play *Soldiers*, which insinuated that Sir Winston had tacitly acquiesced in the plan to murder Sikorski by arranging the plane crash at Gibraltar, Randolph exploded. It was suggested that the allegation might be 'technically inaccurate'. 'It's not technically inaccurate, it's a bloody lie,' he shouted.

The barristers who faced him may have been acclimatized to the courtroom, but none of them could lash out with as much enthusiasm as Randolph. And as well as this, they might, unlike Randolph, have sometimes grown tired.

Peter Carter-Ruck, who often acted for him in the legal world, describes the impulsive generosity of Randolph. No sooner had he won a case than he would hurry the solicitor who had acted for him from the law courts into a taxi and drive him to Asprey's in Bond Street. 'I want you to choose something really good to remember this case by,' he would insist and his legal friends knew that he meant it. They had to choose a beautiful present. Randolph adored *giving* things. He only wished that he was richer than he was – but money was not the thing that mattered to him. It was the *feeling*.

Unfortunately after winning the libel case Randolph became overbold. He thought that he understood completely the laws of libel and within months of his triumph over the *People* Randolph used a nearly identical phrase on TV concerning a certain leader writer on his own paper the *Evening Standard* who, encouraged by Randolph's success, decided to sue. Lord Beaverbrook wrote a brief note to the embarrassed Charles Wintour in which he astutely remarked, 'Possibly by this time both the young cocks will want to settle.' They did, and the matter never came into court.

What fun Randolph had when in April 1957 he found himself on his feet again making a speech at Miss Foyle's Literary Luncheon at the Dorchester Hotel. He had recently published a small book entitled *What I Said About the Press* which W. H. Smith refused to sell. Having some thousands of copies on hand Randolph had arranged stalls containing *his* book in front of the W. H. Smith stalls (heaven knows how he got the Dorchester Hotel to agree to this) and he ordered his friends to sell them any way they could. Laura, always a gallant comrade, found herself ordered to display them on the counters of the fashion boutiques she had opened. 'But it's so difficult to force people to buy a political book along with material for lampshades,' she demurred, but Randolph didn't care. 'Of course the ex-Countess of Dudley can sell anything anywhere,' he argued, and Laura found that crates of books were arriving at her shops. She did her best, though clients became rather bewildered when they thought they were buying the latest fashion gimmick and found they'd got to improve their minds about the Press as well.

Randolph's speech at the Dorchester Hotel lasted twenty minutes and indeed the audience who had paid to attend this luncheon must have felt they had their money's worth. 'I believe,' Randolph began, 'that every human being in this country of ours, whether he be a politician, a journalist, a plumber, a carpenter, a bricklayer or even a member of the royal family, is entitled to some genuine privacy in his private life, and that it is complete abuse, in the name of the so-called freedom of the Press, for rich men to try to get richer by allowing their editors to send underpaid reporters into people's houses in order to ask impertinent questions. . . . '

Randolph continued, 'Meanwhile what about *The People*? I don't mean the public. I mean the pornographic newspaper which is published by Messrs Odhams to celebrate each Sabbath. Did you see their leading article of April 7th? I expect not. I don't suppose educated and cultured people such as we have at this gathering would condescend to read such drivel – but this leader is a corker and deserves to be put on the record.'

Randolph went on, 'I would like to express my thanks to the many distinguished editors and journalists who have given friendly and in some cases flattering reviews to my book, though there have been some papers which have failed even to mention it. Among these must be noticed the *Daily Telegraph*, the *Sunday Times* and the whole chain of Beaverbrook newspapers. I imagine the *Daily Telegraph* overlooked the book in order to give pleasure to Lady Pamela Berry, that the *Sunday Times* did not review it because Lord Kemsley does not like me and that the neglect of the Beaverbrook newspapers is because Lord Beaverbrook is again in this country – I'm going to see him after lunch – and he is thoughtful about encouraging libel actions. . . . Despite this and despite the wrongful and monopolistic boycott applied against the book by great firms like W. H. Smith and Rymans I am glad to be able to tell you that it is selling like hot cakes. . . . '

Randolph was a natural for TV but he flared up rather too often and this habit did not always entertain spectators. There was an awkward incident in America when in front of an audience of millions he stormed out of the studio. Tactlessly the interviewer brought up a subject which was causing the Churchill family great pain at the time. This was the illness of Sarah, Randolph's actress sister, whose pathetic bouts of alcoholism had ruined her own stage career and eventually resulted in arrest. Randolph had thought the interview was to be entirely political and was taken by surprise. He had not expected family tribulation to be brought up as a topic. Randolph lost his temper and the interviewer lost his prey. An empty studio was the result and no one knew how to fill in the time.

Back in England Lord Boothby describes one morning when Randolph came to the TV studio to do a programme. Michael Foot was there, enjoying a special lunch provided for the elite. 'For God's sake don't bring Randolph in here,' he said while tucking in to the lobster and hock. Boothby went back to the room where Randolph was making do with more prosaic rations. 'Spam!' exclaimed Boothby naughtily, 'how nostalgic. It takes me back to the war.' Randolph lifted his head suspiciously. 'What are you having in that other room?' Boothby couldn't resist the temptation of mentioning the lobster and Randolph's face fell like a child's. It seemed too bad he should not be allowed among the super stars. But he had to finish the spam alone.

Suez offered splendid material for the press. The *Evening Standard* flew Randolph out to Palestine and there in Tel Aviv he met Anne Sharpley, the girl reporter who was in charge of gathering hard news while Randolph telephoned 'his opinionated articles' to the Paris office. Of course what interested Randolph was the political drama, not the cold facts. The Israelis, always anxious to butter up a Churchill, put a pretty young secretary at his disposal and Anne viewed him for the first time when he was scolding this girl because of some mistake which she had made in her nervousness. Anne informed him crossly that she was prepared to stand no nonsense. A short time later they had to leave for Cyprus and Randolph, treating her like an army batman, ordered her to pack his suitcase, she hesitated but decided to do so. It wasn't worth ruffling up the *Evening Standard*'s political commentator at this stage. So she packed his clothes but at the top she laid his huge tube of shaving cream with the top off and wrote a note 'Maybe it should travel like this?' Randolph took the hint. He never tried to bully Anne again, and their friendship lasted for many years.

After Eden's resignation everyone expected R. A. Butler to take his place. The greatest 'scoop' Randolph ever made for the *Evening Standard* was his article predicting that Harold Macmillan would become Prime Minister instead. The leader writers had all produced articles saying the next man would be R. A. Butler. Randolph found this period much to his liking and lived on the telephone day and night, chiefly night. He used his extensive sources of information to announce with certitude who would be chosen. The result of Randolph's inquiries was that the Beaverbrook newspapers knew the result at almost the same time as the Queen. While the reporters of Fleet Street were trying to guess who the next Prime Minister would be, Randolph dropped a hint to Anne Sharpley who was still working with him on the *Evening Standard*. She rang up Lady Dorothy Macmillan who was in her bath but came dripping to the phone. 'Is it out already?' Lady Dorothy asked and then realized that she had inadvertently confirmed her husband's appointment. Randolph and Anne and the *Evening Standard* had good reason to be cock-a-hoop at having discovered this secret.

Later on, when Harold Macmillan made Lord Home his Foreign Secretary one of the journalists who expressed a sense of outrage was Randolph. Lord Home has described the occasion:

He wrote to tell me my selection was intolerable, and that he intended to denounce it with suitable invective. . . . He invited me to luncheon in the Ritz Hotel so that he could confirm his impressions and improve his copy; and he told me that he had to hand in his script by 5 pm on the day he had chosen for our meal. Knowing his lazy habits and his liking for food and wine, I strongly suspected that he would not have written anything by lunchtime, and would be hard pressed to meet his editor's deadline. I therefore wrote out, in the form of question and answer, my own appreciation of myself, and described the main lines of my approach to British foreign policy. I took it to the luncheon and when we arose at 3.30 I said, 'Randolph, I have made you a few notes on how I see my task ahead in the next two or three years, and something of my philosophy which will underpin foreign policy. In case it is of any use as an *aide-mémoire* put it in your pocket!' The result was better than I hoped, for the document came out virtually verbatim.

The *Evening Standard* sent Randolph to write articles in Cyprus when trouble broke out there in 1958 and it was pleasurable for Randolph to discover that his friend the Hon. Julian Berry, son of Lord Camrose, was there commanding the Household Cavalry. Julian had travelled out to the Middle East with Randolph in No. 8 Commando. Although only a subaltern at the time, he had kept his eyes open and knew him well. From Nicosia Airport Colonel Berry as he now was, received a phone call from Randolph saying that he was on his way and would like to stay, 'But you can't get through the military barriers,' said Julian, 'Find a hotel for the night and we'll expect you tomorrow morning.'

'Don't worry,' said Randolph. 'I'll manage'.

An hour later he arrived at Colonel Berry's house having argued his way past sentries and barbed wire.

'I can't think how you managed it,' said Julian, 'No one is supposed to be allowed through after dark.'

Randolph just grinned, 'I know my way around. And I'm not Winston's son for nothing.'

In May 1958, came the famous upheaval in Algiers which led to the installation of General de Gaulle as the French President. Randolph, representing the *Evening Standard*, contrived to get to Algiers via Switzerland in the wake of Monsieur Soustelle, a mystery man at the heart of the Gaullist plot. Randolph got in ahead of the other reporters and inveigled someone to arrange an immediate interview for him with Soustelle himself. How evocative was the drive to the Villa des Oliviers overlooking Algiers where his father had discussed French military plans with de Gaulle during the war! Soustelle was now lodged there, and unfortunately for Randolph several bottles of champagne were promptly opened. Randolph held forth rather more than he listened and omitted to take notes during the brief moments when Soustelle was permitted to speak.

Next morning Stephen Barber, who was covering Algerian affairs for the *Daily Telegraph*, breakfasted with Randolph on the balcony of his hotel room overlooking the harbour. This meal consisted of a curious mixture of fried eggs and Veuve Cliquot (Randolph had made a great favourite of that saying about a hair of the dog that bit you) and Barber knew he must help his friend invent a good story for the *Evening Standard* which was due to ring up at any moment. The trouble was that Randolph couldn't remember what Soustelle had said! Not even the date of de Gaulle's probable arrival in Algiers.

The inevitable phone call came through and Randolph sat down on his bed seemingly at his wits' end as to how to produce a good story. For a few moments he held forth on the privilege which had been accorded him. No one else could have met Monsieur Soustelle at all, but Winston's son naturally had gained admittance to the very villa where his father had discussed things with de Gaulle during the war. ... Then Randolph paused for breath, and thought up the next bit, 'I wish I was at liberty to tell you exactly what Monsieur Soustelle told me – but my lips are sealed. ... ' He went on to describe what *he* had told Soustelle and how deeply he agreed with him about civilians controlling the military etc.

Lord Beaverbrook was so enchanted by this interview that he caused it to be printed not only in the *Evening Standard* but in the *Daily Express* the following morning, and Randolph had reason to be pleased with himself. Later on he chartered a light aircraft to fly him and his friend Barber to the rebellion in Corsica. Arrest by French paratroops meant nothing to Randolph when he was out for a story, but the authorities eventually decided it would be less trouble to expel than to impound. As Barber said, 'Randolph had the knack of getting hold of the only telephone around that could be coaxed into reaching London or Paris to enable him to dictate copy.' A very dramatic version of the uprising appeared in the *Evening Standard*.

Suez continued to offer plenty of grist for Randolph's mill. The incredible stupidity with which that campaign had been conducted showed up Anthony Eden's lack of understanding of the military enterprise. As the *débâcle* rolled to its unhappy conclusion Winston, who had always liked and defended his successor, had been forced to say to Randolph, 'But *I* would have told the Americans exactly what we were going to do.' Randolph's political commentary grew vindictive, and in November and December 1958 Beaverbrook published in the *Daily Express* six articles by Randolph covering the Suez crisis. As a result of these Mr Anthony Head, who had been Secretary of State for War and then Minister of Defence, stood up in the House of Commons and made a speech defending the operation. In it he said:

This biography or whatever it is called, which has been written about Sir Anthony Eden is a very peculiar document. I do not know what was the purpose behind Mr Randolph Churchill's writing it. Mr Churchill bears what is perhaps the most illustrious name in England today, and the very fact of his bearing that name gives a certain authority to his book. I would say that this life of Sir Anthony Eden, particularly those parts which have been published [the six articles which were in fact the last chapters of the book], is a smear not on Sir Anthony, but on Mr Randolph Churchill as the son of our greatest statesman.

I believe that history, looking back, will regard this episode in Mr Randolph Churchill's journalistic career as a disgrace to the proud name that he bears. . . .

When Mr Head remarked, 'The operation is now regarded as a failure – Why?' there were cries of 'Because it failed'. Randolph of course had lots of puff with which to answer what he called 'this graceless and unconvincing intervention in the House of Commons'. He had supposed Anthony Head to be his friend and wrote, 'I am naturally taken aback that he should prefer to correct me publicly rather than privately.'

Meanwhile Randolph was discussing publication of a full life of Anthony Eden with his literary agent, Graham Watson, and in a short time the volume entitled *The Rise and Fall of Sir Anthony Eden* was published by MacGibbon and Kee. Graham Watson raised an eyebrow when asked to join author and publishers at lunch at the Savoy and both eyebrows when he read the preface of the book which began thus:

One week after I had agreed to embark upon this work, Colonel Nasser nationalized the Suez Canal. Nineteen weeks were to elapse before Sir Anthony Eden's ill-planned, ill-timed and abortive invasion of Egypt and twenty-five weeks before the regrettable abandonment, through ill health, of his political career.

The events which supervened in these six months have added considerable interest to the story, but they have inevitably affected the way in which it must be told. When I agreed to write this book Sir Anthony was the most powerful politician in the land. After a long, laborious and successful career he had risen to the eminence of power which he had long desired and for which he had long been earmarked. What would have been a simple success story has become tragedy on an almost classical scale. . . .

The fact that it was a breakdown in his health which led to Sir Anthony's withdrawal from public life naturally evoked the sympathy of every generous mind, and since this objective appraisal may be thought by some people to be of a critical nature, it is only right to state at the onset that it is my firm conviction that even if Sir Anthony had never been the victim of ill health his tenure of power could not have been prolonged for more than a few weeks. Even before the Suez misadventure there were many of his colleagues who felt that he was inadequate for the task and that he would have to be replaced as quickly and kindly as possible. . . .'

When Brendan Bracken died in the summer of 1958 Randolph forgot his many hates and wrote a splendid obituary of the mysterious red-headed young man who had attached himself to Winston way back in the past. 'He has died before his time, and despite the promise of his spectacular youth, he never achieved the summit in any field. Yet he was greatly loved and esteemed. He performed unnumbered acts of kindness for every sort and condition of his fellow humans. And I rather think that someone will "sound a trumpet for him at the other side".

'Despite the ups and down I had with him over thirty-five years, I have no hesitation or lack of breath in this valedictory fanfare: "You were always on the good side: you loved truth and honour: you hated cruelty and injustice: fare thee well, my gifted, true and many-sided friend." '

All went well with Randolph and the *Evening Standard* for nearly five years. He continued to prove himself a discerning journalist. Occasionally when he drank too much and could therefore not remember what he intended to write, his editor Charles Wintour had to reprimand him, but on the whole he was the most interesting and original man in Fleet Street.

Then came a somewhat too-good luncheon at the Savoy Hotel with Sir William Carr, owner of the *News of the World*. The offers made went to Randolph's head. He wanted at that moment to go to America and the *Evening Standard* refused to send him, and he wanted his telephone bills paid at Stour and elsewhere, and he wanted a car to rush him around to all the excitements. The *News of the World* seemed ready to provide all these amenities.

By the end of the meal, Randolph, puffing a big cigar, decided he must change masters. Charles Wintour wrote to Lord Beaverbrook on 5 September 1959.

I am disappointed that Randolph Churchill has left us at the moment when he might have repaid some of the time and money we have spent on him. His election reports might have been quite entertaining because he would have buckled down to the subject. But apart from that he was a rapidly diminishing asset.

Mr Blackburn has probably passed on to you my note about the reason for his departure. You may like to see the drivel that Randolph submitted as an article on Monday. At the time he was very annoyed indeed that I refused to publish it, but I think he now recognizes that it was no good.

He had a fair amount to drink that day and wrote a piece on the TV broadcast that was only passable and contained several irrelevancies that I cut out.

This also annoyed him, but the real factor is that he wanted to go to America, and the *News of the World* offer showed him it could be done.

To this Lord Beaverbrook replied, 'I am sorry that Randolph Churchill's gone away, but there were advantages and disadvantages and I got most of the advantages and you got most of the disadvantages. I don't mind if he blows up against us on TV. He will sooner or later, but it doesn't make any difference.'

Wintour chuckled when he received this note. He knew only too well what Beaverbrook meant by 'advantages'. Randolph could be fascinating as a conversationalist at a dinner table. It was a very different kettle of fish when he rang his editor in the early hours to discuss some abstruse point pertaining to a future article.

One of Randolph's first assignments with the *News of the World* was to fly to South Africa. Having obtained the lucrative job of Chief Foreign Correspondent, he stopped en route in Kenya and made a brief excursion into the wilds.

Before leaving Nairobi he hired a jeep and guide and drove out to the game park. To his annoyance the lions they came across had killed the night before and were therefore placid and sleepy. 'Call yourself lions?' Randolph shouted at them. 'I wish you could hear a British lion roar! You're no good – you sissies!'

Next day he embarked for Johannesburg and found himself sitting next to another correspondent in the plane, Stephen Barber, who was also going to report on the South African situation. The journey was not without humour. As usual the stewardesses handed around immigration forms which had to be filled in before landing. These forms seemed unusually long and Randolph took umbrage at the question concerning his 'proposed means of financial support while in South Africa'. He wrote, 'This is an impertinent question but you may take it that I am most generously treated by my employer.' Worse was to come. When Randolph read the question concerning race he got really angry and began to write furiously, filling up the small space allotted for answers and spreading himself down the margins of the paper. Peering over his shoulder Barber read, 'Race: human. But if, as I imagine is the case, the object of this inquiry is to determine whether I have coloured blood in my veins, I am most happy to inform you that I do, indeed, so have.' Randolph then explained that his great-grandmother on Jennie Churchill's side had been a Red Indian, and whether or not her tribe counted as 'coloured' at the airport Randolph's passport was impounded. What fun he found it to stir up the Johannes-burg officials! Randolph's South African friends who came to meet him had to promise to keep him under control for two nights if the passport were given back, and after a fortuitous interview with Dr Verwoerd, leader of the Nationalist Party, Randolph flew back to England laden with material. By great good luck (for Randolph) Verwoerd was shot and severely wounded within a week and this added pith to the Churchill column.

But the allure of the *News of the World* soon faded. On 28 November 1960 Charles Wintour was writing to Lord Beaverbrook,

Randolph Churchill rang yesterday to ask if the *Evening Standard* was inter-ested in taking him back. The *News of the World* had refused to publish an article he has written (now going to the *Tribune* I understand), and he feels anyway that the *Evening Standard* is a far more suitable medium for his writings than the *News of the World*.

He believes that he can now get out of his *News of the World* contract if we would take it over.

Personally I would like to see Randolph Churchill back in the *Standard* although he is of course, the most troublesome contributor I have ever met. He does bring news into the paper, and he is someone who creates interest in the paper.

At the same time I think that if we went ahead, we should *not* simply take over the *News of the World* contract which is very advantageous to Randolph. I believe he gets £5500 plus telephone bills plus a car with no minimum of articles to be written.

(Actually Randolph had signed a contract after much champagne which the directors had inadvertently worded wrongly. Instead of making Randolph liable for the production of *at least* forty-eight articles a year they had written out *under* forty-eight. Randolph had grown jubilant when he realized that legally he'd pulled a fast one. But of course he had been ready to produce the forty-eight articles. He was honest.)

Lord Beaverbrook contacted Randolph and three days later he informed Wintour, 'Randolph Churchill would prefer to stay with the *News of the World* if he is not allowed a car and £500 worth of telephone calls a year.'

It turned out that Randolph did not really care what paper he wrote for because at the end of 1960 the long-awaited telegram arrived.

— 22 —

Natalie Bevan describes the great moment. She had driven over to tea with Randolph (not to advise on his garden – the last thing he wanted was advice) but to see if a set of pottery elephants she had modelled and baked in clay suited his dining table. After tea, as she left the house and started to drive away, Randolph came running after her waving a telegram. So eager was he to show it to her that he fell down in the drive as he stopped her car. 'He's asked me,' he panted. 'He's asked me at last.' Natalie drew to a halt and got out to hug Randolph. He couldn't speak. It meant so much to him.

Winston had finally decided that his son could do it. The first-class reviews evoked by *Lord Derby: King of Lancashire* had certainly affected the final verdict that Randolph should be chosen for the job.

Natalie Bevan was the great and final love of Randolph's life. He had met her three years previously and from the moment of their first encounter Randolph did his utmost to change himself, to be that which she desired.

Natalie was the wife of a naval officer who lived four miles from East Bergholt. Bobby, her husband, was the son of Robert Bevan, the great artist of Sickert's Camden Town group.

The Bevan home lay only fifteen minutes' drive away. Natalie had come to Stour for the first time in May 1957 to see her friend Lord Kinross who happened to be staying with Randolph. Patrick Kinross opened the front door and Randolph had walked across the hall to greet her. He stopped in his tracks and stood looking at Natalie for a long time in the strangest way. And she looked back at him silently. The rapport was instantly established. After a moment of what one might almost call extraordinary recognition Randolph stepped forward and took her by the hand. 'Come out on the terrace,' he said, 'and smell the roses.' Then without more ado he addressed her almost tearfully, 'I've been waiting for you so long. I love you.' And wildly he began kissing her. Randolph had always been a pouncer but this was not his usual way at all. He felt the love of his life had arrived at last and although it was late in the day he was profoundly grateful.

Natalie was the same age as Randolph – forty-six – and as well as being beautiful she was a most unusual woman. She had first married Lance Sieveking and had two daughters. Then after the war she had married Bobby Bevan and come to live in Essex. In her Randolph recognized something he had always been searching for. It was a curious liaison but she admitted the strength of it and Randolph was overwhelmed from the start. Natalie accepted the sudden link – and still remembers the scent of roses that night.

Winston and Clementine were due to celebrate their golden wedding anniversary in the following year – on 8 September 1958 – and their children wished to show their feelings in an unusual way. Randolph thought not only of planting an avenue of roses at Chartwell, but also of giving his parents a 'Book of Golden Roses', each page of which was to consist of a painting by some famous artist.

Soon Natalie and Randolph were driving off to the Colchester Nurseries gathering new beautiful roses of every shade of gold and yellow while artists were being asked, or rather ordered by Randolph, to produce water colours of the lovely honey-coloured blooms.

The first to say 'yes' was John Nash. He went into the garden at Stour, saw a yellow rose, plucked it and went off home to his paint box. He said that he loved the work. He felt as if he was returning to his mistress each day when he entered his studio!

Then a bunch of yellow roses from Stour was sent to Cecil Beaton in London. It was no good Mr Beaton complaining he was just going off to Greece, the roses would not last and he must produce a painting overnight. Cecil got no sleep before his plane flight. Paul Maze came down to Stour with Arabella and they got to work side by side. Then Margaret Birkenhead, the widow of Winston's great griend F. E., rang up to say that some fine yellow roses were just coming into flower in her garden. Could she paint them?

Brushes and water colours were kept at Stour so that no artist could get out of the allotted task. As time ran short Randolph paced up and down the terrace galvanizing everyone into action. R. A. Butler, Home Secretary, (who had been persuaded by Winston five years before to take up painting as a hobby) came over to Stour to fetch his rose and examine what had already gone into the portfolio. The result of RAB's labour was returned by car next day. He said it was done in tempera but the picture smelled strongly of oil and Natalie reckoned he must have got muddled. 'Oh well,' he acquiesced. 'A tube of vermilion oil paint did get mixed up in the tempera box – that's what comes of being an amateur – it's so difficult to handle one's media.'

Perhaps the greatest triumph came when Augustus John was persuaded to paint a cluster of Golden Emblem roses. He had not used water colour for fifty years but it gave him great pleasure to produce this little work of roses in a blue vase.

In fact he drove the whole way from his home in Fordingbridge to see the book after it had been bound. The tome had just been packed up for its journey to the South of France where Sir Winston and Lady Churchill were to celebrate their anniversary, but when Randolph's sister Diana Sandys rushed out to say that Augustus John stood on the doorstep, Randolph went out to greet him. Then he unpacked the book and proudly showed the contents to which by now not only Natalie but his ten-year-old daughter and the renowned Matthew Smith had contributed. Augustus John – a marvellous figure in a black straw boater and red shirt – glanced carefully through everyone's work. 'The important thing in painting is to want to do it!' Then as he left the house he murmured, 'Remember me to your father,' and was gone.

By this time the book weighed 67 lbs and it was a great day when Randolph and Arabella flew off to Nice with it and nine dozen real yellow roses.

In her diary Natalie Bevan wrote, '1958–1959. The most golden of my years.'

In 1959 Randolph made his last bid to get into the House of Commons. Nigel Nicolson had been Tory MP for Bournemouth East, a safe Conservative seat, and because he had protested against the Government over Suez the local association had decided that he should be disowned at the next election in October 1959. Major J. Friend of the 11th Hussars whom Randolph had known so well in Egypt was accepted but then thrown over, after which Randolph travelled down to Bournemouth to make himself available as Tory candidate. He promised not to stand if Nigel Nicolson was readopted but could not resist telling the *Daily Express*, 'I think I would be a better member than Mr Nicolson. I'd be jollier.' Nigel Nicolson was not readopted but Randolph's effort proved a fiasco.

Muriel Bowen was sent by a London paper to Bournemouth to cover the story and she tracked down Randolph to the luxurious Carlton Hotel where he was staying. The head porter told her in sepulchral tones, 'Mr Churchill is on the beach, madame.'

It was an icy day, but Muriel well understood that Randolph might wish to gather his thoughts. She walked over to the high cliff which lay opposite the Carlton and staring down she saw a most astonishing sight.

There down on the windy beach in an overcoat whose collar was turned up around his ears strode Randolph, while at his heels trotted a pack of reporters with notebooks into which they assiduously wrote everything he said. They looked just like a pack of beagles. Finding a lift down to the beach Muriel managed to catch up with the throng. She also got out a notebook, but it became obvious that Randolph was determined to talk about world affairs while the reporters, who mostly came from local papers, kept asking him questions about Bournemouth. However, they jotted down everything he said.

The moment he recognized Muriel from *Evening Standard* days he cheered up, but she had to remind him that what she wrote for London didn't matter particularly whereas what the local press said mattered very much indeed. She also pointed out that his new suede shoes were getting ruined by the wet sand but he did not seem to care. Only Parliament interested him, the place where he could express his views – to hell with his shoes.

Randolph's efforts to capture Bournemouth East were all in vain. The Conservative Association did not choose him and he would not have been human had he not resented the ease with which their eventual candidate rolled home with a majority of nearly 20,000.

Winston took enormous interest in this election and very much hoped his son would be accepted as candidate. He felt that Randolph must have learned something about how to behave with committees and he knew that once he got into the House he would be all right. But Randolph never stood for Parliament again. He had become embittered. Natalie helped him to face the hard fact that he wasn't wanted by the Conservative Party.

Natalie and Randolph had automatically become lovers but now she was forced to think. Into what trough was she leading two men? Bobby Bevan knew about Randolph, of course, and he did not really mind. He had a life of his own. But June was divorcing Randolph and he longed to marry Natalie. Natalie knew that it would be terrible to abandon her husband, it would hurt him so much, and yet, eventually she had to make a decision. Her birthday was on 24 May and Randolph's was on 28 May. On 4 August 1960 he wrote to her:

My own darling Natalie,

There is no need to say much after all that has been said in the last three days. I want you to know that what I said this morning is true: I want you to be my wife as soon as possible. My love for you can stand many afflictions and will, I know, endure. You have had a lot to put up with from me. But I believe you still love me?

Come then. Let us act with courage, conviction and good sense. Let us so arrange our lives that we may start a new and permanent life together on your fiftieth birthday or on mine; or, if you should prefer a compromise on any convenient date between 25th May and 28th May 1961. That only leaves May 25th, 26th and 27th. I see that my birthday falls next year on a Sunday – which wouldn't do so please choose 25, 26 or 27 – Thursday, Friday or Saturday.

Whatever you decide I shall love you, now and forever. Please help me to make us both happy.

Your devoted and unhappy,
Randolph

This then after three years of romantic love was the moment when she had to decide what to do.

She had enjoyed staying with Randolph in Monte Carlo, dining on the Onassis yacht, seeing a lot of Sir Winston and Clementine Churchill and restraining Randolph from foolish gambling. She could not pretend that she hadn't enjoyed basking in the Mediterranean moonlight – until the time came for him to fly off to America to scribble some article. In the summer she could keep her mind occupied by supervising the art exhibition at the Minories in Colchester. All this had become her life. What irked her was the complexity of the set-up. Two men depended on her. She wanted to enhance and not destroy their happiness. Eventually she thought the matter out and she told Randolph that she could never leave Bobby Bevan. They would just have to go on as they were.

From then on, through the years, Randolph would send Natalie six or seven telegrams a night when his brain was at its clearest and these would reach her in a bunch on her breakfast tray. Occasionally she kept them pinned together, and so now one can read at Boxted House: 'Do you suppose that I don't know why your telephone never answers?

You must be very silly if you think I don't know. Love Randolph' etc. The local post office must have enjoyed these messages.

Nancy Blakenham has written me, 'Randolph was as you know, very much in love with Natalie Bevan and we were discussing falling in love. I made some comment to the effect that after a certain age, people didn't really fall in love. He turned on me and said: "Age has nothing to do with it," and added, "I am more in love now than I have ever been in my life before." I was then given a long lecture on the subject. He was obviously referring to Natalie, although her name was never mentioned.'

One did not need to mention it. All who had loved Randolph with understanding, his Mitford cousins Diana and Clementine and Laura whose existence had enlivened him during the war could only say, 'Thank heaven he has found her at last.'

— *23* —

From 1960 onwards Randolph altered his whole way of life and started at Stour the organization which would result in Volumes I and II of his father's life, which he always referred to as the 'Great Work'. That telegram from his father meant that at long last he could get going. Researchers and typists had to be recruited and he started to build a 'strong room' which was to house important documents in the yard. Stour became the centre of a sort of cottage industry.

One has to wonder why Winston had hesitated for so long. If only he had decided on his biographer two years earlier that much more of his story would have been written by Randolph, who had waited so longingly but could never have brought himself to ask for the job.

After Randolph had definitely been selected, the C & T Trust was formed (incorporating the names of Chartwell and Telegraph). The *Telegraph* owned the serial rights while Graham Watson had arranged for Heinemann to publish the book in hardback. Winston's own writings could seldom be improved upon and Randolph chose Lockhart's words, 'He shall be his own biographer' for the front page.

The enthusiastic young men whom Randolph chose as research assistants were headed by Michael Wolff the most brilliant of the historians who came to see Randolph and finally settled with him without what Randolph called 'allowing lawyers to waste money by vetting the correspondence'. Michael's letter of 25 January 1961 reads,

My dear Randolph,

I write to confirm our agreement that I should be your principal assistant in the preparation of your life of Winston Churchill at a fee of three thousand pounds per annum, payable by you in equal monthly instalments. . . .

Our agreement is to take effect on February 1st 1961, and to remain in force unless otherwise agreed by mutual consent until July 31st 1962. After that the agreement may be terminated on either side by six months previous notice.

Yours ever,
Michael Wolff

Randolph really hated to be businesslike. What charmed him about Michael Wolff was his first-class brain and his delicious wife Rosemary and his two little daughters Lucinda and Claudia. Of course, they must all come down to Stour frequently – at that moment the garden was snow-covered, but as soon as the first flowers appeared he would be picking bunches for Michael to take to London.

When Rosemary went to America her husband would write her wistfully: 'Sweetheart – it was a trying week for me. The worst thing was that I simply could not get any work done. Not only have I not written a single word of the Book, but I could not even get on properly with the article. . . . I am only half a man without you. Enjoy yourself but hurry home. . . . ' Neither Randolph nor his staff could survive without the ladies and, as no war was on, why should they?

Secretaries and typists and Miss Harryman, the archivist, were to be kept busy on the top floor at Stour, and to all the employees Randolph explained the honour and excitement of discovering some previously unknown detail of Winston's life. Randolph planned five volumes of 200,000 to 300,000 words with 'companion volumes' following each containing letters and documents to be published separately.

The organization of the Great Work was tremendous. In the Strong Room the documents were housed in steel filing cabinets and original unpublished papers began to arrive which had to be sorted, assembled, photostated and filed. Not only Chartwell and Blenheim were to donate material but the Royal Archives, the Admiralty and Home Office Archives had to be combed, and the papers of Asquith and Bonar Law gave the background to Churchill's early life. Michael Wolff, ordained Chief Researcher, had under him other 'Young Gentlemen' researchers who quickly acquired the habit of throwing tantrums. However, their frequent outraged departures 'for ever' usually terminated at the gates of Stour. Alan Brien, Robert Rhodes James, Michael Molian, Martin Gilbert, Frank Gannon, Tom Hartman took their turn. They became exhausted after a few days work and eventually they would each give angry notice, think better of it and decide that the experiences they were enduring compensated for brainstorms.

Soon after Michael Wolff had been elected to his post, Randolph told him they must drive off to Blenheim Palace with his son, young Winston, to see what the archives there could produce.

Bert Marlborough, the 10th Duke, welcomed them to the house, but he himself had not got particularly good manners. Michael Wolff was led to a freezing cold bedroom and had his bags unpacked by a supercilious footman who even placed Wolff's silver in little arranged piles. At dinner, which took place in a small room called the Library although it boasted neither books nor shelves, it became obvious that cousin Bert was intent on watching TV throughout the meal. 'Your bloody library isn't a library and TV isn't meant to replace conversation,' Randolph shouted.

As a result the two Mr Churchills and poor Michael Wolff had to pack their own bags (the footman must have gone to bed) and drive angrily away to a hotel in Woodstock where they spent the night.

'But we haven't seen the archives,' Michael Wolff complained next morning. Randolph laughed. 'Never mind. I'll get everything sent over to Stour. Bert is so ignorant he doesn't even know he's got archives.'

So that was that.

When Martin Gilbert, a knowledgeable young historian from Oxford arrived, Randolph gave him to understand that he was to drive around England calling at all the big houses announcing that he was 'Mr Randolph Churchill's assistant' and that any papers that might be of interest in compiling a life of Winston should be forthcoming. Bewildered owners of huge mansions, who scarcely knew they *had* archives welcomed anyone with knowledge, and Martin Gilbert found himself invited to go through numerous libraries. His host would often lead him back to the front door saying, 'Take away anything you like.' Martin Gilbert was then packed off to America to look for titbits. When he cabled that Winston's early correspondence with the statesman Bourke Cockran revealed rich treasures and looked 'meaty', Randolph wired his congratulations as if to a victorious general.

Happily the Strong Room at Stour had now been completed and on its shelves all documents pertinent to The Life could be stored. When the papers had been carefully filed and arranged after photostating, they gave a wonderful background to Winston's tempestuous life. Miss Harryman had her work cut out but she loved it.

And then, of course, there was Mrs Sexton, the cook, to be cajoled into producing what Randolph called in a favourite phrase of his 'a notable soup'. When Mrs Sexton had first arrived, Randolph had thrust Escoffier's cookbook into her hands. 'This will tell you how to do everything.' The bewildered Mrs Sexton was unaccustomed to reading but she took the book away and did her best.

'Living as I do entirely in the country and largely in the eighteenth century . . .' Randolph would begin many dinner tirades but Anne Sharpley noticed that friends were starting to drop by the wayside. They came to Stour still for occasional weekends but they had not the stamina to stand up to him. When he noticed their absence he grew wistful.

Occasionally he took Anne Sharpley to local Conservative fetes. Eventually an unknown Tory MP named Enoch Powell, writer of a pulverizing article in *The Times*, was lured to Essex. Randolph was curious to know Mr Enoch Powell, but after a long session with him in a tent Randolph appeared muttering in his special way to Anne, 'I'm not sure I like that gent'man.' She took him home before a worse encounter occurred.

And to this day she will try to explain the unexpectedly delightful guest Randolph could be when lunching in her flat. Although so demanding at his own table, when he came to town and took a meal alone with her (and she did not pretend to cook well!) any plate of pudding would be consumed with relish. She says, 'No schoolboy taken out for a holiday treat could have been more appreciative – that was his charm really – the charm of a schoolboy.' Those were the two sides of Randolph. He was unutterable and endearing by turn.

Alan Pryce-Jones, the author – and Randolph's Eton friend – gives a hilarious account of the day when he was staying at Stour and Randolph arranged for a TV series entitled 'Conversation in Country Houses'. In the middle of the night Randolph, as was his wont, had rung up his friend Frank Pakenham asking him to arrive and be amusing, but Lord Longford sleepily protested that he was always busy on Fridays and Randolph petulantly remarked, 'Oh, if you are going to make difficulties we will have to do without you.' Frank Pakenham heard no more.

A crew of twenty technicians arrived and Randolph told his house guests, Ann Fleming (the wife of Ian Fleming) and Vanessa Jebb (whose father had been Ambassador in Paris), to chat away on interesting subjects. Cameras, lights and coils and coils of wiring filled the house.

Lunchtime came, but there was nothing for anyone to eat. (At that time the cook had left and Randolph happened to be having tiffs with the local shops who refused to deliver to Stour.) Eventually Natalie Bevan arrived with a basket of tinned soups and there was much opening of tins and search for mugs. Unfortunately while the conversants greedily consumed their soup Randolph stuck to a tumbler of Scotch whisky. By the time he had reduced the TV crew to a frenzy (they had brought their own sandwiches) Miss Jebb found herself tongue-tied, and as the one thing forbidden on TV is 'dead air' the conversation in country houses languished. Randolph became angry, 'Can't you open your bloody mouth?' he asked Vanessa who had become paralysed and speechless. Randolph then placed himself just in front of the camera and proceeded to hold forth in the vein he thought suitable. Unfortunately he failed to notice that nothing could be seen on the screen except a large square of his own white Aran-Island sweater. Timorously the crew pointed this out to him. 'Oh, fuck,' said Randolph loudly. This was not what country-house conversation was supposed to be and the episode never reached the public, although it was kept for private consumption. Doubtless the director thought the vast sums spent on this project were compensated for by their mirth.

Randolph's TV programmes often went awry. Alan Brien describes one evening when he took Randolph and Aristotle Onassis to record a 'chat show' together. It had been well advertised, but on the day Randolph and Onassis got paralytically drunk and when they arrived at the studio the TV organizers seeing their state (instead of photographing and keeping what would in time turn into a unique record) put them in a room together and *pretended* that cameras were working. Onassis left the country next day but for a long time Randolph kept saying, 'It's most extraordinary. No one seems to have seen that TV conversation and we were in terrific form. It must have been brilliant.'

Brien never revealed the truth to him.

Meanwhile the garden slopes were being steadily cleared; daffodils and aconites filled one space, azaleas another, snowdrops were planted everywhere. Polyanthus, primulas, foxgloves and bluebells arose and Randolph discovered that big splashes of the same colour were more effective than if plants were just dotted about. A blue river of polyanthus weaving between the trees was a spectacular delight. The terrace was expanded and a delicious leafy colonnade constructed outside the dining room so that meals could be taken *en plein air*.

It was a blow to learn that the three hundred rose bushes had got to be replanted elsewhere because after twenty years they had taken all nourishment from their patch, but Randolph supervised the moving and used terms like 'rose-sick soil' with knowledgeability. 'We'll plant the rose garden with larkspur – it has different needs,' he cried joyfully after reading a gardener's manual. Then came a herbaceous border and a bank of peonies. Pleasure could be had by all those willing to work.

In November 1962, Randolph departed for Norwich to help Ian Gilmour (who had been his editor on the *Spectator*) stand for Parliament in a by-election. On arrival in the town the Duchess of Buccleuch, Ian's mother-in-law, found herself put in charge of Mr Churchill the Younger as he was then called. She did not like electioneering but accepted with good grace this somewhat onerous role. 'If you won't knock at doors and argue with people, your job had better be looking after Randolph,' Ian had said. She settled to the task and Randolph, who liked nothing better than to be 'looked after' by a handsome duchess, bustled around from hall to hall doing, she feared, as much harm as good.

In vain Mollie Buccleuch tried to stop him tanking up. But he was out to enjoy himself and he knew his stuff politically. Eventually she crept away leaving a note for him suggesting they should meet in a hotel that evening. Much ruffled by her absence Randolph eventually arrived. 'Don't you understand that I depend on my friends being *present*?' he asked.

And then because Mollie was kind and warm as well as beautiful Randolph opened his heart to her. Lady Churchill snapped his head off when he tried to explain his feelings towards this older woman. 'But Mollie is of a different generation,' she said.

'I don't care,' said Randolph, 'I need her, she's maternal and you're not.' It was a terrible outburst and reminiscent of what Clementine Beit had told him in the past.

The shortest visit ever paid to Stour, said Alan Brien, was that of Randolph's very old friend, Alastair Forbes. 'Ali arrived from London in his fast car,' said Alan, 'churning up the gravel on the drive.' Randolph greeted him at the door with cheers and embraces. 'Come into the library, dear fellow.' Mr Forbes followed him into the library. What transpired is today debatable, but three minutes later Alastair Forbes came out, white with fury, jumped into his car and drove off. 'Once again,' says Alan, 'churning up the gravel.' 'Whatever did you say to him?' Alan asked, but Randolph just seemed puzzled at his friend's departure.

It's too late to unravel it all now, Alastair Forbes just says he suddenly felt that a certain young lady might be waiting for him in

London and he realized that an evening with her would be much more satisfactory than hours of political argument with Randolph.

As Tilly Losch used to say, 'Finish Good – All Good.'

— 24 —

By now young Winston had grown up, spending holidays between his two parents and his four grandparents. He had been educated at Eton and then Oxford University. When eventually Randolph could take him along to White's Club he felt a glow of pride that this good-looking young man could be introduced as his son.

In March 1961, Randolph and Winston left Libya for a luxury safari arranged for fourteen people. They started from Benghazi, the town that Randolph had not seen since the night of the famous raid in 1942 with David Stirling and Fitzroy Maclean, and he lost no opportunity of describing the port. The trouble with Randolph was that he remained incapable of imagining himself in someone else's shoes. On this occasion he happened to take a fancy to two American married couples who were on the expedition. The jaunt has been amusingly written up by the wives.*

This morning I go to help the Churchills with their list of supplies, in case they have forgotten something or need help with their shopping. At 9.30 am Randolph is in a shirt without trousers or shoes. He shows me his neat package of clothes and equipment, and insists that Winston put out a camp-bed so that I can be zipped up in one of their new mummy-style sleeping bags. He is proud of his cooler – his Magical Box, as he calls it – which he says will be kept perpetually full of ice to chill his *pâté de foie gras*. Ice in mid-Sahara is a novel idea, but Randolph, if anyone can, will surely manage it. Over breakfast which Winston ate but Randolph drank, we discuss supplies, and Winston decides that all he needs is deodorant. His father explodes that he's been seeing too much television, but Winston and I go shopping and buy two jars. We also buy ten kilos of charcoal for camp-fires.

*The Great Saharan Mouse Hunt by Miggs Pomeroy and Catherine Collins.

'We shall,' Randolph says, 'sit around a jolly camp-fire and talk.' As he is a great conversationalist, we shall more likely sit around a camp-fire and listen. The first contretemps has reared its ugly head. Randolph insists that the 'other ranks' [i.e. the military] members of the Safari will have their own little camp-fire elsewhere. When Catherine and I protest at both the unfriendliness and inefficiency of this system Randolph's voice rises two full octaves of irritated authority.

Miggs and Catherine, as chosen friends, listened somewhat doubtfully to Randolph's insistence on separating themselves from the rest of the safari: 'They won't understand our jokes you know. Let them have their own camp-fire. Every now and then we'll send them jolly little presents. . . .'

Meanwhile young Winston was tinkering with the Churchill Land-Rover. 'The boy can take one of these cars apart,' his father says proudly. Then he reads them poems and they realize that he reads beautifully – 'a gifted man who should have been spanked more frequently in childhood,' they decide.

When the rest of the party seemed to dawdle Randolph started ahead one morning in the Land-Rover singing loudly, 'When the roll is called up yonder I'll be there.'

At Agedabia Randolph and Winston waited for the rest of the safari to arrive. Miggs and Catherine recorded their meeting that evening. 'Ahead of us first a dot on the horizon and then looming as a road block, is a Land-Rover mounted with a great six-foot flag; white emblazoned with a blue UN. In the middle of the road Randolph sits with refreshments laid out. Winston stands beside him with a gun at the alert. They both wear tin helmets on which have been painted blue bands and large UNs.

'Stopping all cars,' shouted Randolph, intent on fun. The five Americans applied their brakes. 'Stopping all cars. I've been sent up from the Congo to investigate. The UN is worried about conditions in North Africa, identify yourselves.'

Soon they were all delightfully intoxicated and toasting the success of the expedition, and the wives remarked on Randolph quoting his daughter Arabella as saying, 'Papa likes to see women work. . . . '

They found a camp-site in a eucalyptus grove and Randolph claimed the right to cook the first dinner. 'What, no flowers on the table? This is the age of the common man and the commoner woman. . . . '

Cold roast beef, potato salad and tomatoes had been brought by the Americans but Randolph added *pâté de foie gras* and lobster bisque. The two Dutchmen who had appeared from a nearby oil rig had been invited but when they tried to help the wives Randolph forgot his manners and shouted, 'Leave the women alone – bugger off . . . . ' Whether they understood that phrase or not they were never seen again!

'The stars were bright and the night cold and we awoke in the morning to find ourselves covered with pools of icy dew.' Hot tea had a restorative effect, so did sausages but Randolph wanted bacon and eggs. 'So two eggs were carefully cooked but Winston ate them because Randolph then said he could not swallow eggs unless he had tea to wash them down.' (What a nuisance he must have been in the Army!)

On the next night camp was made in real desert, sandy scrub with sage bushes and the Americans laid out fifty mouse traps to catch the special breed of mouse which the expedition had been mounted to investigate.

On 15 March, Catherine Collins wrote in her diary, 'I scramble eggs for breakfast which everyone pronounces delicious except Randolph. "My dear girl," he says despairingly, "You've obviously never read Escoffier. It is essential to beat the eggs well first, then add the seasoning. Don't just throw a hunk of butter into a frying-pan full of unbeaten eggs." '

All next day the Churchill father and son continued to drive ahead searching for new routes to the south. 'Randolph passes the time of day while Winston scouts the terrain or naps under the car. The other cars in the party [those Army blokes who aren't allowed to share the jokes!] disappear on the horizon.' Randolph thought they had overshot Gialo but all he cared about was having his evening drink. 'Give me the binoculars. . . .'

Later that evening by extraordinary chance Randolph found Gialo on his own and drank tea with the Madir. Then Randolph and Winston disappeared. 'On our own we have a quiet supper and as darkness falls we assume the Churchills must be dining at the rig and pack away the kitchen. Late at night the Land-Rover roars into camp and we are berated for not having hot soup in language that Randolph's nanny never taught him. So the kitchen is unpacked, and Winston and I cook up a second supper. We have a difficult passenger in this great creature with his commanding presence, his brilliant wit and rough manners. It has reached the point where we relish the peaceful moments when he is sleeping and yet we all recognize his sweetness. . . .'

On 16 March, Randolph decided that as the *pâté* and caviar were finished he might as well fly home.

He had spent £60 on tulips at Stour and he longed to see them come up. Also he wanted to be there when his pug produced her pups. 'Very irresponsible of me to go away from home for six weeks.' Young Winston could keep the Land-Rover and continue the safari.

By 17 March he was back at Stour coping with the Great Work and telephoning Natalie all through the night. Money was pouring in by now and Randolph was having fewer tiffs with the village shops. As Martin Gilbert was to remark, his highlight was generosity rather than honesty.

— 25 —

During the rest of 1961, the biography of Winston progressed and Randolph divided his time between Boxted House and Stour, where he launched a company which could print pamphlets and enjoy legal privileges, he called it Country Bumpkins Ltd.

At the house Captain Boycott (named after the famous Boycott who had stymied Randolph in an American TV 'Brains Trust') and his mate Annie were the pugs-in-chief, they and their puppies gambolled around together with a spaniel named Orlando. Before he went to bed at night, at two or three in the morning, Randolph was wont to take them all out for a last run in the garden and Annie always acted good as gold. But Boycott showed a malevolent streak. He preferred to lift his leg on his return over the yellow velvet curtains and so a most unlovely hemline showed at their base. He was very quick at it and no one could believe that any dog who had just been out would take the trouble to lift his leg . . . but Boycott did.

Liza Dietz asked if Randolph would contribute an article to her husband's newly opened magazine and Randolph, who did not much like her husband, asked her to come to Stour alone and discuss it. 'You might still find it difficult to have me – I have two small dogs,' she parried but Randolph tossed aside this excuse, 'My doggies adore visitors. Do bring them.' So Liza arrived with a Pekinese and a Griffon, one under each arm. The pugs rushed out yapping. 'Put them down,' ordered Randolph. 'My doggies only want to make friends.' So down she put them and the pugs kicked up such a row that her darlings, deeming discretion the better part of valour, made off like streaked lightning into the garden with the pugs in hot pursuit. This wasn't at all what Randolph had intended and Liza could not help but worry at the disappearance of the 'doggies' – hosts and visitors alike. It was a long time before they reappeared and whether Randolph's article was worth the strain remains a moot point.

Although no longer interested in food himself, Randolph was very intent on entertaining and feeding well his 'Young Gentlemen'. Michael Wolff always had a good appetite and Randolph remained anxious that the dishes served at his table should be of a standard with those produced by Rosemary Wolff, who was a superb cook.

In the summer a new researcher arrived to join the team and he immediately saw that Randolph himself needed looking after. Andrew Kerr adored Randolph, he said to me that to be with him was like going to a university, everything he knew he learnt in Randolph's company. So Andrew worked less with Michael Wolff and Martin Gilbert than with the fragment of a man who knew now that it would be all he could do to ward off the reaper until his job was done. Robert Rhodes James disappeared to write a book of his own on Lord Randolph Churchill, and Andrew, although once or twice he left the house at midnight feeling unable to face yet another row – grew to love as well as look after his strange master.

In December 1962, Tilly Losch came to stay at Stour. Now Countess of Carnarvon, she had retained her loveliness, the great green eyes still slanted up at the corners, her figure was as good as ever and, as her deposed lord had remarked, 'At least her legs can't age.'

Natalie liked Tilly and did not mind when Randolph went off to Paris for a few days with her. It seemed only natural that such old friends should want to be alone together talking about the past, Randolph talking about *himself* and Tilly about *herself*. The last thing that Natalie wanted was to have to listen.

Arabella came to Stour that Christmas holiday when the 'Great Snow' started. Every bush and tree lay deep under a white blanket and Natalie moved over from Boxted House to look after Randolph's young daughter while he was away in the USA.

Charles Wintour, who still often came to Stour for a weekend, made oblique remarks about the two gardeners who were paid by the *Daily Telegraph*. 'How do you manage it, Randolph? One man with a broom to sweep the leaves away is perhaps understandable but how do you manage *two*? I'd love to see your expense account.' On one occasion Charles Wintour remembers reading aloud an article written by Malcolm Muggeridge which appeared in the *New Statesman*. Muggeridge was an old friend and Randolph had poured out his heart to him.

The resulting article stressed Randolph's failed ambitions. Wintour was reading aloud when suddenly he looked up and saw that tears were streaming down Randolph's face. 'It's too true,' he said in a choked voice. 'All he says about my ambitions is so terribly true.'

Despite the knowledge that he would never now get into the House of Commons it was not often that Randolph collapsed emotionally, and he had after all achieved the status of being his father's biographer. Had he been a Member of Parliament he could not have given sufficient attention to this work. As it was Michael Wolff said to me, 'He always gets it right after a night's sleep – the rephrasing of some idea or what to leave out as irrelevant. We've done all the research in the office and laid out the gist and argued about it till late at night – but next morning it's he in the end who comes up with the answer that is always right.'

Apart from the Great Work Randolph continued to have fun with press lords. He started to write pamphlets in eighteenth-century style and these he paid to have printed for a list of 400 picked persons. The press referred to him as a 'self-appointed scourge of politicians.' When all was quiet in East Bergholt the papers considered it ominous – as before a thunderstorm. They wondered doubtfully if Randolph's spleen could be completely immersed in the massive task of writing his father's life.

In 1962, his first pamphlet was printed. It contained three letters between himself and Hugh Cudlipp, the joint managing director of the *Daily Mirror* and *Sunday Pictorial*.

This first pamphlet which sold for a shilling will give the flavour.

To Hugh Cudlipp, OBE
Daily Mirror Newspaper.   31 August 1962
My dear Cudlipp,

I have just been reading your recently published book *At Your Peril*. I notice that you are at pains to refute an allegation I first made some years ago that there was in Fleet Street a 'dog don't eat dog' rule which protected the proprietors of newspapers from criticism. You cite a number of examples in which rival newspapers have been attacked by you, where you have mentioned the name of the proprietor.

What I had in mind (as you well knew and well know) was the immunity enjoyed by press proprietors from intrusion into, or attacks upon, their private lives; particularly by those papers which themselves intrude into the private lives of those who are not fortunate enough to own a newspaper. In this connection I wonder whether the Royal Family could obtain some measure of privacy for their private lives if they bought a newspaper and joined the Newspaper Proprietors' Association?

I can think of six or seven newspaper proprietors whose private lives have been, and in some cases still are, absolutely fascinating. Of course we Country Bumpkins hear about these petty scandals by word of mouth. But I cannot recall having ever read a word about them in the many newspapers that I read. These men may enjoy a measure of immunity in their private lives shared by no other members of the community, with the exception of some important advertisers.

Yours sincerely,
Randolph S. Churchill.

PS You may print this if you will.

To this Hugh Cudlipp replied with equal slickness. In his letter, after the date 3 September 1962, he grandly addressed Randolph as 'MBE', at Stour, East Bergholt, Suffolk, to say that he had received 'my dear Churchill's' communique of 31 August and hastened to say that if Randolph could 'think of six or seven newspaper proprietors whose private lives were absolutely fascinating' he personally could not do so. But then of course Randolph lived in a village where his knowledge as a prominent biographer or voyeur exceeded his. Perhaps it would be as well if he, Hugh Cudlipp, tried living in East Bergholt, for every item of gossip did not reach Strand-on-the-Green, W4

Cudlipp went on to say he was greatly in favour of the Royal Family buying a newspaper and joining the Newspaper Association because few others could afford to do so. It was certainly an interesting idea.

He ended up assuring Randolph that as he had asked him to *think* about his letter he would certainly do so.

After the normal ending 'Yours sincerely, HC' he added as a PS, 'you may print this if you wish'.

Stour,
East Bergholt,
Suffolk.   7 September 1962
My dear Cudlipp,

Thank you for your letter of September 3. I am sorry to think that in Fleet Street or Grub Street or wherever you earn your living, you are so ill informed about the lives of newspaper proprietors. I doubt if you could add to your knowledge by coming to East Bergholt. I think it would be simpler to have a word with your boss, Mr Cecil Harmsworth King. I am sure he could tell you a lot about this and thereby obviate a visit by you to East Anglia, which would be painful to me and my neighbours.

Of course you burke and obfuscate the issue. Your reference to Lloyᵥ George's private life is very wide of the mark. It was not written about in his lifetime. It is true that, as Lord Francis-Williams states in his book, *Dangerous Estates*, Lloyd George 'spent £1,600,000 of the money he had gathered from the sale of honours' on buying the *Daily Chronicle*; but this was only in 1918 and consequently would not have protected him before that year. What did protect him was his ennoblement of so many newspaper proprietors, including Lord Northcliffe and Lord Rothermere, the uncles of Mr Cecil Harmsworth King.

You still make no answer to my allegation that the private lives of newspaper proprietors enjoy a special immunity. Naturally you don't because what I said is true and unanswerable, and therfore unpalatable to the sort of newspapers you are allowed to run.

I note that in the 'Affluent Age' the writing paper available to the executive staff of your newspaper is a good deal more sumptuous (with its deckled edges) than the writing paper used by the Royal Family, and a great deal more expensive than that on which you print your shoddy papers.

Yours sincerely,
Randolph S. Churchill.

PS I shall take advantage of your permission to print your letter. I have not the same facilities that you have, but I shall do the best I can.

Other pamphlets continued in this vein and doubtless by now they have become collectors' items.

In the year 1963 Randolph pressed Natalie to accept £1000 a year for searching out and arranging the illustrations for his father's life, but she had her own fortune and she preferred to work for nothing. As time passed she grew only too thankful that she possessed her lovely home only four miles away. It suited her to drive over to Stour, keep her own room there, work with the researchers and always be free to leave. In a way she felt that it was this possibility to walk out whenever Randolph became tiresome that kept their affair enduring.

On 1 April, which was Lady Churchill's birthday and always alluded to humorously by her, Lady Churchill came to lunch at Boxted, and after the meal she discussed with Natalie Randolph's forthcoming flight to Washington, where he was to accept for his father the Honorary Citizenship of the United States. Kay Halle had striven for years to arrange for this honour to be conferred on Winston Churchill, and in the end her persistence resulted in the passing of a unique Bill through Congress.

So tangled were his feelings about her that Randolph could never relax in his mother's company. Perhaps he remembered his craving for her as a small boy, perhaps he remembered the one time she had seemed to grow close when he wanted to marry Kay Halle and when the coldness of Clementine's beauty shut him up. How deeply he had once longed for those blue eyes to light up with admiration for him alone – for her little son. It had never happened. And now it was too late.

When a fortnight later the Honorary Citizenship was presented at the White House, Randolph stood on a balcony reading out a message from his father to the American nation. Beside him stood his son, and President Kennedy and his wife. Jackie Kennedy wore a navy blue suit with a giant diamond pin. White House guests drifted around the lawns while Winston Churchill's oldest friends – the famous financier Bernard Baruch and Alice Longworth – added their vintage allure.

In August, Randolph stayed with Jack and Jackie Kennedy at Cape Cod, and there he found Laura. Remaining a good loser and in this case unshakably devoted, Randolph whisked her off on the evening picnics given by Bobby Kennedy, the President's brother.

He had returned to England when, in November, President Kennedy was assassinated. In December Randolph flew back to America to attend his memorial service. The death of his own sister Diana Sandys took the edge off the intense emotion he felt when Jack Kennedy was shot. For the first time he had to realize his sister's inner loneliness and regretted hiding from her in the garden with Tom and Diana Mitford. If only they could have understood as children what she was going through – now it was too late to make amends. She had not been able to hold her husband Duncan Sandys, who had remarried after a divorce and had a child by his second wife. Although she worked gallantly for the Samaritans, Diana felt that she was not needed there and she left the society. She took an overdose in her own house in Chester Row.

Sombre indeed was the end of that year, and it was hardly relieved by the reception of the book which Randolph published, *The Fight for the Tory Leadership*. Quintin Hogg, who was Randolph's choice, had not become Prime Minister. However, the press was not kind: the *Evening Standard* reviewed the book critically, saying, 'The result is entertaining but not a great book of revelations. Of course this has not deterred him from having a go with the help of his considerable skill, his sackful of newspaper cuttings and – by the look of it – the confidences of Mr Macmillan himself.'

Hugh Trevor-Roper (Lord Dacre) to whom Randolph sent an advance copy, wrote him on 31 December 1963.

Chief's Wood
Melrose
Scotland
My dear Randolph

Your book arrived yesterday. I thought I would read it before going to bed last night. I like going to bed fairly early in these rural solitudes but I couldn't sleep. I simply could not stop reading and went to bed at 2 am having finished the book.

You are incomparably the best political journalist writing in England today.

Yours ever,
Hugh

Randolph thought so much of Trevor-Roper's letter that he kept it.

Clive Irving the journalist (who became managing director of the *Sunday Times*) has described several visits he paid to Stour.

By that fire there were two very deep armchairs, one each side, and a pouffe in the middle, possession of which was frequently fought for by a gaggle of pugs and usually held by the favoured Boycott. All night long Randolph and guests would sip large and misleadingly diluted glasses of whisky and water. Occasionally, Randolph would rise to seek a reference in the library, or to produce the manuscript of a coming article or papers from his file . . . more to elaborate than prompt, for he had a remarkable gift for total recall. At other times we would be jerked back to the present by a bout of his telephone calls. . . . Whatever the reasons, people did answer the phone at any hour, as I saw in a set piece demonstration of his technique during the scheming for the leadership of the Conservative Party after Harold Macmillan's fall in 1964. Randolph had been waging a misguided and foredoomed campaign on behalf of his friend Lord Hailsham, (Quintin Hogg). This, as Mr Hogg must have realized, was the kiss of death. Although Randolph's support was well meant and robust, it was, in the current jargon, counter-productive. . . . One night he got word that the pro-Hailsham lobby was disintegrating. At about 12.30 am Randolph rang Mr Selwyn Lloyd, said to be wavering. The somnolent Mr Lloyd was instructed to remain 'steady on parade'. . . . Other leaderless Tories were pursued, and the last name on the list was that of Lord Home. Randolph reached him at about 2.30 am. The phone rang, and an understandably distant peer replied. Randolph was taken aback. It was, he felt, a terrible sign of the attrition of the aristocracy's living standards that Lord Home himself had answered directly. Without bothering to reply at once, he put his hand over the speaker and said, 'Goodness how sad. They live like bloody coolies these days.' He then opened the conversation.

'Is that you Alec? Randolph here. Look here, I hope you're advising the monarch that it should be Quintin. It's said that you yourself might be in the ring. I trust that is not so. . .?'

Lord Home was three days later to become Prime Minister. He remained remarkably polite, and patient, and utterly enigmatic.*

This was one of the rare occasions on which Randolph's political antennae let him down, but with many other commentators backing the wrong horse, it was perhaps forgivable.

It was typical of Randolph that when he needed a secretary he should word the advertisement himself. 'Mr Randolph Churchill requires an extra resident secretary at his home in the country, excellent shorthand and typing essential. . . .'

Barbara Twigg, a young girl who had just passed a secretarial course, thought she might have a try. With her father, and in some trepidation as to what tests might be demanded, she travelled by train to East Bergholt and Randolph 'interviewed' her. It was not at all what she expected, he took one look at her fresh lively countenance, demanded no tests in the shorthand notebook which she carried in readiness, assured her father that she would be 'quite safe' in the cottage a mile away, where secretaries were supposed to live, and Barbara found herself engaged there and then. It was May 1963 when she took up her duties and she soon learnt that fast shorthand would have been no use whatever. 'His pursuit of the apposite phrase, the stinging comment, the unusual word made his dictation exceedingly slow, and I eventually evolved an abbreviated form of longhand which only I could understand.' Randolph had however supreme confidence in himself as a secretarial judge and when he heard there was to be a 'Secretary of Britain' contest he ordered Miss Twigg to enter. Barbara was horrified at the idea and managed to wriggle out of it – but her boss remained quite certain that *his* secretary would have won had she only tried.

Barbara Twigg had to get used to a timetable unlike that of any ordinary secretary. At 2 in the morning, just as she had got to sleep, the phone in her cottage might ring, 'Could you come please. . . . ' She learnt to disentangle trivial requests by phone – maybe Randolph just wanted her to fix a radiator that had gone cold, or to find an article mislaid or to make soup for an unexpected guest. But if it was necessary

* *20th-Century Magazine*, Vol. II.

to get something off to an editor's desk by 9 am she would dress and drive back.

When the cook left – and every now and then Mrs Sexton would toss her head and storm out – then Barbara knew how to produce a reasonable meal. And despite the fact that Randolph himself did not appear to eat any longer, he liked to see good food appear at his table – above all what he called that 'notable soup'. Barbara became adept at producing versions which could be called 'notable' and gradually she discovered that the one thing which Randolph never refused was her plum cake! It was 'complan and plum cake' only too often now, while the guests tucked into chicken and those vegetables which burgeoned in the walled garden.

$$-\ 26\ -$$

In 1964, Randolph was told that he would have to undergo an exploratory operation on one lung. The lump which the surgeons intended to remove might perhaps be cancer. Randolph, fearless about tribulations of the flesh, refused to get fussed at this possibility. He thought it would be exhilarating to fly to Marrakesh before going into hospital, and on 3 February he took off with Michael Wolff and Andrew Kerr and Miss Harryman to stay at the Mamounia Hotel and work a little more on the book. Later Natalie arrived. The drive from Casablanca airport wasn't too jolly because the car lights were working badly, and poor Andrew at the wheel got the rough side of Randolph's tongue. However, Natalie's diary described rapturously the following morning. 'Woke in golden sunshine. Randolph called and we breakfasted on his balcony. Cold chicken delicious. Then as he had to work I went forth to find goat-tweed in the Souk. Had a row with him but he said he was sorry.'

Back in London, well cossetted by Natalie, he entered the Brompton Hospital for his lung operation. When he came to after the anaesthetic, a nurse whispered a happy verdict. The lump removed had not been cancerous. Although he could not speak, a look of satisfaction crossed Randolph's features.

When the news reached White's Club, Evelyn Waugh made his famous remark: 'So they've cut out of Randolph the only part of him that *isn't* malignant!' When these words were repeated to the patient he trembled with laughter. He couldn't laugh out loud but he revelled in Waugh's wit and wrote back as it was Eastertide. 'I hope *you* have a happy Resurrection.'

This was the time that Lord Lambton came to visit Randolph. Before arriving he telephoned to ask if Randolph would like to see him and demanded, 'What shall I bring?' Randolph answered without hesitation, 'Champagne.' Lord Lambton ordered a case of champagne and took it with him. Randolph's eyes sparkled. He rang for the nurse and said, 'Put three bottles of this in a bucket and bring it back to us.' The nurse went off with three bottles and came back having poured them into an enamel slop pail. Randolph and Tony's faces fell. How did one scoop up tepid champagne with tooth glasses. And such a *vintage*. Mrs Michael Foot was also among the friends who visited him at this time. She found Randolph angrily complaining to the doctors, 'Stop treating me like an invalid.'

Alan Brien went to see him several times and even now, when he knew him so well, he could not help being impressed by Randolph's cavalier attitude to the nursing staff. On the first occasion Brien was shown up, the matron happened to be in his private room. Randolph waved her away – as no matron had ever been waved away before. The good lady was after all on her own territory – but such was her surprise at being treated in this peremptory fashion that she started to sweep out. Randolph did not notice her indignation. As the matron reached the door he asked if two cups of tea could be sent up, and then to make matters worse he started to describe how tea should be brewed. 'First you heat the pot . . . ' began Randolph. 'I do not need to be told how to make a pot of tea,' replied the incensed matron. Alan Brien felt himself growing weak at the fury of this storm. Two cups of very tasteless tepid tea finally appeared. 'Most extraordinary how they won't learn,' muttered Randolph as Alan Brien sipped nervously.

On the next occasion Alan arrived when the surgeon was in the room. Randolph felt rather well by now and to the doctor's surprise he announced, 'I think I can be discharged from hospital tomorrow.'

'I don't think so,' interjected the surgeon.

'I pay you to cut me up. Not to dictate my whereabouts,' riposted the insufferable patient.

The surgeon stamped out of the room. Later he sent a bill for the operation totalling £750 – an enormous sum for those days. So the doctor came out best in the end, but Randolph *had* asked for it!

To recover from his operation Randolph went first to Tanis Guinness's house in Biarritz, which was always open to him. In his thank-you letter, penned on 3 June, he boasted that all his friends said he looked far better after the trip. Then he joyously told her about his garden which had blossomed during thirty-six hours of heavy 'gardener's rain'. 'The pansies are distinguishing themselves,' he wrote, 'and the roses are just bursting. . . . ' He fussed because the wisteria was being eaten by the birds and one can see how happy the troubles and tribulations of the earth kept him.

Then to finish off his 'cure', Randolph flew to Capri where Mona Harrison Williams owned a lovely house. She had always remained a friend of his, this society beauty older than himself with whom he had been in love – or so he thought – all those years ago before the war.

While Randolph was in Capri, staring at what should have been a blue sea, Michael Wolff continued working at Stour, and he wrote to Rosemary about his chores there – the picking up of files from the Public Record Office, etc. And then Randolph phoned from Rome to say he was coming home on Saturday. 'Poor fellow, he had no sun in Capri and is feeling rather sorry for himself. The truth is he has done very well after such a major operation, but he cannot possibly be physically or mentally fit for many months to come.' Yet the magical quality remained and people forgave his abominable behaviour because of the effect Randolph produced on them.

That summer Randolph was able to enjoy the marriage of his son to Minnie d'Erlanger, daughter of the late Sir Gerard d'Erlanger. Sir Winston attended this festivity, the last one at which he was to appear.

— 27 —

In January 1965, Sir Winston Churchill went into a coma at his London home in Hyde Park Gate, and all those who had loved him most dearly, even his wife Clementine, longed for him finally to depart. It was a painfully long-drawn-out drama for the family which gathered round, wondering when that extraordinary spirit would finally give way. Winston's words had put stuffing into the British people during their darkest hour, he had been the greatest war leader in history, but he had not, as he ardently wished, dropped dead while making a speech in the House of Commons. Now he had to lie unconscious while the whole country held its breath. Death had never frightened him but this slow going was not the one that he would have wished for.

During the long wait Randolph moved to London where he took rooms in the Hyde Park Hotel. Natalie had her own flat in nearby Lowndes Square. The Churchill family, Clementine and her daughters Sarah and Mary, kept vigil in turn. Winston, whose wife Minnie was about to have a baby, and Arabella came and went. Diana Sandys' three children and Mary's four called on their grandmother almost daily.

Lady Jean Campbell, journalist daughter of the Duke of Argyll and granddaughter of Lord Beaverbrook, arrived for dinner with Randolph and Anne Sharpley attired in a red velvet evening gown. Randolph considered her outfit over-sumptuous for the evening on which his father was expected to die. After midnight she grew sleepy and lay down on the sofa. Anne Sharpley fussed around wondering how the Lady Jean could leave the hotel next morning clad in red velvet.

After breakfast, Lord Moran, Sir Winston's doctor, called in to say, 'It is unbelievable that he is still breathing, he hasn't had anything to eat for ten days or anything to drink for five. What a heart he must have to keep on breathing!' Anne then dressed Jean in Randolph's clothes and sent her back to the Ritz Hotel with her red evening dress under her arm in a paper parcel.

Towards eleven o'clock on this fantastic day June arrived with a black coat which she thought Arabella could wear. Arabella, however, deplored the idea of not buying a *new* black coat of her own. Then a message came from Lady Churchill saying the grandchildren were not to wear mourning, just black armbands. 'But I'm not a child,' expostulated the sixteen-year-old Arabella. Randolph blew up. 'My daughter will wear what I say!'

The protracted wait ended on 25 January. It was lucky that Randolph was well at the time, and could play his part in the tremendous state funeral given to his father. For three days Sir Winston Churchill lay in Westminster Hall, built long ago by the Normans, and, after thousands of people had filed past, the coffin was drawn to St Paul's through silent streets. It was a freezing winter's day. The wind seemed full of daggers of ice, and Randolph walked with bowed head behind the gun carriage which bore his father's coffin covered by a Union Jack and towed by sailors. Londoners stood waiting for their Winston to pass by.

After the trumpets had sounded at the end of the ceremony in St Paul's, and the pipers' lament died away and the cranes bowed in homage, a launch carried Winston's coffin away down the Thames. It seemed as if England was burying its own heart. So it was that, with only the family as mourners, Winston Churchill returned to Blenheim where he had been born.

A curious stillness fell on the frozen country. We all sensed that an era had drawn to its close. Winston Churchill's voice would never again ring forth. And his son, his only son, whom he had so cherished, lifted his head with a final pride. He had determined to do well the task allotted to him. He had walked unswervingly through the streets, he had followed the coffin to the very end. Wherever he was, Winston would surely now understand the tempests that raged in his son's blood.

After the funeral was over, Randolph again went to Marrakesh, where he'd taken a villa. Natalie, Michael Wolff, Andrew Kerr and Miss Harryman went with him. Already he felt that he might not have time to finish his father's biography before he himself died, so 'the team' were galvanized into action. Meanwhile Arabella flirted with Jean, the sixteen-year-old son of Boul de Breteuil who owned that intriguing Moroccan palace where Winston had stayed during the war.

On 27 February 1965, Michael Wolff wrote to his wife:

My darling,

I write this in my morning 'office' at a large millstone at the bottom of an avenue of cypresses, a dozen stand at each side of the rose garden. Some of the cypresses are as tall as 13 Holland Park's. The sun rises at 7 am and I shortly after the sunrise and I get to this seat by the millstone at about 7.30 am when the sun is beginning to warm things up, down the rose garden and over the cypresses one can see the snow-covered Grand Atlas Mountains, with one particular peak shimmering in the morning sun. All around are the noises of early morning life – the labourers pushing carts or beating their asses, the swallows and starlings and robins, the doves in the dovecot, the peacocks and the storks, not to mention the bull frogs – Hardly any poultry I'm glad to say so we don't have everlasting cock crows – nor a mosque with its clangings and shoutings. We are I suppose about four miles west of the centre of Marrakesh. Inside, the villa has very high ceilings and huge stone-paved rooms – everything is designed to keep one cool in days before air conditioning was invented. Although it is all one storey, the spaciousness is such that no one need get in each other's way. . . . The servants consist of the admirable Hamid who is major-domo and speaks French: I say speaks but actually he only whispers and hides behind pillars to make himself scarce. Then there is Zeonib – which means the beautiful one – an ugly elderly woman who is an adequate cook provided one does not overtax her ingenuity. . . . We live on hot crois-sants (from a local bakery), coffee and fresh fruit juice for breakfast. (There are four acres of orange and grapefruit trees on the estate, and Randolph had bought two of each, so every morning one of the under-gardeners goes out to pick our day's supply.) For lunch we have *hors d'œuvres* with a lot of charcuterie, and some meat or fish dish. Randolph, of course, doesn't eat at all, but we will survive.

Zeonib the cook lives on the premises (in a hole in the wall), so also (in another hole) does the head gardener who also acts as night watchman with a big stick. Sundry women, men, gardeners and hangers-on appear at suitable times.

Randolph has not been well and the smooth French doctor whom he had when he was last here drove up in his fast, red two-seater and pronounced high blood pressure. Natalie is sweetness and light, and is really looking after him – Andrew has been most amusing – you must get him to give his own account of the journey. . . . When Jack Profumo* could not resist 'christening'

---

*Jack Profumo had caused the famous scandal in Lord Astor's house Cliveden when he was Minister for War and he and Christine Keeler were accused of a swimming-pool flirtation.

the swimming pool by diving in and Randolph could not resist the comment, 'Really Jack I should have thought you'd learnt your lesson and given up all that.' [The Profumos arrived in Marrakesh after the Astors had left!]. . . .

Randolph goes to England March 31 for his mother's birthday in April and to see his dogs and bulbs at Stour and Her Majesty at Windsor. He returns to Casablanca April 6 bringing Arabella with him.

Randolph made no bones about his dislike of sightseeing. I have two accounts of the 'fantasia' arranged to welcome the King of Morocco on 1 March 1965 – one written by Michael Wolff to Rosemary and one by Natalie Bevan for her diary. They are very different. Natalie enjoyed every minute. She writes,

I was taken by some lively beautiful French friends of Randolph's into the crowds and we walked by the tents of the chieftains who had come with their horses and entourage to camp outside 'les Ramparts de Marrakesh' to welcome their King.

It was very medieval, with thousands of people and horses moving slowly into position. A very high wind blew and there were flags flying. No one knew, neither police nor soldiers, when the king was due to arrive but the beautiful stallions, brilliantly decked out in gorgeous trappings of gold and silver and exquisite colours, were kept to one side of the route and us spectators were kept to the other. . . . Eventually we were manoeuvred into position by a soldier who seemed to like us for he led us to the front of the crowd and told us to sit down. So we all sat in the dirt while the wind blew straw, paper and dust in our eyes, in our hair, in our teeth, but the scene was so fascinating, the crowd so colourful and dignified, the wild music so penetrating that two hours passed like a few minutes. Then the King drove by in a closed car surrounded by motorcycles! Then we were jostled past the rows of carpeted tents to the 'Field' where the horses were gathering for the 'fantasia'. Young men on wonderful horses kept challenging each other, and they would race down the stretch of turf shouting and shooting their long guns.

Michael Wolff's letter to his wife gives a more sober account:

The weather has been a disappointment. We have had two days of high winds, dark clouds and occasional showers – not at all nice – and we spend most of the day indoors by the fire. This morning however it looked as if it was going to be fine and I am out at 6 am at my 'desk' on the millstone! Randolph is better but his state changes. Yesterday we did 11 hours work . . . slow but sure and quite good. We spend nearly all the time at the villa, hardly ever venturing out. . . . The Mamounia [the big hotel of Marrakesh] is as bloody as ever, and you can see the Souks and Arab places just so often but no more. The great excitement in the town are the preparations for the Fête du Throne – the 4th anniversary of the King's accession – (Days off for all the servants and shops closed. If it isn't Ramadan it's something else). Anyway, for the past few days hundreds of horsemen from all over Morocco have been arriving to take part in the great 'fantasia' or ride past the King. You've seen the sort of thing on the movies . . . lots of horses and men in white and *feux de joie*. They have camped just outside the walls and the Mamounia Hotel in beautiful bell-shaped tents, each lined with different gaudy hangings, each with its own beautiful carpets, copper kettles etc. It really is a sight to be seen and some 400,000 Marrakeshians seem to be doing nothing else. When not watching the horsemen rehearse they go into the tents and listen spellbound to the stories of the horsemen, sipping the while mint tea. It is like a tale out of the Arabian Nights . . . but when you think of it, nothing has really changed here much in 2000 years.

A few days later Michael writes excitedly about his homecoming which was drawing near and one gets a taste of these working trips to Marrakesh. 'Randolph is better but not well, hardly goes out and doesn't like sightseeing so that means (à la Beaverbrook) that no one else can. I will change all that when *you* come out . . . but to be honest I don't feel like sightseeing myself. Composing, which is what we are doing, takes a lot out of me, and after working solidly all day I don't feel like anything else. We are all in bed by 11 and I sleep solidly for 8 hours a night.'

After flying back to England in April, Randolph and Lady Churchill were summoned to lunch with the Queen at Windsor Castle. After the meal they handed back Sir Winston's Garter Standard. Randolph found himself enchanted by Her Majesty and thought he had made a great hit with her. 'She took a fancy to me,' he said afterwards. One has to wonder how much of the Queen's affability had been royal good manners or if she had seen into Randolph's inner nature.

Less stimulating was the dinner recorded by Natalie at Boxted House on 25 June, 'Randolph to dine. He will talk to me about his money troubles and cook troubles.'

Cook troubles were worse than money troubles because Randolph was unusually happy-go-lucky regarding finances. Generous by nature he could not understand that small tradesmen wanted to be paid on the dot, and he always returned from his American lecture tours (which brought in a great deal) owing rather more than he had actually earned. Every time he gave a successful lecture he threw a dinner party to celebrate and as the mathematics of bills bored him the final result was sometimes disastrous.

Laura occasionally came to stay at Stour, and on one occasion when she drove away she noticed that her fuel tank was empty. Seeing a petrol station in the village, she drove in and ordered several gallons. Then she saw her purse contained only a few coins, and so she told the man, 'Fill me up and I'll reimburse Mr Churchill who must have an account with you.'

The man's face fell. 'But he owes us a fortune already.' So Laura had to drive back to Stour and ask Randolph to lend her a fiver before she could actually leave.

Money troubles were to become worse when Boul de Breteuil arrived to stay at Stour.

Randolph lost his head. He confided to Natalie that he couldn't help enjoying Boul's company 'because she isn't swanky' (which Natalie wasn't and Randolph was). Then he couldn't resist boasting further. 'Boul seems rather keen on me,' he remarked hopefully of the pretty blonde widow.

The result of all this was that Randolph set off to show Boul around London where he insisted the sights were as interesting as those in Paris. Although Randolph had, under Natalie's strict supervision, given up gambling for stakes beyond his means, when he took Boul out he talked glibly of the city's hot spots and wanted to show them to her. Boul spoke little English and certainly did not understand that Randolph was trying to impress her. When they went to dinner at Annabel's in Berkeley Square, Randolph had to explain that it was the most famous nightclub in England. And then he himself, after a few drinks, got muddled with the gambling counters. Eager to show off and demonstrate how much he could afford to lose at one throw, Randolph placed what he imagined to be £500 of chips on the tables. He lost and the chips represented £5000, which was much more than he could dredge from his own coffers. Next day, head hanging, he had to own up to Natalie that he'd lost £5000. The money would have to be found somehow and puddings must be reduced at Stour.

One of the few people whom Randolph listened to and obeyed without question was Dr 'Terry' Marshall who attended many patients around East Bergholt. I happened to be there on the day that Dr Marshall told Randolph·that he would die within months if he did not give up drinking spirits. Randolph nodded quietly and never touched whisky or brandy again. These were his favourite beverages and Dr Marshall could hardly believe that he would have sufficient self-control. But it was easier for a determined Churchill to. abstain completely than just to cut down. Henceforth Randolph, who wanted to live long enough to finish his father's biography, only consumed beer. But he had already developed cirrhosis of the liver, and that organ never recovers.

Occasionally Dr Marshall did a kidney test on Randolph. Apparently all birds and fish have a high *serum urea* because they do not urinate. At the end of the paper attached to Randolph's sample the laboratory pathologist wrote a query, 'Are you sure this isn't a fish?' That was the terrible thing. Randolph sweated a lot, and was already using his skin as an eliminating organ instead of his kidneys.

During that summer of 1965 I went to Stour several times, for Randolph was assiduous in helping me to write the life of his grandmother, Jennie Churchill, who had been my great-aunt. With pride he would lead me to the Strong Room where the papers were kept and there, having pointed out the shelves neatly arranged by his researchers, on which Jennie's letters and those of her correspondents were kept, he would leave me with the door wide open and the sunshine streaming in. I would sit scribbling away on the doorstep, for it was a hot summer and I felt averse to missing any sunshine that could brown my legs. And then I began to notice the negligence with which Randolph went out, leaving the key in the lock! Maybe Michael Wolff would come to rootle through some documents himself. 'We took everything from Blenheim,' he would say, and then seeing me struggling to decipher King Edward VII's letters to Jennie, he would hearten me by adding, 'Hasn't His Majesty got hellish handwriting? It's the worst kind of all because it looks neat until you try to make out what he really writes. *Chère amie* at the start of each letter is easy but then one realizes that all the vowels look exactly the same, and it's no good taking a magnifying glass. You just have to keep staring and eventually the sense may reach you.'

Miss Harryman the archivist and Barbara Twigg also helped me. Thus it was that I managed to pick out Jennie's early letters and so, using also my own memories of her and my grandmother's stories, I wrote her entire life.

Sometimes Randolph asked me to bring my twelve-year-old daughter Leonie for the weekend and I well remember how he always made us walk to Mass on Sundays.

'I wish I had your discipline,' he'd remark wistfully. 'Light a candle for me.'

As we walked we would pass the great unhung bell in East Bergholt churchyard about which Randolph often held forth, for it had been cast for Cardinal Wolsey before he fell on evil days and could not afford to build a church tower for it. 'You must never take good fortune for granted,' Randolph commented.

Then he would cross-examine Leonie when we came home, 'You aren't really a pagan,' he would say. 'And you did light a candle for me, didn't you?'

'Yes I did, and said a prayer too,' she'd answer truthfully. But I couldn't ever quite bring myself to light a candle for Randolph. I felt he must light that candle for himself.

Often, at meals, during that summer, the conversation would turn to the splendours of Winston's funeral. Randolph did not feel that anything more could have been done for a great Englishman.

I remember one evening when the garden had been open to the public for some charity. Dusk was falling, and still visitors trooped around. Dinner time came and my daughter appeared primly in her best dress. We were all seated at table when some of the garden visitors pressed their noses against the window panes.

'A pound extra to watch me at mealtime,' roared Randolph and my daughter who took his remark quite seriously looked up in astonishment. 'Of course they've got to pay extra to see the family eat,' he comforted her. 'No, don't pull down the blinds – just make them pay when they go out,' he told the Young Gentlemen who were in charge. With one eye on the gaping throng my daughter chewed away. She was thinking no doubt of Versailles.

Randolph was not really good with children but he yearned to be. Lucinda Wolff has preserved one letter he wrote her from Stour on 25 July 1965.

Dearest Lucinda,
Thank you for your charming letter. It was delightful to hear from you out of the blue.
I am dictating this as my handwriting is not as good as yours: and you might not be able to read it. Do come here again soon. My love to your mother.
Your affectionate
honorary uncle,
Randolph

That summer my father and stepmother Iris came much to Stour and Natalie says that the first time my father met her he thought she was a beautiful new cook and throwing his arms around her covered her with kisses! My father cared little for food but yet another crisis was going on in the kitchen and the appearance of this fascinating person filled him with hope that more than a mug of cocoa could be expected.

Having met Natalie, my father and Iris often stayed at Boxted House and drove over with her to Stour each day. In the long ago my father used to stay with his elder cousin Winston and so he had many boyhood memories some of which could be slipped into the book.

In November 1965, Frank Gannon, the only American research assistant joined the group of Young Gentlemen. Since he was not British born, although a graduate student from Jesus College, Oxford, he had to apply for a work permit. Randolph had to write to the Home Office explaining why he did not employ an Englishman. Randolph ended his letter saying, 'Incidentally, since my father was half American, and an honorary American citizen, I do not really regard Americans as foreigners.'

Once Gannon had grown accustomed to Randolph's ways he loved the work. He was fascinated by the endless stories, anecdotes and reminiscences concerning Winston. 'In the early evenings, as we would sit reading from the galleys or chapters in progress of the Great Work, he would punctuate the reading with remarks, epithets, jokes and excessive grunts, just as if he were hearing it for the first time, and just as if it were a report of contemporary events. He could revel in the perspicacity which his father always showed.'

It was Randolph's habit to have everything read aloud to him. He said that hearing words gave him a better sense of their value.

Gannon wrote, 'Everything, however, revolved around one book: the Great Work. He was determined that his life of his father would be so complete and so magisterial that it would stand unassailable. . . . He really could not believe that anyone working on the Great Work could have a life independent of it. When I finally had to return to Oxford to work full time on my thesis he wrote to me, "I am indeed grieved that your stern masters require you to leave me. . . ." '

Before Frank Gannon left, a curious incident befell us both. We happened to be walking together away from the house through the tangled garden and we were rejoicing that Randolph's political life had never come to fruition so that in the end he had been ready to take up his father's biography.

As we walked, a sudden smell of cigar smoke caused us to stop and stare around incredulously. We went up to a heap of decaying tobacco plants and sniffed but it was not that; then we came across two gardeners digging and Frank asked them if they had been smoking cigars – they stared at us blankly and shook their heads.

'No,' they said. 'We don't smoke at work. . . . '

This happening never recurred. So strong had been the smell and so curious the manner in which it smote our nostrils that we could not think of any explanation. It was as if someone from another world had breezed in to agree with our conversation, 'Yes. Isn't it lucky that Randolph is free. . . . Only he could understand the beginnings of my life.'

— 29 —

Natalie has described an evening in November 1965 when, after a long day's work arranging the photographs for Volume I, she got back to Boxted exhausted and Randolph telephoned her, 'Can I come to dinner and spend the night? Barbara Twigg will drive me over and you can drive me back in the morning.'

Natalie's diary records:

I made a delicious dinner in the kitchen. As we had all had late nights we decided at 11 pm that we would take the dogs for a walk and go to bed. Randolph took the pugs to bed with him. I only had the cat. I gave Randolph a sleeping pill and took one myself. I remember nothing more till about 4 am when there was a thud and a moan. Bobby and I both leapt out of our beds and I said, 'Oh God, it's Randolph.' We looked over the top of the stairs and there he lay spread out like a Hieronymos Bosch. Bobby rushed downstairs. Randolph murmured, 'I must have fallen.' Bobby said, 'Take it easy old boy,' and they crawled up the stairs together. Randolph went to the loo and when he went back to his bedroom I went in. His knees were badly cut and so was his elbow. He seemed quite calm so we bandaged him up and went back to bed, leaving the doors open and the landing light on. At about 7 am I heard Randolph calling and groaning, 'I am in excruciating agony. You must get a doctor and an anaesthetist at once. I must have broken my arm.' After which he started uttering the most ghastly groans which so paralysed Bobby and myself that we could hardly remember which doctor to call. We tried Dr Marshall who was away on holiday and eventually we got Dr Slee at Dedham.

Dr Slee said, 'What's he done now? Can't you bring him over to me?' I asked Randolph if he thought he could manage to go. 'Good God no, and tell him to bring an anaesthetist with him.' With my hair in curlers and covered with night cream, I collected the dogs, comforted them and let them out. Bobby made a cup of tea and we both got dressed trying not to listen to Randolph's moans of

'Oh my God. . . .' I went in and suggested an aspirin.

'A spoonful of brandy. . . .' Randolph whispered.

At 8.30 Dr Slee arrived. I heard him say, 'What have you done to yourself?'

'I've broken my arm. Don't touch it.'

Dr Slee gave him an injection of morphia and came downstairs saying, 'He's got no resistance to pain at all. Nothing can be done until we have an X-ray.' So I telephoned Barbara Twigg to come over with a suitcase packed for the hospital.

Bobby had to leave at 9 am to see some moated house miles away. Barbara Twigg arrived and we all tried to wait calmly for the ambulance, which finally appeared at 11 am. Two strong men in navy blue uniform got out. 'Can we go up and see "the victim"?' they asked. They leant over the low bed in which Randolph was lying and said, 'Well, sir, where does it hurt you most?' Then came a long altercation. 'Don't you touch me,' cried Randolph.

'We've got to get you to the ambulance.'

'I would like to be laid on a stretcher.'

'We can't get a stretcher down the stairs.'

'Why didn't that bloody doctor do what I asked and give me a real anaesthetic. . . . '

After ten minutes of such talk the blue-coated men say to me, 'Can you get a doctor, Madame?' So I phone Dr Slee to come back but he is out on another emergency call. Mrs Slee the doctor's wife says she will try to get in touch with Mr Dunn who is to do the X-ray at 12.30. The ambulance men get fussed about possible accidents in their absence. They cannot get through to their HQ by wireless because of overhanging trees outside our door, so they drive off and try to get their machine working outside the gates. In their absence Mr Dunn telephones from the hospital and I explain to him what a terrifyingly difficult case R is. Mr Dunn is exceptionally understanding and says, 'Look here, Mrs Bevan, we must get this thing sorted out. I have some patients here, but I could be with you by 12.30. Do you think he will be all right till then?' As the ambulance returns and then drives away a neighbour comes rushing up the drive. 'Oh, Mrs Bevan, I'm so glad you are all right. We saw the ambulance leaving your house and thought it must be *you*.'

Natalie then had time to remove her hair curlers and to send Boycott and Annie back to Stour with Barbara Twigg. At noon Dr Slee returned and gave Randolph a very strong injection. Almost immediately Mr Dunn drove up and the two men, after talking quietly as doctors do in the drawing room, went upstairs.

The sedated Randolph behaved quite differently and obeyed their orders. When Mr Dunn said, 'I want you to do this. . . .' he did it. A fascinating operation then took place. Paper was spread over the floor and bed, plaster of paris was mixed in bowls, the arm placed in position, the plaster soaked and placed from shoulder to wrist and bandaged on. I held R's hand and Mr Dunn held his elbow while the plaster set. Five minutes later the second ambulance arrived and another lot of blue-coated gentlemen mounted the stairs. This time Randolph agreed, under the directions of Mr Dunn, to get into the ambulance chair and be carried downstairs. Then he was moved onto a stretcher in the hall and was lifted into the ambulance where I sat with him. I waved to our gardener but one of the blue-coated gentlemen said, 'You can see out but he can't see in.' I had never before realized this! So all the smoke-glassed ambulances we see are full of waving patients! We reached the hospital where Mr Dunn had organized everything perfectly, a nurse accompanied Randolph's trolley straight to the X-ray room. I sat outside the theatre listening to the conversation of those unfortunate folk who had been waiting hours for their X-rays.

At about 4 pm, R was wheeled to his room and Mr Dunn said to me, 'If you like to settle him in, I've got another patient but I could take you home in half an hour.' As it was Saturday this seemed to me a most gallant offer, and as I had had no breakfast or lunch and was feeling a bit shaky I gladly accepted.

So that was Natalie's day, and it was likely to be the day of anyone who allowed themselves to get caught in the Randolph net. But Natalie was different. She really cared.

Within a month Randolph was back at Stour in rather good form. It was Natalie and all his staff who remained weak. They could but be thankful that all this happened after the final arrangements for Volume I had been made.

— *30* —

In the following spring there came another sojourn at Marrakesh where Randolph took a villa once more instead of staying in a hotel. He drove Natalie, Michael and Rosemary Wolff mad with worry, because here in this romantic but medically untested Moroccan oasis he insisted on having all his teeth pulled out. His English dentist had said it was time for this operation, so Randolph suddenly decided that Moroccan dentists were just as good and probably cheaper than the homegrown variety.

Volume II of Winston's life was due to be handed to the publishers within months, and Michael Wolff, whose brilliance enabled him to retain the position of Chief Researcher while keeping his sanity, knew well how to handle not only boxes of documents *en voyage* but also the other researchers who had to be towed around.

Randolph returned to England toothless but refreshed. His English dentist was ordered to set to work on healing gums and to devise the right set of 'snappers'.

At the same time Randolph knew the pleasure of becoming a grand-father, for a son was born to Minnie and young Winston and named Randolph. Edward Heath stood as godfather and Randolph drove to the church escorted by Andrew Kerr.

In January 1966, Randolph went to Switzerland with Natalie and Arabella, more for the sun and air than for the skiing. Arabella was now seventeen and very lovely. Randolph would often say, 'Arabella will not *come out*. She will *emerge*.'

From Vercovin Michael Wolff wrote to Rosemary and his letter gives a picture of what life in Randolph's entourage had become:

Darling. . . . It is Sunday morning, cloudy as usual, but the dentist who plays the church bells is trying to pick out *Marlbruk s'en va-t-en guerre* and it's not bad considering the organ is lacking a vital note. Andrew has still not come back from the village where his weekly night of nameless orgies takes place. I've met his Swiss Miss and her companions. His is certainly the pick of the litter. But they are little puppies with puppy-dog faces (and complexions) and *figurez-vous* as they say, only one comes of this Canton – anyway you have nothing to fear! Martin [Gilbert] has come for the weekend and started work on the South African chapter which he had originally prepared. . . . Randolph has been in a very sad decline. If I did not have a stubborn belief in the immortality of these Churchills I'd say he was a dying man and give him six months at the outside. He is exasperating and at the same time infinitely pathetic. Last Sunday he got up at 1.45 pm, and it's been later every day since. Yesterday he got up at 4.15 after 15 hours sleep. . . . Actually last night we had a reading of Chapter I and he perked up. Clearly he lacks stimulus here and when the spark goes out it is very difficult to relight the fire. It is very sad. All this is *very secret*. I work hard, but not too well, that is I am making errors of fact and judgement.

After this party returned, Lady Churchill (now a life peeress with the title Baroness Spencer-Churchill) had to come to Stour several times to identify people in early photographs, and this she often found difficult. Randolph may have resented his mother's lack of affection when he was a little boy, but now he raged when she hesitated. 'That looks like dear Eddie,' she would venture, 'But give me my spectacles I can't quite see. . . . Oh no it's a Zulu chief . . . quite different.' Randolph's newest Young Gentleman, Tom Hartman, had to choke back his laughter on very many occasions.

Volume I of Winston's biography appeared. It received marvellous reviews in every paper in the world. Such a story could hardly *not* be noticed. Randolph turned the launching luncheon party into a near disaster by making a long speech about his latest *bête noire*, Lord Thompson of *The Times*, who was nothing to do with the book. Also he got cross when people lined up with books for him to sign rather than thank his lucky stars for so many eager buyers. The fact remained that Volume I was out and no one could have done it better.

While Michael Wolff worked assiduously on Volume II, Andrew Kerr and Barbara Twigg concentrated on looking after Randolph, who was incapable of 'minding himself'. Natalie could inspire, but it wore her out to cope with mundane matters.

Tom Hartman says he will never forget his first morning at Stour. He came in ready for work to find Randolph speaking sternly to

Captain Boycott, whom he had just found peeing on the sofa. He swept the pug off angrily saying, 'Don't you know better than to do on the cushions what you are supposed to do on the floor?'

A few nights later Tom watched Lady Diana Cooper sitting on the same sofa wearing a gorgeous evening dress and gleaming with jewels. He saw her sniffing and looking around at the cushions, but she could not guess what had so often occurred there.

At this time Randolph employed an extra typist who happened to be very ladylike. The other secretaries lived out, but this one had a room upstairs and she grew furious because her supper was always sent up to her on a tray. After a short time she told Tom Hartman she wished to give notice. Randolph refused to see her, 'I can't be bored with these wails. *You* accept her resignation.'

'No', said Tom, 'I won't.'

So finally the lady stormed into Mr Churchill herself and said her piece. 'I'm not accustomed to being treated like a housemaid.' Randolph blinked, 'Oh I never knew you were one.'

Tom also had to sit through a very puzzling dinner when Randolph never ceased to rant to his main guest concerning the iniquity of giving up Singapore during the war. 'There were 90,000 British troops and only 30,000 Japanese – how could our precious Eastern base be simply handed over?' Hartman noticed the gentleman who was being addressed cowering beneath the onslaught. At the end of dinner Hartman whispered to Randolph, 'What was all that about Singapore?'

'Don't you know that General Percival was the man who gave it up and that was he.'

'But it wasn't,' said Tom. 'That was the Assistant Editor of the *Sunday Telegraph* who had travelled down specially to see you. His name rather resembles Percival.'

'Oh God,' groaned Randolph. 'What a waste of breath and I had so many questions to ask that editor.'

Tom Hartman soon perceived that Randolph did not really like the arty types who were Natalie's friends. She often brought them over and one evening at dinner Randolph found himself forced to make conversation to two gentlemen who had been living together in bliss for some twenty years. Eventually he asked what part of England they came from. 'Essex,' they answered, and Randolph looked across the River Stour which was Suffolk's border with Essex. 'How strange,' he said, 'I thought only buggers lived there.' After this Natalie found it difficult to keep the conversation going.

Anecdotes of these days fill her diaries. Randolph was sent a salmon from Scotland and, as there was at that moment no cook, he asked Miss Harryman to grill it. 'I'm not a kitchenmaid,' she riposted, and flounced out of the room. Randolph's own efforts to cook were however calculated to melt a heart of stone, and later she relented. Delicious salmon with cucumber from the garden appeared on the dining table for a week.

In July of that year Natalie went with Randolph to Beaverbrook's villa near Monte Carlo. Her diary cites the joys of speed boats and of water skiing, and there is one telling observation about the gambling habits with which she had inculcated Randolph. 'Won £17 in the casino and came away with it. First time in my life I've ever done that,' he said.

At that time Natalie wrote me a letter describing Randolph at Monte Carlo. 'It was glorious golden sunshine and Randolph became better immediately, really much better. He hasn't drunk any whisky or gin or spirits, only beer, and he has been getting up earlier and working with Andrew on the "Board of Trade" chapter and going to bed earlier. He says he doesn't miss whisky and is never going to drink spirits again. Eating is not good yet, but better, and will get much better I am sure ... he showed me the letter of yours that came to Cap d'Ail and he was very moved and pleased by it; "Read this fan letter," he said.' I had written to Randolph to say I thought he was doing the book magnificently and I still feel the truth of my words ... no one could have felt the pathos of his father's childhood as he did.

Natalie came back early from the South of France, leaving him there because she wanted to take Arabella to a ball in Essex. 'I had promised a long time ago that she and a French girl could stay at Boxted and we would all go together. So we danced till 4 am on my first night back, and then Arabella went to breakfast in the tent and Bobby took them all to the station for more balls in the Isle of Wight.'

In August Natalie, who was preparing Randolph for a TV series which could run alongside the books on Churchill, drove my father and his wife over to Stour for luncheon. Randolph and Michael Wolff were working on Volume II on the terrace. 'Give us another half hour and we'll finish the Board of Trade chapter,' Michael pleaded, so Natalie kept my father walking around the garden while he racked his brains for tales of Winston.

A few days later a big red helicopter picked them up at Stour and within fifty minutes 'suddenly we see this curious prosperous red brick town on a hill surrounded by fields which is Harrow', writes Natalie in her diary. And her personal account of this making of a documentary film for TV is so vivid that I quote it verbatim.

They traipsed around the school which Winston had so hated and examined the panelled room covered with the names of boys carved through the ages and stared at WSC's letters kept in the library.

Cameras. About 10 men, lights etc, and they start shooting quite quickly. Cameraman reloading camera – pushes his hands out of black cloth which has elastic round wrists and reloads *all by touch*. It looks like a doctor poking his fingers up and examining someone's inside. Randolph as usual seems like a pro, absolutely at ease (and of course he is full of suggestions as to how the whole thing should be done). After shooting R and I go and sit on a bench in the tarmac quad overlooking the chapel and library. The *Harrow Observer* sends up two photographers to take R against the background of the school. . . . A coffee break is organized in the quad yard for the cameramen. The lamps on the gates are being reinstalled. The town seems very peaceful sleeping in the sun.

11.30 am R starts second shooting. Randolph looking at photo of WSC leaning over stairs. . . . 'Excellent' they say and start filming. Randolph looking at WSC's name carved in panelling. (It's very small, just in the beading between the two top and bottom panels and next to it is Jack's name.)

Winston S. Churchill 1892

Jack S. Churchill 1896

12.15 RSC looking at names on panelling. Walks up very slowly and points at names.

12.45 Connecting shot walking down steps from school towards Headmaster's House. Drove to King's Head Hotel where R says, 'Mrs Bevan deserves a bottle of Pol Roger '59' – lunch for 19 people. I have lobster. R has scrambled eggs, doesn't eat them. A pint of bitter does for his lunch. . . .

2.35 Poor R has to walk in and look around – he seems very solemn but there is hardly any space for 'ACTION' which they keep calling for – it is difficult to believe that all this effort goes into a 30-second TV shot. The cost will be £5000. R is standing up heroically to all the waiting about in the hot sun. . . . I have felt very well and quite useful. We have finished with the shooting and waiting for the helicopter to return.

5.00 Take off from Harrow for Oving and Blenheim.

5.30 Passed over Oving, beautiful house, statues in grounds, Palladian swimming pool. R says, 'We've beat up Overegging Hall.' [But they dared not land and allow Lady Pamela Berry to chase them away!] Blenheim looks absolutely wonderful from the air in the golden evening light . . . the river and all the lakes. We go in taxi from Blenheim to the Bear in Woodstock; a charming hotel in a lovely village. I feel very happy. R has been absolutely charming, amusing, cheerful.

Back at Blenheim the flowers smell absolutely filthy. We think it's the 18 hundred people who have been around but the Custodian discovers it's the dahlias.

In the dusk they drifted through the state rooms, lingering by Stubbs' Tiger and the Joshua Reynolds portrait of the Duke of Marlborough.

Next day they continued filming at Blenheim, and Natalie finds the camera crew most endearing as they carry heavy lights around the room where Winston was born. In the evening they fly back to Stour in one hour thirty-five minutes. 'We land on the lawn. Very exciting.'

Randolph was preoccupied after his visit to the churchyard at Bladon. He could not decide whether it would be a mistake to lie there at his parents' feet. 'Would there be room for *me*?'

When again they had to visit Blenheim to check over the TV Randolph was determined all should be done his way. Natalie left him there to drive back to Essex. This was Randolph's last visit to Blenheim, and history repeated itself when Bert Marlborough insisted on keeping the TV going throughout dinner. Randolph argued that TV was not intended to replace conversation and eventually he got up and pulled the plug out of its socket. In doing so he broke the plug and in vain the butler tried to mend it.

Very late that night, Randolph and Andrew Kerr drew up at Hertfordshire House in Buckinghamshire where Laura and Michael Canfield lived, and banged on the door. The servants had gone to bed but eventually Michael Canfield appeared in pyjamas. 'Do you realize it's two in the morning?' asked Michael, who rather liked Randolph despite his appalling ways.

'Never mind the time. We've come to spend the night. Stop the dogs barking.' Without awakening her domestic staff Laura found sheets and Andrew at any rate fell into a heavy sleep.

On 28 October, Natalie flew with Randolph to Stockholm with Charles Pick of Heinemann to do publicity for the book. Her diary recalls the day.

'8.30 wake Randolph. Find him already immersed in sex book. 10.00 am. He has acupuncture while telephoning to the newspaper about the book.' Meanwhile Natalie goes out to buy toothpaste! 'At 12.00 Charles Pick of Heinemann arrives with car and we drive to the airport.' Natalie happily records 'VIP treatment. Nobody asks about money or passports. Drinks in BEA private room. On board the plane

Randolph kept on reading, apparently fascinated by *In Praise of Older Women*. I will get it away from him tonight. I'm delighted to be "older"!'

Randolph ate his lunch on the plane and Natalie and Charles Pick quaffed champagne. She hoped she wouldn't get 'champers poisoning'. When they arrived at Stockholm the plane was met by Georg Svensson of Bonnier, the publishing house. Charles Pick lost his suitcase ('some fool has taken it by mistake') so after form-filling they set off for Stockholm and reached the Grand Hotel at about 6.30. Randolph became less sweet after a fracas with photographers and Natalie, who knew him only too well, felt let down and craved a good dinner! To her rage he wouldn't look at the full moon silvering the Palace and bridges and opera house and for two and a half hours solidly read his book. Natalie wrote:

I get very bored indeed and go for a walk and find out what time on the morrow the Queen Christina exhibition opens. Examine bar and restaurant. Pretty deadly. We are not allowed to drink Snapz in the bar. Lots of local drinking rules so I have ½ bottle of champagne upstairs. At dinner R only eats soup. Me smoked eel and scrambled eggs. Very good but I feel let down. R seems OK upstairs. Continues reading his sex book. . . .

I go out for another walk. Rotten! I must remember things *do* seem difficult when one first arrives. I wish I hadn't come but I can see I'm useful. 'Whatever should I have done if you hadn't been here?' says R. 'You wouldn't have come,' I reply. Anyway they are going to make him work hard but it's enjoyable work for him and he is wonderfully well.

Next morning was a Saturday. Natalie hadn't realized she had to put her watch forward an hour and so she woke Randolph only a few minutes before his first TV interview.

He is very agreeable when I explain it's the fault of my watch and that he must get up at once. 'That's all right,' he says, 'I'm very good at getting up quickly.' He is. Pick rings to say, 'Don't rush. The cameras are not ready.'

11.00 am. Pick collects him and I go off to Christina Exhibition. Georg Svensson joins me there when he has got R started on his TV stuff.

12.00 Two more newspaper reviewers.

1.30 Over to the Opera Restaurant for Smörgasbord.

3.00 Back to the hotel for more interviews. I go off exploring old town and churches.

5.00 Back to rest.

6.00 R on TV. Not very clear but he looks all right walking about outside hotel. Oh, well, I really wouldn't have Randolph any different!

8.00 We walk around to the Strand Hotel where Contessa Kerstin Berna-dotte resides with her husband. He was one of the Swedish Prince's entourage until his unfortunate alliance. Now he is an attractive Conti of something. She was drunk and ghastly and we had a real old Randolph evening. I quite enjoyed it really – so I suppose did he. But what a waste. We went on to a nightclub taking her with us and most of the time she spent leaning across me telling Randolph what fun they'd had in bed together 21 years ago. Rather boring for me really.

Then came photographers and she pushed me to one side and tried to get them to photograph her leaning all over R. I got up and walked away from the table. R followed me and we stayed in another bar until the photographers were gone. I expected her to remain at our table but when we went back to explain that R did not like being photographed she had vanished.

Next morning, which was a Sunday, Natalie went back to the Christina Exhibition with Randolph and Charles Pick.

Randolph has been busy reading about Christina in the night and knows what he wants to see.

2.00 Luncheon.

3.00 Bateau round some of the islands.

4.00 Back to tea and rest.

7.30 Grand dinner with all the nobs. I am the only lady present but I don't in the least mind. Red-headed Bonnier makes a speech of welcome and R replies very well indeed. After dinner we adjourn and talk for a bit and then R and I excuse ourselves and escape to bed. I'd forgotten to say that I have rather a poky room. R and Charles Pick have done much better.

Monday 31 October. Late morning. But it is grey so it doesn't much matter – Some woman (as usual!) who met R 20 years ago asks Svensson if he would tell R she would like to see him. R asks her to lunch and to the Press Reception afterwards, so at 3 pm we make our way into a gilded red plush room where there are about 80 men and women standing about eating titbits and drinking various concoctions. Lots of photographers. They look a well-dressed, respect-able but dull lot . . . one woman in black flowing robes and a low cut dress and one very beautiful young girl.

During all this Natalie sat silent. She thought of Michael Wolff and Martin Gilbert slaving away. Later Gilbert would pay her the heartfelt compliment that 'Natalie Bevan was the catalyst who kept us all together.'

After the press reception there was a sort of political interview. In her diary Natalie wrote:

R thinks that Charles Pick has worked very hard in Stockholm. I personally think he has had quite a good time too and is extremely glad I came along to be Randolph's Muse. Svensson said, 'We will gladly pay Mrs Bevan's expenses. She has been so very helpful.'

Tuesday 1 November 1966: I had a glorious sleeping pill from R last night and slept like a log. Packed, and at 10 am R rang to say he was awake and at breakfast. We listened to his 'Radio Talk for Children'.

Painless drive to the airport.

Painless flight home.

But it had been long enough. Natalie accepted her role of Muse and Catalyst. She loved Randolph but his stalwart physical constitution was weakening, and every journey abroad was full of terror as well as triumph.

One can but be thankful that he had a sleeping pill to spare.

— *31* —

Perhaps the most striking thing about Randolph was his sense of wonder. He never lost it. He lived in a magic world where each day amazed and excited him.

In January 1967, Randolph wrote to Natalie, whom he had known now for over ten years, 'My dependence on you for my whole life and happiness is so entire that I am frightened of saying anything that could make the future more difficult. . . . You were an angel to come to Stour to see me off. Goodnight darling and wait for me. . . .'

But Randolph remained full of surprises. In April he telephoned Natalie after they had lunched together at the Savoy Hotel. 'Fasten your seat belt while I explain. . . . You know that pretty girl we kept looking at in the restaurant? Well, she came over to my table after you had left and asked for my autograph. She had a ticket for Paris this afternoon but I made her change her plans and she is coming to Stour for the weekend. She'll travel down with Arabella and we'll all lunch with you on Sunday. I hope you don't mind?' Here Randolph paused for breath, 'Meeting *me* has made all the difference to her life . . . see what I mean?'

'I see,' said Natalie in an icy voice.

'And guess what her name is. . . .'

'I really can't,' said Natalie furiously.

'Well it's most curious,' Randolph continued, 'It's Natalie too!'

'So we'll be two Natalies on Sunday?'

'Yes,' said Randolph jubilantly.

'L'Affaire des deux Natalies' was coolly written up under that title in the diary. She really couldn't be cross for long. He was *too* impossible.

That summer of 1967 I frequently came down to Stour, and during one of my visits Randolph met me looking distraught. Captain Boycott had been killed. In a way it was Randolph's fault: he had procured a Jack Russell terrier whom he had named Lord John Russell. Meanwhile his bitch Annie came into season. The two males fought, and as pugs aren't much good at that sort of thing, poor Boycott had suffered a severe neck wound and died. Randolph telephoned frantically to the vet, 'Please come and put down the murderer. . . .'

But by the time the vet arrived Randolph had had second thoughts. 'Let there be a stay of execution,' he announced. 'We need time to think it over.'

Secretaries hid. Researchers hardly dared enter the room to ask questions and Annie sat moping. It was a hideous weekend and one was glad the whole household had the biography to fall back on. But the Jack Russell terrier survived, the 'stayed execution' remained stayed.

This was the summer of the Six Day War, in which Israel beat Egypt, Syria and Jordan. Randolph sent his son Winston off to cover it, and to add to the speed with which they could produce a joint book, Randolph suddenly decided to install a telex machine at Stour. To get this in place quickly Tom Hartman was ordered to telephone to the Postmaster General, but as he gently remarked, it happened to be a weekend and all offices were shut. 'No matter,' said Randolph. He was longing to get off messages and show how *up* in the world he was.

Anything but pleased at his orders, Tom Hartman set to work and tracked down the Postmaster General at his Sunday luncheon. Perhaps in response to the outrageousness of Randolph's demands, there was a general scurry, and a telex machine did indeed arrive at Stour in record time. But by then another weekend had come.

The official telex installer worked until midnight on a Saturday to get the machine going. But it still proved difficult to send out messages and poor Barbara Twigg had to listen to Mr Churchill instructing the instructor, 'Do not come into *my* house and tell *my* secretary how to type. She already types 150 words a minute.'

The exhausted man gazed at Randolph sourly. 'Rum chap,' he muttered and the words he used to Tom Hartman were reminiscent of the Army's view of Randolph.

I can see Barbara Twigg now, sitting in the early hours gazing at the new toy with a very long face. The machine resembled a small piano and she did not like it one bit.

'Mr Churchill, it's quite different from a typewriter,' she explained wearily. 'It has three keys instead of four.'

However, after frenzied calls to the Middle East, the book *The Six Day War* was finished and rushed into print both in hardcase and paperback. But this excursion had seriously held up Volume II of Winston's life, and the publishers were torn between printing a topical bestseller and keeping Randolph glued to his main job. The researchers, who by now resembled a small army, had all been made to concentrate on Israel and Egypt, and several of them crept away with brain fever.

The Times Literary Supplement chose to be particularly slow to review *The Six Day War*, and Randolph composed a furious telegram to the editor, 'Six days to fight it. Six weeks to write it. Six months to review it.'

This was the summer of 1967. At this time I noticed with a fresh pang how terribly Randolph had ruined his body. He was skin and bone now. His clothes just hung on him. When I sat in the chair opposite his green velvet one I tried not to let him see the expression on my face. He was so intelligent still, he knew I was making an effort not to catch his eye. It was unbearable to see him thus, remembering what he once had been. He would suddenly raise his head and catch me turning away and he knew why I turned.

My daughter Leonie did not come to Stour that year. Once when Xenia Field came down and took me off to plant something in the garden, she tried to explain things. 'He knows what a mess he's made of his life,' she said, 'no one knows it better than he.' I tried to think of arguments. If he had become a figure in Parliament then he would not have been free to concentrate on Winston's biography. Xenia stood up with earth-covered hands holding her trowel and said, 'But no one knows what a splendid friend Randolph always is, and the things he does. To people who do him a good turn he remains faithful forever, like a little boy hanging on to his nanny. You have to love him if you know him. You couldn't not.'

Then I remembered the time I met Rebecca West and she talked about Randolph. The story she told was, to me at any rate, very revealing. Randolph had a mistress who moved on to some rich protector and then she suddenly got cancer. She telephoned the news to her new lover and he merely replied, 'I detest illness. It disgusts me. Our affair is finished.'

When Randolph learned of her plight his reaction was totally different. He came to see the person who had once been his girl, and sent flowers every day until she died. Automatically he held out a hand to other human beings if they were in trouble.

During this summer of 1967 Randolph could no longer walk in his enchanting garden but he liked everyone else to go out, wander around and return indoors to tell him what was in bloom. In his mind's eye he could see everything he had planted. I remember the polyanthus that had so excited him when it came up in a flood of brilliant blue beneath the trees. He took me out to sit on the terrace. 'Talk to me about my immortal soul,' he ordered. I couldn't. I sat tongue-tied. Randolph must work that one out for hmself. I knew he had never injured another human being. He had only lost his temper and been rude. This mattered to those who could not answer back but it had been good for his superiors. It made the blood course faster through their veins, and cleared away poisons. The harm he'd done was to himself alone. He'd been his own worst enemy.

As he became aware of the shadows drawing in he said to several people, 'I just want to snuff out suddenly.' But he remained uneasy wondering about the next stage. If total darkness did not descend where was he going to?

He had destroyed everything of himself except his brain. That kept ticking still, but only just. He needed hours of sleep and he doubted if he would live long enough to finish Winston's biography. He was now reconciled to the fact that he had never debated in the House of Commons, yet feverishly he knew how important it was to write his father's life well. He wanted to create a unique work and it would have been impossible to do this if his writing was a sideshow. And yet – and yet – to be a Prime Minister would have been very pleasant too.

Randolph hardly ate at all now. Barbara Twigg's plum cake seemed the only food he could swallow, and she left her typewriter more and more often to mix the ingredients.

Then, a week before he was due to fly to the South of France, he had a haemorrhage. Dr Marshall, who alone seemed able to impose his will on Randolph, came to see him. 'Can't you give me a pint of blood so that if I get ill in the plane I can pump it into me?' asked the impossible patient. 'I don't want to die in front of Arabella.'

'Look here,' said Dr Marshall, remaining magnificently calm, 'I'll give you not a pint of blood but a medicine you can take if necessary during the flight. But remember if you touch alcohol you'll be dead in a week.'

Randolph had stuck to his previous promise: he never drank any alcohol except beer now. But it was too late for improvement. His organs were all packing up. No human body could stand the treatment he had given it.

Natalie, Anne Sharpley and Arabella flew out with him to the Cap d'Ail where the Villa Capponcina had again been lent to him by Lord Beaverbrook. On hearing that Mr Randolph Churchill and party were arriving the entire staff walked out, and Natalie wrote me a piteous account of her struggles in the huge deserted kitchen. She knew that Monte Carlo possessed the most wonderful of markets and there she drove to buy every kind of food, but on her return she almost cut her finger off trying to chop it all up with a large vegetable knife. Blood poured. A doctor had to be summoned. And no more work was done.

Randolph realized how important it was to procure a cook quickly. He racked his brain and finally decided to cable Aristotle Onassis who was far away. 'He has lots of good cooks. He'll send one of his own chaps,' Randolph smugly decided.

As a result of the cable an under-chef from the Hôtel de Paris in Monte Carlo finally arrived. '*Monsieur Onassis m'a commandé de venir*,' he announced.

So Natalie with her bandaged finger retreated from the kitchen and had only to preside in the dining room. Meals began to appear again. In the meantime Anne Sharpley went out early every morning to buy croissants. Everyone knew how to make coffee and so breakfast became the one sure meal. Luncheon and dinner had to depend on the whim of the under-chef.

That winter when Randolph's health was none too good, Natalie had to leave England for a time, and in January 1968 he wrote what was to be the last letter she would ever receive from him. She kept it, although it concerned only the water tanks in her house which had burst and deluged the rooms. Randolph had been left in charge of Boxted House and he wrote very sensibly assuring her that everything had been done.

Stour
Natalie darling,
    You will have received my letter about the misfortune at Boxted. Andrew did the necessary in his usual competent way. He is writing you the details by the same post. I don't think much damage has been done. It rather depends on how it dries out. The central heating has been kept on for this purpose.
    The snow melted miraculously on Sunday night. Since then we have had floods and gales. . . . I have no news except that I miss you very much. I miss

not even being able to ring you, morning and evening. . . . Hoping to see you soon darling. I miss you more each day.

Your devoted
Randolph

As spring approached Randolph suddenly noticed that he was beginning to put on weight. (Apparently this often happens when the kidneys cannot eliminate properly and liquid accumulates in the tissues.) To Tom Hartman he remarked, 'I must have cancer, I am getting heavier.'

'But surely cancer is a wasting disease?' queried Tom.

'Nonsense,' argued Randolph. 'Cancer consists of lumps and lumps are heavy. It must be cancer.'

He wasn't afraid of death. He just wanted to fight on as long as he could. Above all he wanted to finish that book. Dr Marshall helped him and visited the house daily, but no doctor could reverse a trend started by a boy in his teens. And Randolph was fifty-seven that April.

Laura, who had for so long kept his spirits up and had had him to stay every Christmas when Natalie was busy with her own family, came to visit him by train. She reached the station four miles from Stour and was horrified to see Randolph coming along the platform waving his arms in welcome. Pulling an overcoat over his pyjamas he had got out of bed and driven himself to meet her. 'Tom Hartman is away and no one else seemed to be around, so I hopped out of bed and found my car.' Hopped was not the word for he could hardly drag himself along.

In early June, Randolph went to stay with Harold Macmillan for the weekend. Even before Mr Macmillan had been Prime Minister, Randolph had adored him. When he returned to his own house Barbara Twigg noticed what a state of over-excitement this visit had created in him. He expressed special amazement that Mr Macmillan had himself looked up the railway timetable instead of making a minion do it.

Natalie and Andrew conferred about his state of health, and Dr Marshall now came twice a day to give Randolph potions to keep his blood pressure down. The doctor said that it was impossible to guess with Randolph's sort how long they were going to live. On his last visit he told his patient of Bobby Kennedy's assassination and Randolph's face crumpled. 'What stupid people,' was all he said.

On the evening of 7 June Natalie and Andrew Kerr dined with him quietly off trays in his bedroom. Barbara Twigg had made her famous plum cake but Randolph only picked at it. The dogs usually slept on his bed but that night he felt they might disturb him and sent them downstairs. Before midnight, early for him, Randolph seemed to grow sleepy and Natalie decided to go home.

'You only have to telephone me if you want me back, it rings right beside my bed and I'll come immediately,' she promised. Randolph enjoyed the feeling of proximity that bedside phones gave. But on this one occasion he said to her, 'I shan't call you tonight. I won't need you.' It was the only time he had ever told Natalie he would not phone, and those were his last words before she switched out the light beside his bed and went silently out of the door.

In the morning when he did not ring, Andrew Kerr, knowing that Randolph often slept late, did not call him until 11 am. Then he carried in the usual cup of tea and saw him lying on the floor. He was quite cold.

Andrew rushed to the telephone and summoned Dr Marshall who arrived within half an hour. He looked at Randolph and lifted the body back on to the bed.

After the usual examination Dr Marshall said hesitatingly to Andrew, who had loved Randolph and merited a truthful explanation, 'I will have great difficulty in writing out this death certificate to avoid an inquest. A doctor has to write the *cause* of death and with Randolph the answer is *everything*. His liver and kidneys and lungs and guts have all packed up. He's worn out every organ in his body at the same time. . . .'

Randolph would have enjoyed that statement. And although one can never know exactly why he wanted to look out of the window in the early hours, it was as if he had been drawn by the beauty of his garden in the lonely light of dawn. Death filled him with curiosity. He knows now what happens.

Bibliography

Allen, Warner, *Lady Houston, DBE*, Constable, London, 1948

Amory, Mark, (ed.) *The Letters of Evelyn Waugh*, Weidenfeld & Nicolson, London, 1980

Boothby, Robert, *Recollections of a Rebel*, Hutchinson, London, 1978

Churchill, Randolph S., *Arms and the Covenant* (Winston's speeches), 1938

They Serve the Queen, Hutchinson, London, 1953

The Story of the Coronation, Derek Verschoyle, London, 1953

Fifteen English Houses, London, 1954

What I Said About the Press, Weidenfeld & Nicolson, London, 1955

The Rise and Fall of Sir Anthony Eden, MacGibbon & Kee, London, 1959

Lord Derby: King of Lancashire, Heinemann, London, 1959

The Fight for the Tory Leadership: A Contemporary Chronicle, Heinemann, London, 1964

Twenty-One Years, Weidenfeld & Nicolson, London, 1965

A Book of Gardens (one chapter by Randolph), Cassell, London, 1965

Winston S. Churchill, Vols. I and II (and Companion Volumes), Heinemann, London, 1966–67

Six Day War, Heinmann, London, 1967

Colville, John, *The Churchillians*, Weidenfeld & Nicolson, London, 1981

Cooper, Lady Diana, *The Rainbow Comes and Goes, The Light of Common Day, Trumpets From the Steep*, Hart-Davis, London, 1958–60

Cowles, Virginia, *Looking For Trouble*, Hamish Hamilton, London, 1941

The Phantom Major, Collins, London, 1958

Davie, Michael, (ed.) *The Diaries of Evelyn Waugh*, Weidenfeld & Nicolson, London, 1976

Day, Wentworth, *Lucy Houston, DBE*, Allen Wingate, London 1958

Farran, Roy, *Winged Dagger*, Collins, London, 1948

Foot, Michael, *Debts of Honour*, Davis Poynter, London, 1980

Gilbert, Martin, *Winston S. Churchill*, Vols. III, IV, V, and VI, Heinemann, London, 1971–83

Halle, Kay, (ed.) *Randolph S. Churchill: The Young Unpretender*, Heinemann, London, 1971

Harrod, Roy, *The Prof*, Macmillan, London, 1959

The History of the Middle East Commandos, Research Group, Imperial War Museum

Home, Lord, *The Way the Wind Blows*, Collins, London, 1976

Longmate, Norman, *The Bombers*, Hutchinson, London, 1983

Lysaght, Charles E., *Brendan Bracken*, Allen Lane, London, 1979

Maclean, Fitzroy, *Eastern Approaches*, Cape, London, 1949

Macmillan, Harold, *Winds of Change*, Macmillan, London, 1959

Marlborough, Laura Duchess of, *Laughter From a Cloud*, Weidenfeld & Nicolson, London, 1980

Mosley, Diana, *A Life of Contrasts*, Hamish Hamilton, London, 1977

Mosley, Nicholas, *The Rules of the Game*, Secker & Warburg, London, 1982

Beyond the Pale, Secker & Warburg, London, 1983

Pitt, Barrie, *The Crucible of War: The Western Desert* (Vol. I), Cape, London, 1980

Pomeroy, M., and Collins, C., *The Great Saharan Mouse Hunt*, Hutchinson, London, 1962

Pryce-Jones, David, (ed.) *Evelyn Waugh and His World*, Weidenfeld & Nicolson, London, 1973

Quennell, Peter, *Customs and Characters*, Hamish Hamilton, London, 1982

Soames, Mary, *Clementine Churchill*, Cassell, London, 1979

Sykes, Christopher, *Evelyn Waugh*, Collins, London, 1975

Westminster, Loelia Duchess of, *Grace and Favour*, Weidenfeld & Nicolson, London, 1961

Whicker, Alan, *Within Whicker's World*, Hamish Hamilton, London, 1981

Wintour, Charles, *Pressmen and the Press*, André Deutsch, London, 1972

Young, Kenneth, (ed.) *The Diaries of Sir Robert Bruce Lockhart 1915–1938*, Macmillan, London, 1973

Index

Abyssinia, 32, 51, 55
Adenauer, Dr Konrad, 112–13
Admiralty House, 2–3, 47
Albania, 41–2, 105
Alexander, General, 78, 80, 93, 102
Algiers, R. in, 74, 78–9, 90, 93; 1958
   revolution, 143
America, 71, 76, 85, 118; R. in, 17, 19–21,
   34, 113–14, 119, 141, 147; confers
   Honorary Citizenship on Churchill,
   171–2; Kennedy assassination, 172
Amery, Julian, 105–6, 128, 137
Anderson, General, 74
Asquith, Lord, 2, 4, 5, 157
Asquith, Violet, see Bonham-Carter
Asthall Manor, 8
Astor, Lord, 181n
Astor, Nancy, Viscountess, 9
Attlee, Clement, 108
Auchinleck, Field Marshal Sir Claude, 60,
   61–2
Ava, Basil, Earl of, see Dufferin and Ava

Baldwin, Stanley, 30, 31, 33, 34, 35
Barber, Stephen, war correspondent, 143,
   144; and South Africa, 147–8
Bari, 76, 80–1, 88, 99, 102
Barre, Philippe, ed. Le Matin, 24
Baruch, Bernard, 26, 172
Beaton, Cecil, 34, 43, 151
Beatty, Countess, 73
Beaverbrook, Lord, 4, 49, 107, 141;
   employs R., 21, 26, 33, 34–5, 139–40,
   144; and his defection to News of the
   World, 147, 149; Monte Carlo villa,
   195, 205
Beit, Sir Alfred, MP, 117; marriage to
   Clementine Mitford, 45
Beit (née Mitford), Clementine, w. of above,

117; R.'s relationship with, 36, 37–8,
   44–5, 155, 161
Belgrade, 100; White Palace, 102–3
Bernadotte, Contessa Kerstin, 199
Berry, Col. the Hon. Julian, s. of Lord
   Camrose, in Cyprus, 143
Berry, the Hon. Michael, s. of Lord
   Camrose, 126
Berry, Lady Pamela, 126–7, 141
Berry, the Hon. Seymour, s. of Lord
   Camrose, 28, 47
Betjeman, Sir John, 15, 24, 27
Bevan, Bobby, 150, 153, 189
Bevan, Natalie, 168, 205; R.'s last love,
   150–5 passim, 187, 200, 201; at
   Marrakesh, 176, 180–2, 192; and R.'s fall
   at Boxted, 189–91; 195–9, 201
Birkenhead, F. E. Smith, first Earl of, 2, 11,
   18–19, 35
Birkenhead, Freddie Smith, second Earl of,
   28, 89, 90, 126; in Croatia, 94–7 passim,
   100, 102; and Waugh, 95–7
Birkenhead, dowager Countess of, 151
Blakenham, Nancy Hare, Lady, 155; and
   life as R.'s neighbour, 128–9
Blakenham, Lord, 18, 128
Blenheim Palace, 22–4; search of the
   archives, 157, 158; TV documentary,
   197
Bonham-Carter, Maurice, 4
Bonham-Carter, (née Asquith), Violet, w. of
   above, 4
Bonnier, Charles, 198, 199
Boothby, Lord, 141
Bosnia, 75–7, 82–3, 85–6
Bowen, Muriel, and R.'s Bournemouth
   candidature, 153
Boxted House, home of Natalie Bevan, 154,
   167, 168, 171, 183, 187

Bracken, Brendan, 12, 26, 32, 33, 39; R.'s
  obituary, 146
Braden, Spruille, interviewed by R., 114
Breteuil, Boul, Comtesse de, 181, 184
Brien, Alan, as R.'s assistant, 122–7 *passim*,
  160, 161; encounter with Waugh, 122–3;
  and R. in Brompton Hospital, 177
Brownlow, Lord, 49
Bruce Lockhart, Robert, 26
Buccleuch, Duchess of, 161
Buckley, Christopher, 118
Butler, R. A., Lord Butler, 137; and
  Premiership, 142; and 'Book of Golden
  Roses', 151–2

Cairo, 52–5 *passim*, 61, 77
Campbell, Lady Jean, 179–80
Camrose, Lord, 28, 47; buys Oving, 126
Canada, R.'s lecture tour, 16–17
Canfield, Laura, *see* Dudley
Canfield, Michael, 110, 133, 197
Carnarvon, Tilly, *see* Losch
Carr, Sir William, 146
Carson, Stephen, MP, 135
Carter-Ruck, Peter, 139
Castellorizo island, 51 and n
Castle Leslie, Co. Monaghan, 135 and n
Castlerosse, Lord, 27 and n
Catholic Church, Great Schism, 90
Chamberlain, Neville, PM, 35, 41
Charteris, Laura, *see* Dudley
Chartwell, 8, 9, 12, 19, 22, 133, 156, 157
Chequers, 49, 50, 75, 108
Churchill, Arabella, d. of Randolph and
  June, 117, 125, 164, 179, 180–1, 192,
  195, 205; at Stour, 132, 134, 152, 168
Churchill, Clarissa, engagement to Anthony
  Eden, 121; marriage, 136
Churchill, Clementine, w. of Sir Winston, 1,
  12, 13, 34, 115, 161, 179; and
  Dardanelles, 3; in US with R., 20–1, 172;
  Golden Wedding, 151–2; at Stour, 171,
  193; life peerage as Baroness Spencer
  Churchill, 193
Churchill, Diana, *see* Sandys,
Churchill, Lady Gwendoline, w. of Jack, 3
Churchill, Jack, brother of Winston, 3, 10,
  13
Churchill, Jack, commando, 81
Churchill, Jennie, *see* Churchill, Lady
  Randolph
Churchill, Johnny, cousin of Randolph, 4,
  15, 16
Churchill (*née* Osborne), June, second w. of
  Randolph, 115–17, 134, 153; at Stour,
  131, 133–4; and Churchill's death, 180
Churchill, Marigold, 5, 7
Churchill, Mary, *see* Soames

Churchill (*née* Digby), Pamela, 107; first w.
  of R., 47–9, 52, 70–1, 109, 112, 115
Churchill (*née* Jerome) (Jennie), Lady
  Randolph, 1, 2, 4, 7, 185
Churchill, Lord Randolph, 2, 12, 70
Churchill, Randolph Frederick Edward,
  birth and childhood, 1–5; prep school
  experiences, 6–7; at Eton, 8–15; journey
  in *Warspite* with his father, 10–11; at
  Oxford, 15, 19, 21, 29; US lecture tour,
  19–21; newspaper journalist, 21, 29,
  34–5; twenty-first birthday party, 28; in
  Germany, 29, 35, 39; Parliamentary
  candidate, 29–33, 48, 105–6, 119–20,
  152–3; at Marrakesh, 33, 176, 180–1,
  192; Spanish assignment, 39–40; military
  training, 41, 57; marriage to Pamela
  Digby (*see under*); with Commandos in
  Egypt, 52, 54; Major in Press Dept., 54,
  60, 61; and access to his father, 54–5, 56,
  58; difficulty of his military placement,
  57, 58, 60; and SAS, 60; and Benghazi
  harbour raid, 63–9; back injury, 68, 70,
  71, 85; war correspondent in N. Africa,
  74; liaison officer in Sicily, 75–6; in
  Malta, 76; and Teheran Conference, 77;
  and Yugoslav Military Mission, 78–83,
  94; relationship with Evelyn Waugh, 90,
  91, 93–8, 99, 100–1; injured in plane
  crash, 91–2, 93; separation from Pamela,
  112, 115; in India, 114–15; marriage to
  June Osborne, 115–17; Korean war
  correspondent, 117–19; relationship
  with his assistants, 122–3, 156; in US for
  his father's honour, 171–2; lung
  operation, 176; in Capri, 178; and his
  father's death, 179; in south of France,
  204–5; last days and death, 206–7; spoilt
  by his father (*see under* Sir Winston);
  obsession with his mother, 1–2, 5, 12,
  39, 43, 45; inspirer of love and affection,
  8n, 13, 125, 138, 159, 203; journalistic
  ability, 9, 29, 34–5, 41, 108, 134;
  garrulity, 11, 12, 26; craving for affection,
  12, 37; outstanding memory, 12, 13, 17,
  34, 63, 173; oratorical and electioneering
  ability, 13, 17, 34, 105–6, 136, 138;
  incurs dislike, 13–14, 49, 56, 71, 107;
  effect on other people, 15, 19, 34;
  arrogant and self-assured, 18, 26, 34;
  alcoholism, 19, 34, 35, 71, 94, 100, 160,
  161; rudeness, 25, 37, 40, 44, 46, 48, 50,
  71, 106, 118, 133; affection for his
  father, 26, 40, 93; brilliant and
  stimulating companion, 34, 36, 37, 63,
  96, 105; desire for military prowess, 56,
  62, 103; courage, 57, 60–1, 86, 95, 118;
  behaviour in America, 113–14: irrational

rages, 114, 129; generosity, 115, 139, 183; secret telephone book, 135 and n; and his dogs, 167, 193–4, 202; skill as an author, 169, 195

Writings: Arms and the Covenant, 40 and n; *A Book of Gardens*, 132; *Fifteen English Towns*, 124; *The Fight for the Tory Leadership*, 172–3; *Lord Derby: King of Lancashire*, 124–5, 131, 150; *The Rise and Fall of Sir Anthony Eden*, 128, 145–6; *The Six Day War*, 202–3; *Twenty-One Years*, 6, 18; *What I said about the Press*, 140; *Winston S. Churchill Vols. 1 and 2*; R.'s concern with the project, 27, 124, 131, 156 ff., 169 ff., 193; *Women and their Place in the World* (thesis), 9

Churchill, Randolph, s. of Minnie and Winston, jr, 192

Churchill, Sarah, later Oliver, 3, 22, 33–4, 36–7, 41, 141, 179

Churchill, Tom, commando, 81

Churchill, Sir Winston Leonard Spencer, 6, 7, 113, 178; spoils his son, 1, 9, 11–12, 19, 34, 39; and Dardanelles, 3–4; his speeches, 16, 17, 29, 34, 40–1, 46, 119; tour of Canada and US, 16–17, 27; and his own biography, 27–8; and R. as Parliamentary candidate, 30–3, 40, 106; and Mosley, 35–6; at work, 41–2; and Second World War, 46, 48; and Orde Wingate, 56; and Fitzroy Maclean, 75, 77–9; and Yugoslav Military Mission, 75; at Marrakesh, 78, 79, 104–5; and Hiroshima atom bomb, 105; defeat in 1945, 106, 107; return to power, 119; and Suez, 144; R. to write his biography, 150, 156; US Honorary Citizenship, 171–2; death and funeral, 179–80

Churchill, Winston, jr, s. of Randolph and Pamela, 40, 49, 104–5; and his father's engagement, 115–16; at Eton and Oxford, 163; and R.'s Libyan safari, 163–6; covers Six Day War, 202; marriage to Minnie d'Erlanger, 178, 179

Clissold, Major, 95, 98

Cockran, Bourke, 158

Collins, Catherine and Pomeroy, Miggs, *The Great Saharan Mouse Hunt*, 163–5 and n

Colville, Sir John, 48, 70

Commandos, 50, 51, 52, 56, 112, 143

Congress of Europe, 112–13

Conservative Party, and R. as a candidate, 29–30, 33, 107–8, 153

Constable, John, 128, 131

Cooper, Sir Alfred Duff, 78, 90, 110, 130

Cooper, Lady Diana, 27, 49, 78–9, 194; in

The Miracle, 44; and Waugh, 90–1; on R. in Algiers, 92; in Rome, 93–4

Cooper, Corporal, 65, 66

Corsica, 93, 94; R. and, 144

Coward, Sir Noël, 121

Cowdray, Lord, 128, 129

Cowles, Virginia, war correspondent, 39, 49, 73; *Looking for Trouble*, 40

Crichton, Commander Michael, 10–11

Croatia, 89, 91; British Mission, 85, 94, 95; Waugh/R. conflict, 90, 93–8, 99, 102; advent of Birkenhead, 94–102 *passim*; German air raid, 96–7

Cudlipp, Hugh, 169–71

Cunningham, Admiral, 80

Cunningham, Lt. Col. William, 93

Curzon, Lord, 36, 76

Cyprus, 142, 143

Dacre, Lord (Hugh Trevor Roper), 173

Daily Express, 144, 152

Daily Mail, 32, 35, 39

Daily Mirror, 169

Daily Telegraph, 68, 141, 168; R. as Korean correspondent, 117–18; and Algerian affairs, 143–4; and R.'s life of his father, 156

Daly, Dermot, 57

de Gaulle, General, 78, 143, 144

d'Erlanger, Sir Gerard, 178

d'Erlanger, Mary Caroline, 'Minnie', 178, 179

Deakin, Capt. F. W., parachutist, 75

Dedijer, Vladimir, 93

Derby, Edward George Villiers, Earl of, R.'s Life of, 124–5

Dietz, Howard, 113

Dietz, Liza, 121–2

Digby, Lord and Lady, 47, 70

Digby, Jaquetta, 115–16

Digby, Pamela, *see* Churchill, Pamela

Dodecanese islands, 51 and n

Dorchester Hotel, R.'s literary luncheon speech, 1953, 127; 1957, 140

Douglas-Home, Sir Alec, 142–3, 174

Dudley, Laura, 46, 86–7, 109, 114–15, 133, 138; R.'s letters to, 72–4, 77, 79–80, 84, 109–10, 114–15; and R. at Stour, 133, 183–4; and R.'s death, 206

Dudley, third Earl of, marriage, 73, 80, 109

Duff Cooper Memorial prize, first award, 130 and n

Dufferin and Ava, Basil, fourth Marquis, 15; death in Burma, 103, 126

Dufferin and Ava, Maureen Marchioness of, w. of above, attacks R., 126

Duncan, Sergeant, 81

Dunn, Lady Mary, 47

East Bergholt, Suffolk, *see* Stour
Eastern Times, 62
Eden (later Lord Avon), Sir Anthony, Foreign Secretary, 52; engagement to Clarissa Churchill, 121; P.M., 135, 136–7; Suez, 136–7, 144–6
Edward VII, 24; letters to Jennie Churchill, 185
Egypt, 52, 60, 76–7
Eisenhower, General, 80
Elizabeth II, 128, 182, 183
Elliott, Air Vice-Marshal William, Balkan Air Force, 80; political dinner party, 80–1
Emery, Frank, Korean exploit with R., 118–19
Eton, 8–9
Evening News, 31
Evening Standard, 33, 41, 128, 143, 153, 172; Winston and 'Londoner's Diary', 41; and Anglo/American Middle East Agreement, 137; and Suez crisis, 137, 141; and Macmillan as PM, 142; R.'s defection, 147, 149

Field, Xenia, 131–2, 203
Findlay, Richard, Parliamentary candidate, 32
First World War, fall of Antwerp, 3; Dardanelles, 3; Armistice, 5; 1919 Peace Conference, 40–1
Fleming, Ann, 159
Fleming, Ian, 159
Foot, Michael, 139, 141; and R. as a candidate, 30, 119–20
Foot, Mrs, w. of above, 177
Forbes, Alastair, visit to Stour, 112, 161–2
Foster, Sir John, 138
Foyle, Christina, 1953 Literary Luncheon, 127; 1957, 140
Franco, Francisco, 39
Franks, Col. Brian, SAS commander, 89; and Evelyn Waugh, 89, 90
Friend, Capt. J. A., 'Jummy', 54, 152
Fulton, USA, Churchill Memorial, Churchill's 'Iron Curtain' speech; 119

Gandhi, Mahatma, meeting with R., 114
Gannon, Frank, 157, 187–8
George V, coronation, 2
Germany, R. in, 24, 29, 35, 46; Nazi movement, 29, 35, 46; invasion of Belgium and Holland, 48; and Greece, 52; Serbo-Croat atrocities, 86 and n; evacuation of Balkans, 96, 99; concedes defeat in Europe, 104
Gilbert, Martin, 51 and n, 157, 158, 166, 168, 193, 199

Gilmour, Ian, 139, 161
Greece, 41; Battle of Crete, 52; Communist rising, 102
Grenfell, Lord, marriage to Betty Shaughnessy, 21n
Grey, Sir Edward, 2
Guinness, Bryan, *see* Moyne, second Lord
Guinness, Tanis, *see* Phillips
Guinness, Walter, *see* Moyne, first Lord

Hailsham, second Viscount, Quintin Hogg, 28, 172, 173
Halle, Kay, 21, 105 and n, 114; R.'s love for, 19–20, 172; and Churchill's Honorary Citizenship, 171–2
Hanfstaengel, Putzi, 29
Hare, John, *see* Blakenham, Lord
Harmsworth, Esmond, *see* Rothermere
Harriman, Averell, 56, 70
Harris, Sir Arthur, C-in-C Bomber Command, 71
Harrod, Sir Roy, 15, 19
Harrow School, 196
Harryman, Miss, 157, 158, 176, 180, 185
Hartman, Tom, 157, 193–4, 202, 206
Harvey-Miller, Kay, secretary to R., 115
Head, Anthony, Minister of Defence, 144–5
Hearst, William Randolph, 17–18, 24
Heath, Edward, 192
Hitler, Adolf, 29, 35; and Mosleys, 36; and Second World War, 46, 48, 76; Stauffenberg plot to kill, 110
Hoare, Sir Samuel, 31, 32
Hochhuth, Rolf, *Soldiers* R. and, 139
Hogg, Quintin, *see* Hailsham
Hore-Belisha, Leslie, 40
House of Commons, 71, 107–8; Winston introduces R., 48–9
Houston, Lady, backs R. as Parliamentary candidate, 30, 31, 33; and aerial warfare, 30; death in 1936, 34
Hudson, Robert 41

Independent Conservative Association, formed by R., 32
India, 30
Irving, Clive, of *Sunday Times*, visits Stour, 173–4
Italy, and Second World War, 41–2, 64–5, 76, 81, 93

James, Edward, s. of Mrs Willie James, 24, 25
James, Robert Rhodes, 157, 168
Japan, 104; bombing of Hiroshima, 105, 108
Jebb, Vanessa, 159, 160

John, Augustus, and 'Golden Rose Book', 152
Jones, Thomas, 9–10
Jordan, Philip, 92

Kemsley, Lord, 141
Kennedy, John, President, 172
Kennedy, Jackie, w. of above, 172
Kerr, Andrew, 168, 192, 193, 197, 207; at Marrakesh, 176, 180, 181; and R.'s death, 206, 207
Keyes, Admiral Sir Roger, 10–11
Kinross, Lord, 150
Kitchener, Lord, 3
Kommer, Rudolph, 44
Korean War, R. as *Daily Telegraph* correspondent, 117–19; Mekong river exploit, 118–19

Labour Party, 1945 victory, 106
Lambton, Sir Miles, later Lord, 52, 176–7
Laval, Pierre, 32
Law, Andrew Bonar, 4, 157
Laycock, Col. Robert, Commando forces, 49, 50, 52, 54, 58–9, 76, 106, 112
Legh, Sir Piers, 21
Leslie, Anita, and R., 21–2, 54; ambulance unit, 55, 62
Libya, 163–6
Lindemann, Professor, 10, 15, 19
Listowel, Lord, 114
Lloyd, John Selwyn, 136, 137
Lloyd George, David, 5, 11
Long, Lady, *see* Dudley
Longford, Lord (Frank Pakenham), 117, 159
Longmate, Norman, *The Bombers*, 71n
Longworth, Alice, 172
Losch, Tilly, 18, 24, 25, 41, 168
Lyttelton, Oliver, Minister of State in Middle East, 56

MacArthur, General, 119
MacDonald, Malcolm, MP, 33
MacDonald, Ramsay, PM, 30, 31, 33
Maclean, Brig. Sir Fitzroy, 72, 128; and SAS, 62; abortive raid on Benghazi harbour, 63–9; head of Yugoslav Military Mission, 75, 76, 81–3; meeting with Winston, 77, 78, 79; and Vis island, 88; with Partisans in Serbia, 99, 100; in Belgrade, 102–3; *Eastern Approaches*, 66–7, 83–4
Macleod, Iain, 138
Macmillan, Harold (later Earl of Stockton), 41–2, 79, 142, 173, 206
Macmillan, Lady Dorothy, 142
Malta, 76

Marlborough, Gladys, Duchess of, 22
Marlborough, John Albert (Bert), tenth Duke of, 158
Marrakesh, 78, 79; R. and friends at, 33, 176, 180–1, 192
Marreco, Anthony, 112, 113
Marshall, Dr 'Terry', 184–5, 204, 206
Maurois, André, at Princeton, 20
Maxwell, Sir Andrew, 85
Maze, Paul, and 'Book of Golden Roses', 151
Melchett, Lord, 44
Merton, Arthur, 68
Messel, Oliver, 34
Middle East, 51, 59, 137
Middle East Commando Research Group, 51n
Mihailovic, General, 75, 78
Mitchell, R. J., 30
Mitford, Clementine, *see* Beit
Mitford, Diana, *see* Mosley
Mitford, Nancy, 108
Mitford, Tom, 8 and n, 21, 103, 108
Mitford, Unity, 37, 88
Molian, Michael, research assistant, 157
Monckton, Sir Walter, 62
Montgomery, General Bernard Law, Viscount, 74
Moorehead, Alan, and the Dardanelles, 130n
Moran, Lord, 179–80
Morrison, Ian, war correspondent, 118
Mosley, Lady Cynthia, first w. of Sir Oswald, 36, 76
Mosley, Diana, second w. of Sir Oswald, 8 and n, 9, 13; imprisonment, 48, 49, 57, 88
Mosley, Nicholas, s. of Sir Oswald and Lady Cynthia, 76
Mosley, Sir Oswald, 35, 41, 46; imprisonment, 48, 57, 88, 108; and R., 108
Moyne, Bryan Guinness, second Lord, marriage to Diana Mitford, 15–16, 35
Moyne, Walter Guinness, first Lord, 36
Muggeridge, Malcolm, *New Statesman* article R., 168–9
Mussolini, Benito, 11, 32

Nash, John, and 'Book of Golden Roses', 151
New Statesman, 168
News of the World, R.'s defection, 147–8
Nicolson, Harold, 41
Nicolson, Nigel, 152
North Africa, 54, 56; Benghazi harbour raid, 63–9; Long Range Desert Group, 61, 63, 68

Nuremberg Trials, 110

Oliver, Vic, 33, 102
Onassis, Aristotle, 160, 205
Osborne, June, see Churchill, June
Osborne, Col. Rex, f. of above, 115
Oving, nr Aylesbury, 196; rented by R., 125;
126-7

Paget, Lady Elizabeth, 27
Pakenham, Frank, see Longford
Palestine, R. in Tel Aviv, 141
Palestine Post, 62
parachute forces, 52, 59-60; and Yugoslav
Mission, 5, 76, 78, 81; Free French, 61
Parsons, Lady Bridget, 117
Pearson, Hon. Nancy, see Blakenham
Peniakoff, Colonel, 76
People, 140; R.'s libel suit, 138-9
Percival, General, and fall of Singapore, 194
Phillips, Edward, 117, 119
Phillips, Tanis, 113, 117, 121, 177
Pick, Charles, 197, 198, 199
Pitt, Barrie, *The Crucible of War*, 59 and n
Pius XII, Pope, 11, 89
Pol Roger, Madame, 110-11
Poland, 108
Powell, Enoch, MP, *Times* article, 159; at
Stour, 159
Preston Conservative Association, and
Amery/Randolph candidature, 105-6
Private Eye, 138
Profumo, Jack, at Marrakesh, 181-2;
Cliveden affair, 181n
Pryce-Jones, Alan, at Eton with R., 9; on
Birkenhead, 95; at Stour, 159-60

Ranfurly, Hermione, Countess of, 125
and n
Redesdale, Lord, second Baron, 36
Richards, Patricia, (later Lady Jersey), and
R. at Blenheim, 22-4
Ridley, Lady, 2
Romilly, Bertram, 4
Romilly, Nellie, 4, 27
Roosevelt, President, 26, 58, 70, 71-2;
Cairo and Teheran Conferences, 77
Rose, Col. Stephen, 52
Rose, Corporal, 65, 68
Rosebery, Lord and Lady, at Dalmeny, 70
Rothermere, A. C. W. Harmsworth,
Viscount, 17, 28; employs R., 21, 29, 30,
34-5, 39
Rothermere, Esmond Harmsworth, second
Viscount, R. attacks his newspapers,
123-4, 127
Rothschild, Lord, 92 and n

Royal Air Force, 30, 60, 64, 68, 84; Balkan
Airforce formation, 88
Russia, 84-5, 95; see also Soviet Union

Sandroyd, prep school, 6
Sandys (*née* Churchill, later Bailey), Diana,
childhood with R., 2, 4, 7, 8; marriage to
Sandys, 32, 33; in Naples, 88; death, 172
Sandys, Duncan, 41, 115; second husband
of Diana Churchill, 32, 33, 172
Schneider Trophy, 30
Second World War, outbreak, 46ff; German
invasion of France, 48; Normandy
landings, 89, 90; Germany concedes
defeat in Europe, 104; atomic bomb
explosion, 105, 108
Serbia, 94; operation 'Ratweek', 99
Sexton, Mrs, cook, 158-9, 175
Sharpley, Anne, reporter, 159, 205;
encounter with R. 141-2; and Winston's
death, 179-80
Shaughnessy, Betty, see Stafford
Sicily, R. as liaison officer, 75-6
Sickert, Walter, 150
Sieveking, Lance, 151
Smith, Matthew, 152
Soames, Christopher, 114
Soames (*née* Churchill), Mary, 7, 32, 34,
179; marriage, 114
South Africa, 51; R. as foreign
correspondent, 147-8
Soviet Union, 71; R.'s speech at Red Army
parade, 112
Spanish Civil War, 40
Spears, Maj. Gen. Sir Edward, 74
Special Air Service (SAS), 63-9 *passim*, 72,
76, 104
Spectator, 134-5
Springfield House, 71
Stafford, Mrs Berkeley, 21 and n
Stalin, Josef, 77; meeting with Tito, 100
Stirling, Bill, and SAS, 78
Stirling, Col. David, Commando, 50, 58,
163; SAS regiment, 59-61, 72, 104; use
of parachutists, 59; Kabrit training
course, 60, 62, 63; and raid on Benghazi
harbour, 63-9; captured in N. Africa, 72,
76; leaves the army, 105
Stirling, Peter, 60, 62; and SAS, 78
Stockholm, R. and Natalie in, 197-200
Stokes, Dick, MP, 129
Stour, East Bergholt, bought by R., 128-30;
its garden, 129, 131-3, 160-1, 168, 204;
visitors to, 138, 150, 159, 173-4, 183-4;
'Book of Golden Roses', 151-2;
organization for 'Great Work', 157 ff,
202-3
Strathcona, Lord, 41

Suez Canal, Eden and the crisis, 137, 144; nationalization, 145
Sunday Graphic, R. and Hitler's election campaign, 29
Sunday Pictorial, 169
Sunday Telegraph, 194
Sunday Times, 141, 173
Sutro, John, 133–4
Svensson, Georg, 198, 200
Swope, Mr and Mrs Herbert, hosts to R. in US, 113
Sykes, Christopher, 15, 54; and June 1944, 89; Operational Intelligence Officer, 90; 89, 133–4

television, 196, 198; R.'s behaviour, 141, 159–60
Thompson, Joan, ATS, 101
Thompson, Lord, 193
Tito, 82–3, 85; Partisans, 75, 76, 78; meeting with Churchill, 80, 82, 93, 100, 128; Vis island escapade, 100; in Belgrade, 100, 102–3; in London, 127–8
Topusko, 94, 96, 100–1, 102
Trevor Roper, Hugh, *see* Dacre, Lord
Twigg, Barbara, secretary to R., 174–5, 185, 190, 193, 202–3, 206–7

Unionist Association, and R. as Parliamentary candidate, 33

erwoerd, Dr, 148
Vis island, HQ Yugoslav Mission, 81, 83, 88; Maclean and, 99; Tito's escapade, 100
von Blömberg, Marshal, 39
von Hofmannstal (*née* Paget), Lady Elizabeth, w. of above, 27

Warrender, Victor, 40
Watson, Graham, literary agent for R., 89, 125, 145, 156
Waugh, Auberon, 107

Waugh, Evelyn, 102, 106–8, 128; love–hate relationship with R., 26–7, 50–1, 76, 93–101 *passim*, 106–8, 119–21; and Commandos, 50, 52; and Pamela Churchill, 70; interview with the Pope, 89, 103; problem of his military disposal, 89–90; and Yugoslav Military Mission, 90–5 *passim*, 103; and Freddie Birkenhead, 95–7, 101; moved to Dubrovnik, 102; letter to June Osborne, 116, 117; and Clarissa Churchill, 121; behaviour towards Alan Brien, 122–3; on *Fifteen English Houses*, 124; *Brideshead Revisited*, 89, 101; *Put Out More Flags*, 89
West, Rebecca, 203–4
Westminster, Hugh Richard Grosvenor (Bend-Or), second Duke of, 11
Westminster, Loelia, Duchess of, on Winston/R. row, 11
Weymouth, Lady, 126
Whicker, Alan, with R. in Korea, 117–18
White's Club, 130
William II, (the Kaiser), interviewed by R., 29 and n
Williams, Mona Harrison, 43; Capri House, 178
Wilson, General Maitland, 79, 80, 93, 100, 125n
Wingate, Major Orde, 55–6
Wintour, Charles, deputy ed. *Evening Standard*, 168; employs R., 134–5, 137, 139, 146–7
Wolff, Michael, 156–8, 168–9, 178, 195, 199; at Marrakesh, 176, 180–3, 192; on life in R.'s entourage, 192–3
Wolff, Rosemary, w. of above, 157, 168, 186, 192

Yugoslavia, British Military Mission, 75–85 *passim*; Partisan–Chetnik conflict, 76, 100, 102; parachutists, 81–5; Drvar casualties, 85–6; German withdrawal, 99, 100; Foggia bomber centre, 102